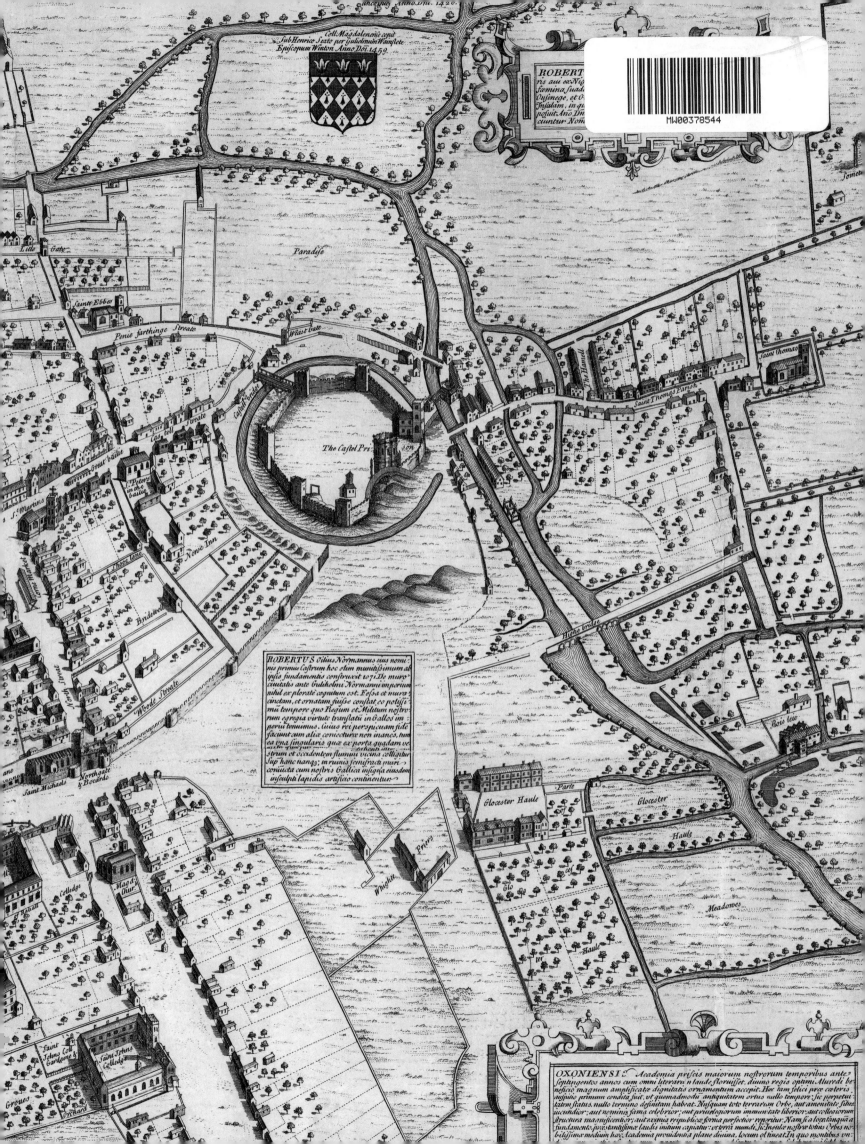

OXFORD COLLEGE
GARDENS

This book is dedicated to the gardeners of the Oxford colleges, past and present.

Frances Lincoln Limited
74-77 White Lion Street
London N1 9PF
www.franceslincoln.com
Oxford College Gardens
Copyright © Frances Lincoln Limited 2015
Text © Tim Richardson 2015
Photographs © Andrew Lawson 2015 apart from those listed on page 319.

First Frances Lincoln edition 2015

A catalogue record for this book is available from the British Library.

978-0-7112-3218-1

9 8 7 6 5 4 3 2 1

Printed in China

The college maps were created and adapted using data from
Open Street Maps © OpenStreetMap contributors.

THIS PAGE Verbena bonariensis in Nuffield College.

OVERLEAF Box balls and ornamental grasses in the courtyard
of the Ruskin Lane Building at Worcester College.

ENDPAPERS The endpapers show Ralph Agas's map of Oxford from 1578.

OXFORD COLLEGE
GARDENS

Tim Richardson

Photographs by Andrew Lawson

F

FRANCES LINCOLN LIMITED
PUBLISHERS

Contents

Introduction **6**

Introduction

So WHERE IS THE university? You will know the answer to that question. The collegiate structure of Oxford University means that there is no central building which might be described as 'the university'. No Oxford student has ever owed their first allegiance to the university itself, because that is not the physical entity they attend. The focus must inevitably be on one of the 38 self-governing and financially independent colleges which constitute the university as a whole. The colleges have developed markedly different characters over the centuries, each with their own customs, reputations and atmosphere. Even the newer foundations quickly seem to develop their own peculiarities, exhibiting fierce independence of spirit and earnest competitiveness – on the river and sports grounds as much as in academic performance. As one graduate reminisced in the 1930s of his time at Oxford around the turn of the 20th century: 'I had little feeling of University – I was at Balliol, not Oxford – there were colleges, all different, with different ways of life and different excellences.'

The question of college character is vexed indeed and is generally avoided by respectable commentators or anyone with a formal link to the university who wishes their *persona* to remain *grata*. But the fact is, college character does exist. It changes over the centuries and even over decades, and is intimately bound up with the personalities and qualities of the human beings who pass through, as well as certain imperishable characteristics which have apparently always been present within the college walls.

An Oxford college is an intense capsule of an environment, a living and working organism that seems to be possessed of its own volition and power. Which makes it a paradox that many of them outwardly look so similar – at least from the street. Even native Oxonians might get muddled around Turl Street, where Exeter, Jesus, Lincoln and Brasenose sit cheek by jowl, each realised in the same honeyed Cotswold stone and each constructed in the approved Oxford Gothic manner. It is only when one penetrates the entrance lodge and starts to wander the quadrangles that a real sense of what the place is about can be appreciated. The quadrangles are by no means uniform in style and tone, and the huge variety of gardens to be discovered in the college's outdoor areas includes the 'private' fellows' gardens (usually open to the public nowadays) or in some cases the groves, walks, lakes, deer parks and meadows which open up once the visitor has breached the forbidding perimeter walls. For college character also has something to do with the physical fabric of the place, which is the matter of this book. If one assumes that a landscape or garden can affect the mind, then the layout of a college – the trinity of hall, chapel and library, plus of course the atmosphere of its quadrangles and gardens – will help to shape its overall feel, its identity.

Topography of Oxford

The colleges are spread unevenly throughout the city of Oxford, often in clusters (which leads to the most intense rivalries). Unlike Cambridge, Oxford has always been an

The War Memorial Garden at Christ Church, with white *Anemone* x *hybrida* 'Honorine Jobert' in the cottagey borders.

important urban centre economically, bureaucratically and militarily. Bounded by low hills – with higher eminences, such as Headington Hill, to the east – it sits at the foot of the Midlands and has historically been a gateway and river connection to the Cotswolds and its riches. Indeed, despite being within easy reach of London, the city habitually looks westwards – not least for quarried stone, architectural style and artisanal skill. The West Country cathedral masons who were often employed in Oxford persisted in the old ways of building even into the 18th and 19th centuries (as described in *Jude the Obscure* by Thomas Hardy, who worked as a mason in Oxford for a period). Perhaps this accounts in part for the Oxford Gothic look which is the house style of the colleges.

The River Thames, known as Isis in Oxford, snakes across the southern part of the city, joined by the tentacular tributaries, running roughly north to south, which are collectively known as the River Cherwell (the place to punt); and by the less significant Trill Mill Stream, which runs past Christ Church. There is also the canal, and various other mill streams. Oxford is thus a watery city, surrounded by flood plains and water meadows, notably the ancient Port Meadow and Christ Church Meadow, arguably the most important ecological sites in Oxford. There are a number of other less significant flooding meadows in the vicinity of the centre of Oxford; these have historically presented limited potential for building and have been accorded low value, with the result that plots of land were left vacant which would later be semi-drained and exploited as garden space by several of the colleges. (Worcester, Lady Margaret Hall and St Catherine's are the best examples of such appropriation.) The watery theme is inherited by the soil near the watercourses, where it can become saturated and claggy. There is clay in some parts (Headington and Summertown, for example) but most of city-centre college gardens are founded on quite good alluvial soil, mixed with gravel in some places. (In the University Parks, for example, there is about 45 centimetres/18 inches of topsoil before it dissolves into gravel.) The climate is what one would expect of the South Midlands and eastern Cotswolds, though it is slightly warmer, with less snow falling. Many of the colleges harbour a form of microclimate

in their gardens because of the shelter provided by high walls and buildings.

The city centre that emerged through the medieval period is quartered around the crossroads known as Carfax, with the High Street running eastwards, and Cornmarket and St Aldate's (formerly Fish Street) north to south. The university first began to take shape in the medieval streets just north of the High, notably School Street, which was knocked down in the 18th century to create Radcliffe Square and the Radcliffe Camera (library). A number of colleges still cluster tightly here, including the aforementioned Jesus, Lincoln, Brasenose and Exeter, as well as All Souls and Hertford on the other side of Radcliffe Square and, across the High Street, 13th-century University College, the oldest of them all. Queen's and St Edmund Hall pop up further east along the High, with Magdalen at the far end by its bridge, and St Hilda's just across the river. North of the High, and parallel with it, is Broad Street, with Balliol and Trinity, and Wadham just around the corner, while St John's dominates St Giles' to the north. Many of the 19th- and 20th-century collegiate foundations – including Somerville, Lady Margaret Hall, St Anne's, Wolfson, Green Templeton and St Hugh's – can be found off the Banbury and Woodstock Roads which shoot away through Victorian Gothic North Oxford, while red-brick Keble is opposite the University Parks a little way to the east. Ancient New College occupies its own territory down the winding New College Lane, east of Broad Street, with modernist St Catherine's a little way north. Noble Christ Church dominates the city south of Carfax, with Corpus Christi, Oriel and Merton to the east, and only lonely Pembroke to its west.

What is now the western part of the city centre was Oxford's earliest focus, with the castle of 1071 on its mound (only the latter survives), the prison and the appurtenances of local government ranged around. This was and is a fairly grim part of town – the gallows here were the scene of 52 public executions in the second half of the 18th century, and the ruins of Beaumont Palace, birthplace of King Richard I and his brother King John, north of what is now Beaumont Street, lent the area a dilapidated and unkempt air. In the 19th century, the canal and then the railway and bus station were allowed to intrude into this sector, as the city's least-loved quarter. Even today this part of Oxford has a somewhat fluid, transient and uncertain atmosphere that is intensified by a one-way traffic system which must be negotiated by visitors who arrive by rail and progress on foot. Of the university, only Worcester, Nuffield and the Saïd Business School have managed to carve out their own spaces here, with St Peter's gridlocked within the modern shopping precincts around St Ebbe's.

From a garden perspective, this is an interesting part of the city as a large chunk of it – formerly the site of the monastery of the Greyfriars in the south-west of the city – became the site of Paradise Gardens, a nursery, inn and attached riverside 'pleasure garden' that thrived during the 18th century when it was known for the quality and abundance of its fruit, which could be enjoyed on a sort of pick-your-own basis. Paradise Gardens appears to have eclipsed the rather shabby Botanic Garden in popularity at this time, though it is almost forgotten today, its site recalled in the name of Paradise Square, which is alas not paradisical at all. It was the particular resort of college fellows (lecturers), who apparently enjoyed the privacy afforded by at least 40 little hedged private garden compartments visible on contemporary maps. It is possible that this particular paradise was not eminently respectable at all times of day or night, given that – right up until the mid 19th century – Oxford's 'bachelor fellows' were compelled to remain unmarried and in theory celibate. The city's more wooded gardens and walks sometimes doubled as de facto red-light areas for fellows and scholars – known haunts at different times were the walks around Christ Church Meadow, Trinity's Wilderness and the Groves of Merton and St John's.

Visitors arriving by coach (both horse-drawn and motorised) would come in to Oxford by descending Headington Hill and crossing Magdalen Bridge – commonly considered the most attractive way to approach the city. The southern part of Oxford around Folly Bridge was always a bit of a backwater (literally, given the number of watercourses and bridges here) while the wide boulevard of St Giles' to the north feels more like an exit than an entrance, somehow – a strangely undynamic zone with its own charms, as described in the *Universal British Directory* of 1791: 'St. Giles's; which is a street of extraordinary

breadth; and, from the trees left before St. John's college, and those in the front of the church, has the appearance of an elegant village.' Of all Oxford's thoroughfares, St Giles' still looks most like it did in the late 18th century.

The eastern approach to Oxford, across Magdalen Bridge, has the other great advantage of presenting the High Street in its best light. 'One of the world's great streets. It has everything. It is on a slight curve so the vistas always change.' So wrote the architectural critic Nikolaus Pevsner in 1974. The secret of its success does indeed lie in the way it curves as it progresses, a veritable Burkean 'line of beauty' in an urban context. The natural elegance of the High is further enhanced by the presence along the way of one or two apparently strategically placed trees – a sycamore and a flowering cherry notably, the former almost certainly there completely by accident as a most salubrious 'weed tree'. The attractiveness of Oxford's streetscape is one of the joys of the city – not just the evocative spires and towers, but the set-piece compositions like the Sheldonian Theatre and Bodleian Library, and the landscape settings of buildings including the Radcliffe Camera and the Observatory (now part of Green Templeton College). As an undergraduate at Oxford, I remember being delighted afresh almost every day as some new perspective opened up, or as the light shone in a new way on a familiar scene. Such beauties add a spring to the step.

As a county town and marketplace, Oxford has always been an intermittently busy urban hub, but from the 19th century it became a centre of light industry, too, with Morris Motors and the Cowley car works providing much employment. Even today, visitors are often surprised by how city-like the centre of Oxford is. It can create the impression that the scholars of the university are hidden away in their colleges, avoiding the hubbub, while normal life continues apace outside. It's a caricature, but not entirely without foundation. Oxford's industrial aspect has also led to a more even balance between 'town' and 'gown' than in some cities (or a more intense stand-off, depending on how you look at it).

Why do the colleges look fortified? The instinct in Oxford has always been to enclose and to make private by means of a quasi-militaristic architecture founded on high walls and imposing gatehouses. It is as if the siege mentality inspired by the overbearing presence of the castle was somehow extended across the city from an early date. Until the mid 18th century, Oxford's walls and its compass-point gateways remained the defining features of the city's plan. A 1702 coloured map by Peter Schenk presents it as essentially a walled medieval city even at this date, packed with churches and chapels but dominated by the castle and city walls. Those colleges situated outside the walls – including Balliol, St John's, Trinity and Wadham – look distinctly vulnerable to attack in this context; the battlements appear to be a sensible precaution. Several colleges in the south and east of the city – Merton, Corpus Christi, New College and Pembroke – incorporated parts of the old city wall into their boundaries, as if each college was its own little castle (quite an apt metaphor in many ways). The siege mentality of the colleges proved to be quite canny, because Oxford – as Charles I's headquarters out of London – was attacked and besieged during the English Civil War at different times between 1644 and 1646, when Magdalen Tower served as a lookout and the colleges' 'mock' fortifications were put to practical use: artillery pieces on Merton's terrace walk, for example, and an embankment dug in Wadham's garden. (It was all to no avail: the Parliamentarian General Fairfax marched into Oxford on June 25, 1646.) Another reason for the fortification of the colleges is the historic enmity between townspeople and students, which in the medieval period spilled over into full-blown riots and lynchings of students on several occasions. The worst riots occurred in 1209 and purportedly sparked an exodus of students who started a new university in a quiet town in East Anglia. A college was a refuge for those escaping the marauding mobs of drunken 'townies' – indeed the name of Oxford's oldest quadrangle, Mob Quad at Merton, is thought to be derived from its historic role as a sanctuary. Merton was in fact the first college to add crenellations to its tower, in 1418, as if to ward off intruders of all stripes.

The obsessive culture of enclosure has also incidentally led to one of the most attractive qualities of Oxford's college gardens – the way that many of them come as a complete surprise. A door is opened and a 'secret' garden is revealed. As the poet and ardent lover of Oxford John Betjeman

commented, 'In Oxford the smallest entrances give on to the greatest wonders.'

The halls from which the colleges sprang

The variety of Oxford's college gardens entirely depends, then, on the existence of physically independent colleges that have developed in different ways and at different times. The college system grew out of the tradition of 'academical halls', which were essentially lodging houses for students dotted across the city. These halls – and there were between 200 and 300 of them by the mid 15th century – formed the wellspring out of which the colleges of the university emerged. As shall be seen, a number of colleges were built over or expanded into land formerly occupied by up to a dozen of these smaller halls. In most cases the old and often dilapidated halls were simply demolished to make way. The main differences between halls and colleges were the financial independence of the latter (due to a necessary endowment), the existence of a teaching body (the fellows), size (they tended to be larger), status (they often had aristocratic, religious or even royal backing), and physical character (a hall, chapel, library, garden and master's lodgings were the aspiration). It was the endowment that made the real difference, since it gave the college a sense of stability and its own land to build on. The term 'college' started to be used generally to describe such institutions in the first decades of the 14th century, after the foundation of Oriel.

According to the most recent multi-volume official history of the university, the first sign of scholastic activity in Oxford was the appearance of a schoolmaster who taught boys of school age in the period between about 1095 and 1125. The custom of educating boys as young as 13 or 14 continued through the medieval period and beyond – there were instances of boys of that age entering the university even in the 19th century. Teachers of law joined the schoolmasters, attracting slightly older scholars and those from further afield, and eventually theology and the liberal arts supplanted law as the main subjects being taught. It is estimated that by the early 13th century there were some 200 to 300 students being taught by scores of masters in the city, all of them living in small groups in townhouses rented out on an annual basis as hostels for students. It became the norm for the master in charge to live with his students in a hostel as 'principal'; he was responsible for the payment of rents and the general upkeep of the building, and in some cases its yard or garden. (The first record of this kind of set-up dates to 1245, when a principal lived with five students, all sharing expenses.) As customs became engrained and their status rose, these hostels began to be styled as 'halls', where youthful exuberance would be tempered by discipline and education, along the lines of a great house or monastery. The principals soon began to work together as a corporation, not least because they needed to control the level of rents being set by the freeholders of the halls, and by 1216 had elected their first leader: the chancellor. In 1230 a statute was enacted demanding that each student should matriculate (formally enter) this corporation, or *universitas*, under an approved master. (Matriculation remains an important ritual for Oxford students, though its statutory significance is generally lost on 'freshers'.) By the mid 13th century, several halls in the High Street had become established as locations for lectures, which were open to students from any of the approved halls. So while it is difficult to come up with a convincing start date, this period – the first three decades of the 13th century – certainly marked the beginnings of Oxford University as a recognisable educational institution.

There was a rich array of academical halls in Oxford from the 13th to the 15th centuries. A hall or lodging could be called an *aula* (hall), *hospicium* (inn or hostel), *domus* (house) or *introitus* (entry), the last the smallest of all – there were only half a dozen 'entries' in Oxford, squirrelled away down passages. A hall would typically lodge between five and 20 young men, either of schoolboy age or older graduates (in some places a mix), with a large communal room serving as the 'hall' itself, and studies and shared bedrooms adjoining and upstairs. The better sorts of building were often owned by the monastic houses, while many of the smaller halls were owned and let by townspeople. Several halls were named after owners of the property – Moyses Hall near Carfax and Jacob's Hall were owned by two generations of the same family. A handful of halls were named after the wealthy student who was

able simply to buy up or rent a whole house: James of Spain at Le Oriole, for example, or William Burnell at Burnell's Inn. Others took their name from a distinguishing architectural feature (Glazen Hall), location (Corner Hall) or physical emblem (Brasenose Hall, named after a door knocker). The names of these vanished halls are spectacularly various: there was an Ape Hall, Sparrow Hall, Mutton Hall, Perilous Hall and a Pill Hall. Some 'halls' had no role in lodging students and were basically pubs: the superlatively named Cabbage Hall and Caterpillar Hall, popular watering holes on the way up Headington Hill, are examples of this. To add to the complexity, halls were often renamed or merged with others over the years, and it is difficult to keep track.

Several of the halls were named in honour of saints, because a good proportion were owned by religious houses such as Osney Abbey, the Augustinian St Frideswide's Priory (which became the foundation for Christ Church) and the Hospital of St John the Baptist (later absorbed into Magdalen). Worcester and Trinity Colleges both grew out of halls owned and maintained by the Benedictines (Gloucester Hall and Durham Hall), while Christ Church itself was partly built across the old Canterbury Hall. St Mary Hall, now a part of Oriel, was affiliated to St Mary's Church on the High Street and was one of the few academical halls to survive into the 18th century; it was unusual in that it boasted a chapel. A handful of other academical halls possessed amenities such as a library – Hart Hall, later the site of Hertford College, was one – or a chapel, as at New Inn Hall, a large house and garden which survived into the 18th century and is still remembered in the Oxford streetscape through New Inn Hall Street. (St Peter's College was later established on its site.) Several of the older and bigger halls were known as 'inns', a reflection of the earliest usage of this term, as a lodgings or hostel, before it came to mean simply a large tavern with rooms for the night and usually stabling. Tackley's Inn, for example, was founded in the 1320s and is today a named part of Oriel, housing students at 106–107 High Street, while Peckwater Inn consisted of buildings forming a courtyard that became the site of the quad of the same name in Christ Church. The inns would originally have been modelled on the example of the Inns of Court in

London, which housed lawyers – and in Oxford too it seems they were generally the lodgings of law students or 'legists'. But the halls which were not 'inns' could be substantially sized, as well – perhaps 30 to 50 of them consisted of more than one building and the majority of halls had a garden or yard. The largest of the halls – such as Deep Hall (now part of Lincoln) and St Alban Hall (later subsumed into Merton) – comprised several ranges of buildings set at right angles to each other to form a court, the type of layout which marked the beginnings of the familiar quadrangle typology. In 1381, for example, one Bartholomew Bishop constructed White Hall on the High Street, with a hall, buttery (servery), kitchen and several chambers arranged around three sides of a courtyard. This ground plan was well established in the case of larger houses or inns in London and other medieval cities. It is clear that some of the academical halls in the 13th to 15th centuries were already halfway to resembling an Oxford college as we know them today. Perhaps the grand example of the livery halls of London proved to be a spur, since several were built around courtyards and some, including Carpenters' Hall and Drapers' Hall, had gardens.

The halls had their heyday in the 1300s and 1400s but afterwards gradually fell away as the colleges came into being; they were also vulnerable to closure following drops in student numbers after bouts of the plague in the city. By the early 18th century there were only seven halls left in existence in their own right in Oxford – though a number were retained in some form as part of the fabric of a college. The last remaining independent academical halls of Oxford were St Alban Hall (now Merton), St Mary Hall (Oriel), New Inn Hall (Balliol), Magdalen Hall (Hertford) and St Edmund Hall (formerly an annexe of Queen's and today the only old academical hall to have achieved college status). *The Gentleman and Lady's Pocket Companion for Oxford* (1747) was quite generous towards the surviving halls even as they waned in influence and popularity: 'These Halls are generally small, and have little to be admired in their Architecture; but the students live in them like Gentlemen in a private Family: There is not so much of that Submission and Ceremony observed as in Houses that are incorporated.'

The tradition of colleges attracting students from specific regions was also established by the halls. This probably arose naturally from the fact that students who travelled to Oxford from the same locality wished to lodge together. Some halls had a reputation as a haven for 'northerners' and some for 'southerners'. Irish law students in the mid 15th century went to Aristotle Hall, Heron Hall, Vine Hall and Coventry Hall, while Welshmen went to St Edward Hall. It transpired that in several cases these geographical ties were inherited by the college that superseded the hall – at Trinity, for example, which as Durham Hall had taken students from the north of England and continued to do so – and the custom has not wholly expired even today: Jesus is still known as the Welsh college, and many colleges offer scholarships to students from specific counties as a residue of this tradition.

The quadrangle: cloister meets city court

The academical halls are important in the history of the Oxford college gardens because the layout of the colleges was influenced by their structure and organisation. It is almost a truism to say that the Oxford college quadrangle was inspired by the form of the monastic cloister, and there are indeed undeniable similarities between colleges and monasteries in terms of ground plan, scale and key buildings. But the cloister tradition is only part of the story. The architectural layout of many of the academical halls was closely related to that of the city court – that is, an area enclosed by buildings which was separated and hidden from the street by the narrow street-side house frontages, but which was still linked to the life of the city via a passageway or entry. (These are the places made notorious as rookeries in the 19th century, painted so vividly by Charles Dickens in *Oliver Twist*.) The college quadrangle was designed to reflect and exploit both the contemplative calm of the cloister and the sociability and busyness of the city courtyard. That does after all seem to capture something of the historic essence of college life, caught as it was between

The recently replanted Merton Borders at the Oxford Botanic Garden, featuring eryngiums, rudbeckias and the tall grass *Stipa gigantea*.

the secular and the spiritual. The entrance lodge or gatehouse can be seen as the equivalent of the 'entry' passage that connects the private to the public realm. And the habit of siting the most important building – the hall in most cases – away from the street and usually raised above ground level had emerged by the mid 13th century, in the typology of the city courtyard house.

It is possible to see these courts, formed by clusters of halls and other buildings, on early maps of Oxford such as Ralph Agas's of 1578 and Wenceslaus Hollar's of 1643. The latter clearly shows Broadgates Hall, which had by this time become part of Pembroke College, with a semi-courtyard design, while halls such as Peckwater Inn and St Mary Hall also naturally developed in this manner. Studying the maps, it can be appreciated that many of the academical halls looked into an open court or across a yard or garden, which was effectively shared space. (It was exactly the same in London, where halls such as Barnard's Inn, Staple Inn and Furnival's Inn, around Holborn, all formed courtyards.) There are a number of 18th-century *Oxford Almanack* engravings based on old drawings of halls; these include images of Great Lion Hall and St George's Hall, both of which bear a resemblance to college design, especially the latter, with its two-storied ranges set in an angle and a variety of doors leading to individual staircases. Perhaps it was this kind of arrangement that led to the staircase system of the Oxford quadrangle, which is arranged vertically not horizontally, so that students and fellows must go outside via the quadrangle itself to visit another staircase. This system helps to make the quadrangle an inherently social space – if not hyperactively so, during term time.

Most quadrangles went up in piecemeal fashion, and this has led to the variety in shape and scale one sees across the college quads. The Oxford quadrangle is perhaps the best example of the benefit of failure-to-complete in an architectural context. There are numerous examples of quads remaining unfinished (Magdalen's New Buildings, for example) or of partial rebuildings of specific areas and blatant new additions in the midst of antiquity (Exeter's 19th-century chapel springs to mind). Rather than being horrified at an unholy mishmash of architectural styles jammed together incongruously, the reality is that the users of the space are continually delighted and intrigued by the clear evidence of historical development – or of simple happenstance – in the college, as a place of antiquity with a rich history of human interaction. (Worcester's Main Quad, where Georgian ranges converse with medieval 'cottages', is perhaps the best example of this.) One sees the same pleasing hybridity in the principal streets of Britain's older market towns, where a sturdy Palladian parsonage might appear to be holding up a rickety half-timbered inn, like a vicar with an incorrigible old drunk.

Gardens and quadrangles

Early maps of Oxford show that the city was filled with green space. Substantial gardens persisted in the very centre of Oxford right up until the early 19th century. (One 18th-century engraving of the area around the new Radcliffe Square shows what looks to be a small cornfield almost in the shadow of the Radcliffe Camera.) In a number of cases there was evidently a productive garden attached to a medieval academical hall. The principal was essentially subletting rooms and providing board as well as an education, so an element of self-sufficiency would have made economic sense. The importance of a garden to many of the early halls is reflected in the 'Aularian Statutes' laid down in the late 15th century as a means of setting academic standards for the halls and maintaining discipline. The statutes specified a fine of 2d for any student who did not help maintain the hall and its garden on the days specified by its principal. It appears likely that these gardens were also used for leisure, with a seat placed in the corner of the vegetable garden, perhaps, or under a fruit tree. (We have no hard evidence for this in the case of the halls, but it was certainly true at several of the colleges, such as Lincoln, early on.) The halls – later colleges – with monastic links tended to have the largest and best gardens; St John's, Trinity, Christ Church, Magdalen and Worcester all fall into this category. This is because they were often situated outside the city walls, where more land was available. There may also have been the influence of the monastic gardening tradition at work, both as a means of self-sufficiency and as a celebration of God's bounty.

OVERLEAF Alliums by the lawn that stretches out in front of the New Buildings at Magdalen College.

A garden was not merely a yard providing vegetables for the table and herbs for the infirmary; it was an appurtenance appropriate to a house blessed by God. Gardening itself was an activity redolent of the innocence of humankind before the Fall, and devotion to it signalled devotion to God.

Most colleges consist of one, two or three quadrangles, the front quadrangle often the oldest and slightly smaller. The transition from quad to quad is one of the greatest joys of Oxford's college gardens for visitors, because one never knows what is coming next; it could just as easily be a tiny medieval courtyard or a spreading lawn overlooked by a splendid Palladian range. The semi-darkness of the passageways which link the quads lends an element of suspense, while the movement from gloom into light only emphasises the sense of surprise (and therefore delight). The experience of movement through the college, its own particular rhythm, is key to our understanding of its character.

The front quad of an Oxford college was never conceived of as a 'garden' and was generally unadorned – either left as mud, partially covered in gravel or hoggin, and at a later date in nearly all cases grassed over in one piece or as quadrants or halves bisected by paths. At most colleges, the front quad is perceived as a 'walking quad', where the grass is off limits, while the second (and in some cases a third) quad is in many cases more of a 'sitting quad'. The idea that the quadrangles were once highly decorated spaces replete with features such as knot gardens is erroneous; only Brasenose ever had anything like that level of decorative horticulture in its front quad, and only a handful of others attempted serious gardening in a second quad (All Souls, for example, may have had an orchard – see page 28). In nearly all cases, decorative horticulture was pursued in the fellows' and master's gardens. If there was any space at all, a separate garden would be made within the college bounds, ostensibly for the fellows. In addition, wherever possible the master would have his own garden. If possible, a college would make three enclosed and discrete garden areas – for master, fellows and undergraduates – all walled off from each other. (Pembroke had the clearest example of a compartmented garden – see page 189). This can be seen as partly a reflection of the university's habitual

and timeless preoccupation with academic rank. In some cases (at Trinity and St John's, for example) the fellows' garden was at first out of bounds to all except the fellows, who were given keys, though at most colleges, over time, all members of the college community roved around the college precincts in a fairly unfettered way. It was not until the late 19th century that some colleges reintroduced the concept of privacy, and locked gates became the norm again. This kind of hierarchical privilege is reflected in the habit that persists in several colleges of allowing only fellows to walk across the grass of the quadrangle.

Masters' gardens are often private in practice – the most secret of Oxford's secret gardens – because in many cases the only way into them is via the master's lodgings. They have traditionally been set apart because for many centuries the master of a college was the only man on site permitted to marry and have children, and the family was deemed to deserve its own space (especially if the principal had daughters). There are some fairly spectacular examples of hidden master's gardens in Oxford, most of them left mysteriously blank and unlabelled on the online virtual tour of Oxford created by the Chemistry Department, which is otherwise fairly comprehensive. At Wadham, for example, the warden enjoys a huge garden, even bigger than the area the public has access to, while at Exeter the Rector's Garden is a mirror image of the fellows' garden on the other side of the chapel. The Deanery Garden at Christ Church – always haunted by Lewis Carroll's Alice – is another substantial garden completely hidden from the public eye (it is behind the library) while the Warden's Garden at New College can only be reached via a bridge across New College Lane. The unconnected member of the public has virtually no chance of getting in to see any of these college principals' gardens, though one consolation is that they can rarely be described as the best or most interesting garden element at a college.

In the very earliest days of the first colleges, it appears the garden was considered a productive space, but quite rapidly the emphasis switched to the pleasure and quietude

it could provide. Several colleges built little pavilions for the students which functioned as outdoor common rooms, while the flowers and fruit of the garden would provide succour and respite from the smells and degradation of the city beyond the walls – the college garden as a nosegay of sorts. A college garden was and still is particularly highly valued on warm summer evenings after dinner in hall, when fellows and students could wander around the paths and terraces to continue their conversations or subdue their animadversions. One foreign visitor, Paul Hentzner, described in 1598 how, 'after each meal, every one is at liberty, either to retire to his own chambers, or to walk in the college garden, there being none that has not a delightful one.' This tradition has waned somewhat now that hardly any fellows live in college or habitually dine in hall in the evening; lunchtime is instead the main social meal of the day, with work and appointments following. This is perhaps one of the reasons why private fellows' gardens appear to be barely used nowadays.

There was formerly much more emphasis on the desirability of exercise in the colleges. Until the mid 20th century Oxford students were encouraged to spend their afternoons out of doors, playing sports, rowing on the river or simply walking in the gardens and groves of the colleges, in Christ Church Meadow, the Botanic Garden, or ranging further afield up Headington Hill or along Magdalen's water walks. The poet Robert Southey provides a good picture of this in his 1809 description of Christ Church Meadow: 'The winding walk was planted with trees well disposed in groups, and all flourishing in a genial soil and climate: some poplars among them are of remarkable growth. Here the students were seen in great numbers; some with flowing gowns, others having them rolled up behind, others again with the folds gathered up and flung loosely over the arm.' Southey also confirms the extraordinary fact that 'gentleman commoners' (usually of the nobility) were distinguishable by the golden tassels hanging from their mortar boards (hats). Walking in the college garden played a particularly large part in the lives of the women students of Oxford University, especially in the period when college rules dictated that female undergraduates could not wander about

the city and university unchaperoned. For many, the easiest option was simply staying within the bounds of the college.

Ball games were (and are) generally banned in the quadrangles, but from the 15th century several colleges had indoor or outdoor ball courts (*sphaeristeria*) where young men were able to burn off their excess energies. The ball games played here were variants on tennis, handball and fives. By the turn of the 18th century these courts had become antiquated and in many cases were replaced by more fashionable bowling greens, which called for far less exertion and may have encouraged gambling. (Joseph Addison penned a revealing poem about the game – he was at Magdalen, where there was a huge bowling green in the Grove.) New College had one of the nicest bowling greens, tucked away under the trees to the side of the Mount, while Lincoln, Pembroke and Queen's also squeezed them in. The bowling green was incidentally the area where the gardeners could show off their skills with sward, traditionally one of the great strengths of English gardening, admired across Europe from the 17th century onwards, where 'English' broderie (patterns) in parterre design consisted of figures cut in turf. These skills were transferred to the grassed college quadrangles from the 19th century. Today, croquet is the main pastime tolerated on the college lawns, though strict rules about it are often laid down by the college deans. Lewis Carroll (Charles Dodgson) at Christ Church was so amused by the seriousness of croquet players that he even published a set of spoof rules.

College gardens have also been put to good use as venues for plays, and there have been several significant theatrical productions at different colleges over the years. (Worcester's lakeside setting has been used repeatedly, for example.) Almost as theatrical is the role played by the garden during college balls. These occasions take on the character of *fêtes champêtres*, with many guests looking at the college garden with new eyes as rosé-tinted dawn rises on the scene of a celebratory bacchanal.

Grass, gravel, groves and decrepitude

The front quad of a college is of course the first impression visitors have of the place, so perhaps it is surprising that for many centuries these were generally left more or less unadorned, and in some places allowed to grow rather unkempt. An 1822 album of engraved views of the colleges shows Jesus's front quad as a mix of rough grass and mud, with some desultory, weed-like shrubs growing against the wall. This is also the impression one gets from early photographs of college quadrangles taken around the turn of the 20th century, where weeds might be growing in the corners or up through paving stones. It is difficult to come to firm conclusions because the documentary evidence is scant, but maps and engravings up to the mid 18th century imply that the surface of the typical quadrangle consisted of compacted mud, perhaps bulked up by hoggin, with gravel pathways cutting across or around it. To judge by the state of the roads until they were paved in the late 18th century, mud was a near-constant fact of life in Oxford. Views of Worcester College, for example, do not shy away from depicting the road in front of it as a mudbath, and Carfax was another notoriously churned-up spot. To combat the quagmire effect, it is likely that colleges started to lay down gravel or paved paths in their quadrangles from an early period, with paving reserved for the newer parts of the college. The gravel needed refreshing every year according to references in the Jesus College accounts from the 1660s onwards (see that chapter for a little more detail). In some cases paving with panels of pebbles was laid across the whole quad – as at Corpus Christi's front quad, which still takes this form today. But it seems this paving was not always laid with elegance of appearance in mind. The author of *The Gentleman and Lady's Pocket Companion for Oxford* (1747), the first guidebook to the city, was not impressed by the quality of the aggregates at Christ Church, and labels Great (Tom) Quad inelegant because 'There are indeed spacious Gravel Walks on every Side; but the rest of the Court is sunk four Feet beneath the Level of the Walks, having Paths, pitch'd with common Pebbles, cross it.' Paths and terrace walks in the fellows' gardens would generally have been gravelled rather than paved.

Grass began to appear in college quads relatively late on. It was probably first essayed at New College in 1789. Most of the college quads were grassed over during the course of the

19th century. As ever at Oxford, however, each college does things in its own way and in its own time, and several did not lay grass in their front quads until the early 20th century.

There were grassy areas within colleges from an early date, but these were sited away from the formal quadrangles, in the fellows' and master's gardens. I shall not attempt to generalise about these gardens here because they were and remain spectacularly diverse, and are covered in detail in individual chapters. Some of the colleges with the largest gardens chose to introduce tree-lined walks into their demesnes, and even a grove-like atmosphere. The definition is a little fluid, but a grove in the garden-history lexicon refers to an attractively wooded area, either natural or planted. A grove is not as dense as natural forest or woodland and therefore more enjoyable to walk around. (A glade, on the other hand, is smaller and generally includes the idea of a semi-formal clearing at its centre.) A grove was seen as a desirable aspiration within the academic milieu of the university because of its reputation as a place of learning in the classical world. Plato's Academy was an outdoor school which contained a sacred olive grove dedicated to Athena, as was Aristotle's Lyceum which was modelled upon it. Other philosophers – notably Epicurus – taught in garden or grove-like settings. So a grove was thought to be a fitting retreat for the thoughtful scholar – the idea of 'seeking the truth in the groves of academe', a translation of a line in Horace's *Epistles* which became current in the mid 18th century. Magdalen, St John's, Trinity and Merton all laid claim to a grove, which came to mean any part of a college garden large enough to be dignified by trees. Sections of the gardens at Wadham, All Souls and Oriel also took on a grove-like aspect, while later Worcester (18th century) and Lady Margaret Hall and St Hugh's (19th century) continued the tradition in different ways. There is no doubt that a grove has since the 16th century at least been something of a status symbol among the Oxford colleges.

The decrepitude mentioned earlier became positively fashionable in Oxford in the mid 19th century and it remained the norm for colleges right up until the late 20th century. The American novelist Nathaniel Hawthorne positively revelled in it in his *English Notebooks* (1870):

How ancient is the aspect of these college quadrangles! so gnawed by time, as they are, so crumbly, so blackened, and so grey where they are not black, – so quaintly shaped, too, with here a line of battlement and there a row of gables; and here a turret, with probably a winding stair inside; and lattice windows, with stone mullions, and little panes of glass set in lead; and the cloisters, with a long arcade, looking upon the green or pebbled enclosure.

Hawthorne notes how the Cotswold stone walls of the colleges might actually crumble away when touched. This often resulted from unsuitable stone being used in the first place, though ivy has often been blamed. Indeed, the whole question of climbing plants in college quadrangles is somewhat controversial, and fashion has ebbed and flowed. There is some evidence that climbers were allowed to smother buildings from quite an early date; one guidebook of 1748 notes how the walls of Trinity College are clothed in evergreens, 'as those in other College Gardens generally are'. By around 1900 the average Oxford quad was almost completely smothered with ivy, a look which was by no means universally popular. Mavis Batey in *Oxford Gardens* (1983) relates the saga of the ivy on Magdalen's tower. A proposal in 1892 to remove the ivy was opposed until 1908, when the scientific arguments put forward by the professors of botany and physiology finally carried the day. Another influence may have been the discovery that the ivy's roots had broken into the wine cellar and its store of vintage port.

As of the time of writing, the vast majority of college quads have been stripped of ivy and Virginia creeper in order to present a 'clean', more modern and polished aspect, perhaps in keeping with the image the university as a whole wishes to present. Only Lincoln College doggedly persists with its creeper-clad quadrangles – and long may it do so, for variety and idiosyncrasy are key to the delight of Oxford's college gardens.

The college gardeners

Gardeners are a near-constant presence in the colleges, where most of their work is done in full view of the master, fellows and students. There survives a delightful historical record of this in the form of an unpublished and uncatalogued series of watercolours tucked away in a volume in the British Library, which probably dates from the second half of the 18th century. Nearly all of these views of the college gardens show the gardeners in action, with their tools (typically a scythe or lawn-roller) strewn around. At Balliol the gardener is chatting with scholars in front quad, while in the view of Magdalen a pair of gardeners are using a ladder to tend climbing shrubs by the old gatehouse.

Today there is not always a great deal of interaction between the college gardeners and the rest of the college (gardeners are often quiet types). A head gardener has nothing like the impact of a head porter on the life of the average student. When the bursar of University College asked one long-serving porter what he thought his duties encompassed, the response was: 'My jobs stretch from cutting a bloke down who's hung his bloody self to finding a safety pin for a lady's elastic knickers that's fallen down.' Who can compete with that? But there are occasional instances of students offering to help with the gardening, and at Worcester for example there is a system where the 'punishment' for certain misdemeanours is garden work.

There is evidence that students value highly the quality of the college gardens, however. On websites and other guides designed for prospective students, both the formal entries and the webchat advice tend to rate friendliness and inclusiveness as the most telling aspect of a college, with quality of accommodation and the appeal of the garden next in importance. (Academic matters barely figure.)

The college gardens today are each run along highly individualistic lines. In most cases a college fellow is deputed as 'garden master' or some similar appellation (at St John's this post is Keeper of the Groves) and their level of influence and intervention varies considerably. The basic responsibility of the garden master is one of financial oversight and the justification of expenditure, though in some cases the academic involved seeks to make other changes, whatever the level of their expertise or experience. At one college, I came across a curiously planted herbaceous bed where the front was all pink flowers and the back was all blue. I was told it was because one garden master liked pink while their successor liked blue. (I felt a little like Alice at this point.) There are cases where the garden master works creatively and respectfully with the gardeners, however.

Garden maintenance at some colleges has been outsourced to the University Parks team (see page 315) but the majority of colleges still employ a head gardener and at least one under-gardener. The larger college gardens might have a team of six to eight, though Wadham for example has until recently had just two gardeners – who between them have worked at the college for more than 80 years. Pembroke and Corpus Christi have head gardeners who prefer to work alone. Most of the Oxford college head gardeners now meet informally once a term, always in a different garden, and compare notes. There is some friendly rivalry but the emphasis seems to be on the friendliness, with head gardeners helping each other out in different ways and also making gifts of special plants or recommending new members of staff to each other.

One of the skills particularly prized in Oxford, for obvious reasons, is lawn care, and a term one hears used by Oxford gardeners is 'quad man' – that is, someone who specialises in turf in the quads. ('Man' is appropriate because it is still the case that nearly all of Oxford's gardeners are male, though there are currently three female head gardeners.) The 'keep off the grass' sign is something of a running joke in Oxford colleges, though it's no joke to the gardeners who are charged with maintaining the sward in pristine condition at all times of year. Another occasional speciality within the colleges is the cultivation of fruit under glass – especially the grapes and other soft fruit so highly prized at the dessert course traditionally consumed in the senior common room, with port and snuff still doing the rounds in some places. Wadham's ancient vine, for example, continues to yield about 250 bunches of grapes annually, while Worcester presses its own fruit juice from apples and pears in its orchard.

Some other college gardens worthy of note

Not every Oxford college garden is interesting enough or substantial enough to have been afforded a whole chapter in this book, but several others are worth mentioning here. St Cross College is tucked behind a modest frontage on St Giles' but boasts two attractive small quadrangles linked by an arcaded passageway; Front Quad is particularly well proportioned while Back Quad features a gravelled seating area focused on an astrolabe. Harris Manchester College is also worth seeking out, with three well maintained interconnecting lawned quadrangles, the last featuring a scallop-edged fountain set in a formal garden with a cruciform of clipped box hedges. Mansfield College, slightly to the north, features wide-open lawned spaces in front of the main college building and also a lawned garden to the west. There are some nice details to be found in Linacre College, where the new, red-brick-walled Rom Harré Garden adjacent to New College playing fields was added on in 2010, partly by way of recompense for a new accommodation block built over the main college garden – it is focused on a sundial in the form of a book (slightly kitsch) and is nicely planted with a range of shrubs and perennials. Garden interest at St Peter's College is focused on a curved raised bed, just two bricks in height, which arcs in front of the modern accommodation block in its front quad. The feel is meadowy, dominated by pennisetums and other grasses, with some flower colour from pink dahlias and white nicotiana, plus the berries of cotoneaster. But the capital stroke is the placement of a *Rhus typhina* at one end of the bed. St Antony's College has made some chic additions recently in association with its new Gateway Buildings (2013), which have transformed the college facade and entrance. These include a 'front garden' with planting beds and box hedging, and a three-plumed fountain bubbling away above a stainless steel-lined pool by the porter's lodge. Another small 21st-century Oxford garden can be found at the Rothermere American Institute on the South Parks Road, where the Princess Margaret Memorial Garden of 2006 takes the form of a gently terraced sunken garden of lawns, cottage-flower planting beds and a central pool. Finally, it is worth looking in to the Saïd Business School, next door to the railway station, built in 2001. Here, the quadrangle features a wooden pergola with a cloistral

flavour, a number of purple-flowered paulownia (foxglove) trees and, poised above, a 400-seat open-air amphitheatre.

It is customary to end the introductions to garden books with some kind of elaboration on the idea that gardens are constantly changing and that this is something which should be celebrated. The cheerfully unsentimental fatalism of the gardener, who knows that all work will be undone over time, was well expressed by George Harris, head gardener of St

Hugh's, on the occasion of his retirement in 1972 after 45 years of service. 'Harris, the garden will never be the same without you,' some high-up said to him. His reply: 'You can't expect it to be.'

All Souls College

T O OUTSIDERS IT'S JUST another college, sitting there quietly, plum in the middle of the High Street, its door always closed. But inside the world within a world that is Oxford, All Souls is a kind of academic Valhalla. Its official name is the College of All Souls of the Faithful Departed, though it is unlikely that anyone who has just been elected to a prize fellowship there will feel as if they have entered a celestial departure lounge – the chosen ones who gain entrance to these portals will most definitely have 'arrived', at least academically speaking.

This is the college beyond the colleges, available only to Oxford's fabled 'first-rate minds', who are also deemed clubbable enough as dinner companions. The 130 fellows comprise invited star academics, plus a couple of new graduates each year who are hand-picked from a small group who have excelled in their final examinations and are then asked to apply for a prize fellowship which necessitates an exam and interview of fabled toughness. (Only one or two get in, and in some years none.) There are no undergraduates to lower the tone and clog up the quads. It has always been this way, ever since the college was founded in the 1430s by an intellectual Archbishop of Canterbury who had been involved in several other colleges during his career and finally saw the need for what we would now call a graduate college. Everyone at All Souls is engaged in research, even if it is incidentally into the depths of the college's celebrated wine cellar (about which a

North Quad, with the Codrington Library – its sundial reputedly designed by Christopher Wren – and the Grand Dormitory, both the work of Nicholas Hawksmoor.

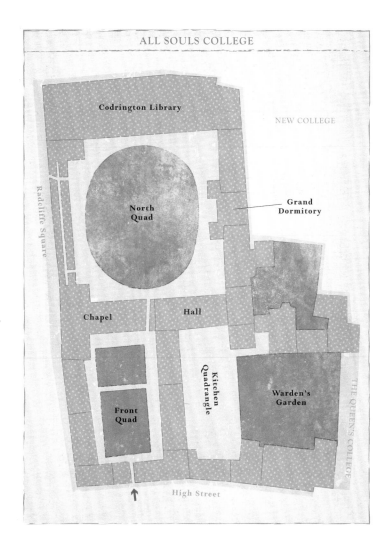

ALL SOULS COLLEGE

Codrington Library

NEW COLLEGE

North Quad

Grand Dormitory

Radcliffe Square

Chapel

Hall

Kitchen Quadrangle

Front Quad

Warden's Garden

THE QUEEN'S COLLEGE

High Street

RIGHT The soaring twin towers of the Grand Dormitory are reputedly the origin of the term 'ivory tower' as a description of academic other-worldliness.

whole book has been written) – for this is a rich institution, to cap it all. The prevailing idea is that the great brains who pace these precincts can think in a pristine and unfettered environment. Indeed, it is said that the term ivory tower was coined to describe All Souls, though in reality the college has always placed a strong emphasis on engagement with the real world, the study of law being one of its traditional strengths. Prize fellows are even allowed to live in London if they wish, as long as they attend a dinner in college hall each weekend during their first year.

It was not always like this; the college slumped, rather, in the 19th century, and even in the 1920s it was 'stuffed with founder's kin, like New College', according to the Cornish historian and long-standing fellow A. L. Rowse, who recalled fellows hacking up from the countryside on horseback to the college. But All Souls eventually roused itself from its port-induced torpor, and its reputation today as a rarefied intellectual hotbed is as strong as it has ever been.

Until recently All Souls was firmly off limits to all but the fellows and their invited guests. That door on the High was not just closed, but locked. Recently, however, the college has opened up to visitors on certain weekday afternoons – a welcome move. Fortunately, in order to gain civilian entrance

to All Souls, one is not required to parse Latin or discourse on incunabula; in fact the porters prove to be among the friendliest and most helpful in the university. As a result visitors are now able to experience one of the most dramatic architectural moments that Oxford has to offer: the transition from Front to North Quadrangle.

Front Quad has little by way of a garden to talk about. It was built more or less all of a piece in the mid 15th century, in classic Oxford-collegiate medieval style. The highlight is the Perpendicular Gothic chapel with its five great windows and tall pinnacles scraping the sky. A pair of immaculate plats of grass offset the buildings beautifully and are in perfect scale with them. There is the usual wisteria (in the chapel bays) and some annuals (often marigolds) planted here and there for colour, but in general the planting at All Souls is more or less irrelevant next to the architectural interest and the way the buildings occupy the space. For without the quadrangle setting, these buildings would be nothing like as effective; they must function cumulatively.

A passage in the top right (north-east) corner of Front Quad tunnels its way past the east end of the chapel. The diffused light becomes brighter and seems to beckon the visitor on. Suddenly one emerges into the most extraordinary vista, one of the most dramatic in all of Oxford, architecturally speaking. This is North Quad, which is about three times the size of Front Quad, a simple enlargement of scale that has a remarkable effect. It also represents an object lesson in how the principle of sudden juxtaposition is key to quadrangle design. Here the effect is enhanced by the fact that All Souls has an empty feel, with so few fellows in residence at any one time. North Quad is also more open in aspect and responds to the architectural extravaganza unfolding around it in the heart of Oxford, including the great spire of the University Church of St Mary the Virgin, which is next door.

Straight ahead is the Codrington Library, designed in 1715 by Nicholas Hawksmoor and one of the university's undisputedly great buildings. Hawksmoor's brief was to work in a Gothic mode in homage to the existing college architecture, especially the chapel. (There may have been a political impulse, too, in that All Souls was a Tory college at

this time, under Warden George Clarke: there was perhaps a desire to avoid the Palladian mode, which was part of the brand identity of the pro-Whig House of Hanover.) The Codrington Library's great procession of tall windows in bays topped by Gothic pinnacles certainly references the chapel's facade, but its sheer scale and magnitude gives it an entirely different air. The sundial which was set atop the middle window in the late 19th century was reputedly designed by Sir Christopher Wren, who was a fellow of All Souls (where his interests were scientific as opposed to architectural).

A huge oval lawn – with mown stripes leading up to the library's bays – unites the other architectural elements of the quad. To the left (west) a modest cloister borders Radcliffe Square, effectively integrating the magnificent dome of James Gibbs's Radcliffe Camera into All Souls' purlieu, while to the right (east) is another remarkable exercise in Gothic-inflected baroque by Hawksmoor, with soaring twin towers that have the thrusting energy of rocket ships. (It is said that these are the original ivory towers.) This building contains the Senior Common Room and accommodation for fellows, and if anything it is even more impressive than Hawksmoor's reworking of the west front of Westminster Abbey, with which it shares some visual kinship. It was given the slightly curious name of Grand Dormitory, which evokes images of academics enjoying pillow fights and midnight feasts in their communal bedrooms. (In fact, fellows at most colleges were expected to share rooms with at least one other colleague well into the 18th century; they were all unmarried, of course.)

Until the mid 18th century North Quad's grass was divided into four rectangles (as depicted in the *Oxford Almanack* of 1728), but in 1765 the great oval lawn was made. As with Front Quad, there is little of floral interest, but the shape of the lawn at its centre decisively affects the tone, for it creates the impression that the ensemble of striking buildings around it, each set apart from the other, have been arranged in a landscape setting. In this sense the central lawn plays a similar role to that of the lake at the great landscape garden of Stourhead, Wiltshire, in the way it lends unity to the scene and cradles its architectural episodes. In its entirety, North Quad makes for a fine example of a quadrangle with a landscape setting. Other examples of attempts at landscape milieux for college buildings at this period in Oxford include New College's Garden Quad and Back Quad at Oriel, where Wyatt's library and a pair of new buildings were also arranged amid continuous greensward, before misguided efforts were made to join up the buildings to create something resembling a traditional enclosed quadrangle.

All Souls is most fortunate in that it possesses a plan called the *Typus Collegii*, or 'view of the college buildings', dated to 1598, which shows how at one time the college had quite extensive gardens. Front Quad was left bare, but the cloistered quadrangle to the north of it – on which North Quad was later built – is illustrated with three stylised trees, while there is a garden farther to the north-east with two elaborate knot gardens. We know that there was an orchard in the earlier college – perhaps it was within the cloister? – and that the garden or a part of it was known as the grove, in typical Oxford fashion. The college rented this land to the north-east up until the early 18th century, when it purchased the site in order to make use of the massive financial bequest bestowed by Christopher Codrington, the All Souls fellow after whom the library is named. The *Typus Collegii* shows one other garden area, and this still survives in a different form. The land to the east of Front Quad was acquired by the college in about 1560 and then built upon under the auspices of Robert Hovenden. This great Warden of All Souls filled out the college account books himself, and his entry pertaining to this reads:

> The Warden's garden was some time the Rose Inn, and being purchased by Sir W. Petre and given ye coll. it lay waste till 1573, when Master R. Hovenden desired the Compy to grant it him and he would enclose it and remove the well which was called Rosewell standg in it (whereof it was said merrily the fellows wash'd every day in Rose water) upon his own charges. The week before Easter 1574 he began to level ye ground, and the whole charge came to £14 2s. 10d, and ye well with ye pump 40s.

It appears Hovenden paid for this garden out of his own pocket; he was careful to itemise the costs out of respect for accounting

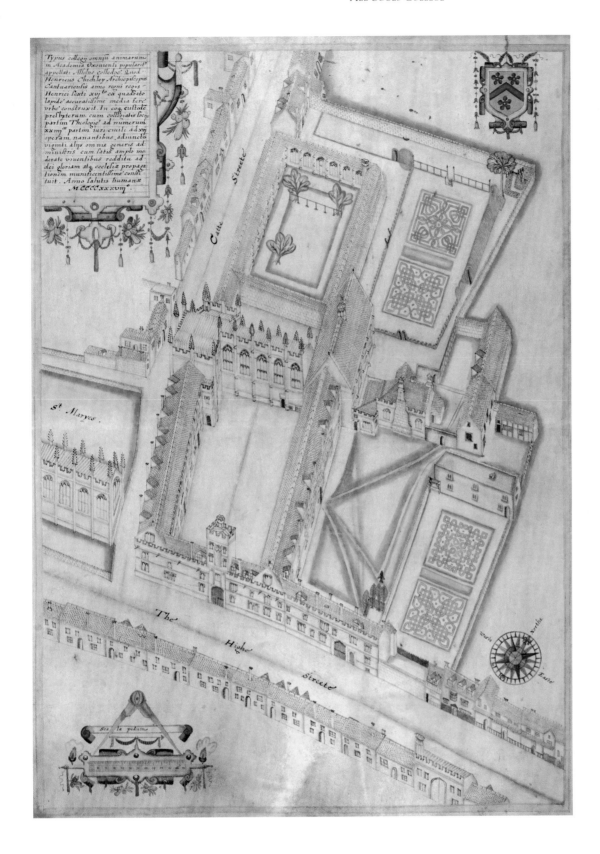

as opposed to memorialising his own generosity. The *Typus Collegii* shows the way this land was divided into roughly equal rectangles and used for two purposes: the western section became a service area traversed by paths, with the aforementioned new water pump (this is now the yard known as Kitchen Quad), while the eastern section was planted out as the Warden's Quadrangle and Garden, overlooked in due course by the new Warden's Lodgings of 1703. The plan shows a pair of knot gardens similar to those in the northern part of the college, though by the time of David Loggan's engraving of 1675 it had become a rectangle of mature trees. The Warden's Garden exists to this day as a lawned space with mature trees, one of the innermost of Oxford University's many inner sanctums.

Balliol College

ASTLE-LIKE IT LOOMS OVER Broad Street, the tower throwing down a metaphorical gauntlet to all who pass by: 'Enter Balliol, if you dare,' it says. 'Do you think you can keep up with us?'

Balliol is, to lapse into corporate-speak, an 'outward-facing' college, politically savvy and in touch with the real world. Indeed, the whole world seems to pass by its door, the Broad being more sociable than the High, especially now it is semi-pedestrianised. The college's reputation for faux modesty probably results from a desperate need not to appear fuddy-duddy. Balliol almost seems embarrassed to find itself in a backwater like Oxford; the train times to London are forever engraved on its heart. It wants to come across as chilled-out, but is in fact uptight and super-competitive. This garners results: Christ Church may have its 13 prime ministers, but Balliol men have probably had a bigger impact on British intellectual and political life than those of any other college. Chilled? This is a hothouse.

It probably all goes back to Benjamin Jowett, the college's great 19th-century master, who put Balliol on the map and made it a place to reckon with, if not to be. It was apparently Jowett who first said (to the Viceroy of India): 'Never explain. Never apologise.' That is now the mantra of power-brokers everywhere, and ambitious, aspiring men-of-the-world are traditionally attracted to Balliol. It was not always the case. One long-serving 18th-century master of the college was elected solely because of a family connection. When his

Garden Quadrangle, where mature trees including horse chestnut and copper beech provide dappled shade for *Narcissus* 'Actaea' below.

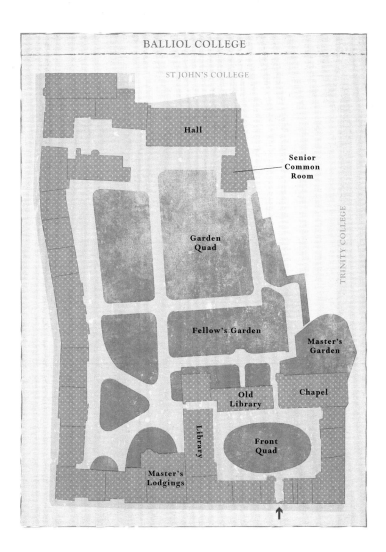

BALLIOL COLLEGE

ST JOHN'S COLLEGE

Hall

Senior
Common
Room

Garden
Quad

TRINITY COLLEGE

Fellow's Garden

Master's
Garden

Old
Library

Chapel

Library

Front
Quad

Master's
Lodgings

RIGHT The Fellows' Garden is situated behind William Butterfield's striped chapel of 1857, where the architectural fragments fancifully known as the tomb of Dervorguilla are planted in spring with cerise and violet 'Triumph' tulips amid orange wallflowers.

Jowett's powerhouse ambitions for the college. It overshadows the rest of Front Quad in every sense. The undergraduate rooms in here somehow feel higher up than those anywhere else in Oxford. James Wyatt's elegant battlementation of the quad (1792) was probably the finest intervention as a means of lending unity to the buildings, which are mostly of 15th-century origin. But that clever stroke was undone by the domineering candy stripes of William Butterfield's chapel of 1857. The great architect of Keble College was not always adept at harmonising his work with its surroundings; in fact sometimes, as here, he seems bent on making buildings go 'clang!' when put together.

The planting of Front Quad helps knit together its disparate elements. Among a variety of shrubs against the old hall, to the left, is an *Azara microphylla*, its yellow flowers exuding a chocolate scent in spring, while to the right a wider range of shrubs and small trees bursts forth, including a holm oak, variegated holly, *Melianthus major* and rosemary. The chapel is toned down (only slightly) by a specimen of *Colletia paradoxa* among others, while a wisteria drapes itself horizontally along the width of the library. Below this is a herbaceous border lit up by dahlias planted at intervals – a vivid magenta specimen that sings out was one of several propagated specially by the head gardener, Christopher Munday, to celebrate the 750th anniversary of the college in 2013, and is to be named in Balliol's honour.

The attractive low tower peeping over the north-west corner of Front Quad, part of Anthony Salvin's mid-19th-century work, seems to beckon the visitor on and through a dog-leg turn passageway and out into Garden Quad. This is an underwhelming transition, with parked cars, asphalt surfaces and a mishmash of generally undistinguished buildings creating the impression of a service area. Garden Quad is actually founded on a clear cruciform path system over large stretches of lawn, though that is not immediately apparent. The quad is extremely large and it is difficult for visitors to gain their bearings. As is so often the case in Oxford colleges, one longs for the intervention of a sensitive landscape architect.

The college's physical development has been quite straightforward: a case of buying up more and more land to

election was contested he did not opt to argue his case; instead he tried to have the holder of a critical vote, a senior tutor whose only foible was having barricaded himself into his rooms on a semi-permanent basis, declared insane. If all such donnish eccentricities were treated thus, Oxford University would have to be declared the largest lunatic asylum in the world.

As befits such a busy and high-functioning place, the compact Front Quad just gets on with it. Here is the chapel, straight ahead, with the old library range next to it, the horizontal energy of its closely aligned, repeating windows creating the impression that one is already on a whirlwind tour of some sort. The old hall (now the new library) is on the left and in the centre lies a simple ellipse of lawn. That is the college at a glance, with only the 'new' dining hall out of sight, up away to the north, on the far side of the mammoth, sprawling Garden Quadrangle. For Front Quad represents less than a quarter of the college's acreage, tucked into its lower right-hand (south-east) corner.

The visitor to Front Quad will naturally have his or her back to the porter's lodge, but somehow the scene is still dominated by the sheer mass of Balliol's Broad Street frontage, looming behind. This range was substantially enlarged by Alfred Waterhouse in 1867 as the physical embodiment of

LEFT The hot border recently created on the eastern side of Garden Quadrangle, near the Senior Common Room. It features a wide range of red, orange and yellow blooms, such as dahlias and crocosmia, offset by large-leaved plants including *Ricinus communis* (castor oil plant).

RIGHT Spring in Garden Quad: the complementary blossom of *Magnolia* x *soulangeana* and pear.

the north and then constructing new buildings around the perimeter. By the late 19th century, the area which became known as Garden Quad was effectively enclosed. It did have a grove-like character at one point, before an institutional atmosphere overwhelmed it, and there are some vestiges of this remaining on the western side, in the form of a handful of mature trees including a copper beech and a pair of horse chestnuts. There are also no fewer than five mulberries in various places. The mulberry is a 'power tree' of sorts, hence its popularity at Balliol, perhaps. It has long been favoured in aristocratic demesnes as a rather superior addition; there is also an association with loyalty to the Crown, since mulberries were planted in the early 17th century at the behest of James I, who envisaged a national silk industry. The author of Balliol's official history surmises that the college's mulberries date from this time.

If the name Garden Quad seems misleading, that is only because it is in fact a reference to the Fellows' and Master's Gardens, whose location may not be immediately apparent to the visitor. These are situated to the right, in the area north of the chapel, the earliest part of the college to be used as a garden. Designated 'private' gardens, they are today the most open of such horticultural inner sanctums, with no formal division or gateway dividing the Fellows' Garden from the rest of the college.

We know that this area had made the transition from being a kitchen garden reserved for vegetables and fruit into more of a decorative space by the end of the 16th century. From the college accounts of this period we can build up an idea of its

appearance. An apple orchard was planted in 1562, and ten plums in 1583. There is an entry of six shillings in 1582–83 for 'making the seates in the Gardin'. A 'little house' needed its lock mended in 1590 and 'poles for the arbor' were purchased in 1595. Gravel was required for 'the walkes in the garden' and an entry in 1608 reads 'Item for plantinge 8 yonge elmes in the backside' – which would not have been as painful a procedure as it sounds. So we have a picture of a tree-shaded garden of gravel walks, with an arbour and a summer house of some kind (unless these were one and the same thing), plus a number of fruit trees. It potentially sounds like a modest 'wilderness' of perhaps two or four compartments linked by paths, each compartment filled with either orchard trees or focused on a summer house. David Loggan's engraving of 1675 shows four distinct garden areas taking up perhaps half the space currently occupied by Garden Quad. To the left (west) was a simple grassed space crossed by a diagonal path flanked by young trees (probably limes). Directly behind the old library, where the Fellows' Garden now is, was a simple grass parterre garden of four compartments and a central roundel, with arches and a corner arbour. Adjacent, on the site of the current Master's Garden, was a much smaller space in a similar style, while a long east-west rectangle of a garden to the north consisted of trees – it looks like they are the aforementioned fruit trees – laid out in a formal pattern.

There is a slightly different formal layout shown on William Williams's engraving of 1733, but the basic subdivisions remain the same; in this plan the northernmost enclosure is named the *Hortus Magistri*, or Master's Garden, and the rest is the *Hortus Sociorum*, or Fellows' Garden. The college archive again reveals something of the garden in 1793–94, when nursery bills detail the trees and shrubs used in a substantial programme of replanting, which would probably at this date have been achieved in a more naturalistic fashion – necessitating the removal of the dividing walls and hedges. The Fellows' Garden was given its current basic form at the time of the completion of Butterfield's chapel in the late 1850s. There is a letter from Butterfield to the college in which he describes 'a private Terrace for the Fellows with a low wall' near the chapel. 'In front of this I have shewn low trees, as hollies and other dark evergreen shrubs.' A little way north he proposed 'a large formal shrubbery' with yew plantings, because 'I feel that the College would be made very much more cheerful in winter by some good dark foliage. It is a mistake to connect yews with Churchyards only.' Butterfield's plan for an atmospheric garden of foliage effects has not survived, if it was ever planted at all. Some sense of the horticultural style of Balliol in the 19th century can be gleaned from a rare engraving of the college's gardens at this period, in J. and H. S. Storer's *The Oxford Visitor* of 1822. This shows the area in front of the Master's Lodgings, in the southern part of Garden Quad, as laid out with several island shrubbery beds, set in grass and cordoned off by chained bollards.

Despite the design shortcomings of Garden Quad, the horticultural quality at Balliol today is among the best in the university, and there is much to enjoy in the planting that bounds the northern end of this lawned space. Big grasses such as *Miscanthus* x *giganteus* and *Stipa gigantea*, together with showy cardoons and feathery pennisetum grass, add up to a border gardened in the contemporary manner. The likes of *Verbena bonariensis*, *Helenium* 'Moerheim Beauty' and *Nepeta racemosa* 'Walker's Low' add summer appeal, while the purple alliums are a strong note in spring. There is a fine *Catalpa bignonioides* (Indian bean tree) here, too, while the height and bulk of the chapel and old library range creates a pleasing sensation of being semi-enclosed. The imposing pile of architectural bits and pieces in the middle of the lawn causes pain to Balliol scholars because it is consistently and erroneously described as the tomb of Dervorguilla of Galloway, widow of John de Balliol and founder of the college in 1282. In fact it was cobbled

together from discarded parts of the old college frontage and chapel during its 19th-century remodelling. It is surrounded by bulb plantings in spring, when tulips and forget-me-nots sprout from the base.

One wonders how much time the master spends in his little garden. It is freely open to the public, but most visitors fail to realise that it is there, on the other side of the yew hedge at the east end of the Fellows' Garden. This is understandable, because the arrangement of tall hedges creating a passageway makes it appear either impassable or private. The theme of this small space is variegation, with euonymus and a kerria by the chapel, and a large itea with its drooping catkins. Here, the chapel looks at its best, as there is no other architecture with which to compete. But the capital stroke in the Master's Garden is the dramatic view up to Trinity chapel's tower, just a few metres away – not so much a borrowed view, more of a pickpocketed one. There are female personifications of Geometry and Astronomy on top of this tower; perhaps visitors need the aid of both to view it from this angle.

Out in Garden Quad proper, the visitor may wish to explore as far as Waterhouse's Victorian-Gothic hall at the northern end, which has an excessively square and block-like appearance. This is in keeping with the generally muscular tone of all of Balliol's architecture, which reached its apogee in the high-Victorian period and seems expressive of the moral and intellectual idealism of that alumnus of Balliol, the poet Matthew Arnold. The dining hall, itself a bully, now looks rather bullied by the modern buildings flanking it. The Senior Common Room is in the north-east corner of Garden Quad, and running southwards from it is an unexpected and dramatic horticultural treat: a fantastical 'hot' border devised in 2005 by the Balliol garden team, with massive *Musa basjoo* plants, crocosmia, variegated cannas, nicotianas, rudbeckias, dahlias, salvias, cleomes, daylilies, persicarias and 'Thalia' fuchsias, all offset by the dark leaves of ricinus (castor oil) plants. A wrought-iron gate ('we found it in the cellar') in the midst of the border, left slightly open, is a welcome touch of whimsy.

Strappy-leaved bananas (*Musa basjoo*) flapping above orange daylilies and several varieties of yellow rudbeckia. A decorative iron gate in the middle of this hot border is almost overwhelmed in late summer.

Brasenose College

THE NAME IS RIDICULOUS, apparently derived from a medieval brass door knocker which now hangs in the college hall. It has been rendered as 'brass nose', 'brazen nose' and in Latin as *Aenei Nasi*. Some say it is nothing to do with noses, but is derived from 'brasen huis', or brewhouse, since the capacity to brew one's own beer was highly prized by the early halls. Is it any wonder many Oxford people just call it BNC? But we should surely treasure this college's name all the more because of its uniqueness: most colleges are named after saints immortal, or else mortal benefactors such as Mr and Mrs Wadham, Lord Nuffield or old man Balliol. It is a welcome change to find one which celebrates an item of door furniture. It's actually a reflection of the unpretentious, workaday origins of several Oxford colleges, growing out of existing academical halls that in some cases were little more than lodging houses or inns owned by townsfolk. The original Brasenose Hall (first mentioned in 1279) would have been identified by its door knocker much as a tavern might be identified by its swinging sign. Other old Oxford halls including Bull Hall and Eagle Hall were also recognised by such emblems.

Brass nose notwithstanding, Brasenose is, quietly, one of the most venerable colleges within the university, founded in 1509 by two men, a bishop and a lawyer who hailed from Lancashire and Cheshire respectively. As a result the college long cherished a strong north-country bias, fielding students on the northern side in the not infrequent street fights between northerners and southerners (and often the Irish) in

Old Quad's sundial is its major adornment, although the doorways are marked by topiarised variegated hollies in terracotta pots.

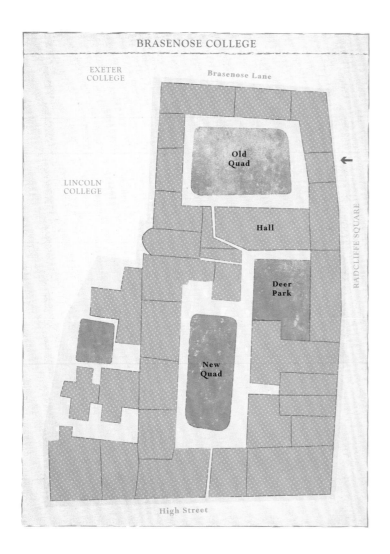

BRASENOSE COLLEGE

EXETER COLLEGE

Brasenose Lane

LINCOLN COLLEGE

Old Quad

Hall

RADCLIFFE SQUARE

Deer Park

New Quad

High Street

ABOVE A view from the Deer Park looking past the trunk of a yew tree towards New Quad, with hyacinths and emerging Fosteriana tulips in the foreground.

RIGHT The dome of the Radcliffe Camera as seen from within the Deer Park, where scented *Choisya ternata* is in flower.

the 16th-century university. The acquisition and absorption of existing academical halls in order to create a new college was a trend begun by Oriel and continued by Brasenose and others afterwards. Brasenose Hall was not the only academical hall to be subsumed into the college in the first half of the 16th century; there were eight other existing halls on its city-centre site, including Little University Hall, Ivy Hall, Shield Hall and St Thomas's Hall. Several of them, including Brasenose Hall itself, were acquired from University College. The college's extent was described at the time the land was bought as: 'the tenements…callyd Brasynose and the little University Hall and all garden lands…abuttyng upon the East parte on the Schole Strete and on the South parte against an hall and garden called Salysurry [Salisbury] and on the North parte against the strete that goeth from Schole Strete toward Lyncoln College and on the West parte against Lyncoln College.' Nearly all of the old and in several cases decayed buildings of the academical halls were demolished over the course of a decade – and the gardens mentioned grubbed up – to create the college's principal quadrangle, today styled Old Quadrangle, which was finished by 1518. The only part of old Brasenose Hall to be retained was the kitchen, which today juts out into the south-west corner of Old Quad.

Like others in that group of colleges squashed tight inside the city centre around Turl Street and Radcliffe Square, Brasenose has never had much room to play with, so a substantial garden was not going to be a possibility. The college did own some land south of Old Quad, which is shown on the Ralph Agas map of Oxford of 1578, and it was probably this that was described as a garden in the 16th century, but it's not clear what form it took – it was never called a fellows' garden as other maintained spaces were at this time.

Old Quad itself is a generous space, ranged around an expansive, almost field-like lawn which is notable for its breadth, proportionally, in the context of Oxford quadrangles. There is some horticultural interest in the form of the variegated standard hollies in pots that have been placed by the doorways. Old Quad also contains a beautiful sundial (1719), a burst of gold against a blue background set into the north wall, as if to emphasise the sunlit nature of the college's precincts. The records show that this was not the first sundial to be placed here.

But a sundial was not Old Quad's most notable characteristic. It was unique among college front quadrangles in that it was heavily ornamented by the late 17th century. David Loggan's engraving of 1675 reproduces in detail the elaborate parterre or knot garden which was made here from box, yew and other evergreens. Many colleges had such adornments, but they tended to be tucked away at the back of the college, as part of a fellows' or master's garden perhaps. This was the case at All Souls, for example, which had more ambitious knots than Brasenose's. Front quads were variously paved, gravelled or latterly laid to grass; nowhere else was the opportunity taken to create such a strident design statement at the outset, as a quadrangle set piece. Perhaps this is partly why the Principal of Brasenose could abide it no more by October 1727, when it was ripped out and laid to grass, much to the consternation of the antiquary Thomas Hearne, who wrote:

Last Week they cut down the fine pleasant Garden in Brasenose College Quadrangle, wch was not only a great Ornament to it, and was agreeable to the Quadrangle of our old Monasteries, but was a delightful & pleasant Shade in Summer Time, & made the rooms, in hot Seasons, much cooler than otherwise they would have been. This is done by the direction of the Principal, and some others, purely to turn it into a Grass Plot, & to erect some silly Statue there.

This statue, known locally as Cain and Abel but in fact a lead copy of Giambologna's *Samson Slaying a Philistine*, was itself almost as unique an ornament as the knot garden had been. The only examples of statues in front quads were at New College, which entertained a Minerva from the 1780s, and at St Mary Hall – a hall adjoined to Oriel College – which also had a statue of the Virgin Mary in its one quadrangle during the mid 18th century. The Samson statue was the gift of George Clarke, a fellow of All Souls who had been an undergraduate at Brasenose and who still took a strong interest in his old college. Along with his friend Dean Aldrich of Christ Church, Clarke was the greatest arbiter of architectural taste in early 18th-century Oxford, with an advisory role on various college building projects. (His greatest monument is Christ Church's gargantuan library.) The decision to remove the parterre was very likely his, as he would have been well aware of the trend towards naturalism in garden design – or perhaps more accurately away from the 'foreign' topiary and clipped figures in box, which the poet Alexander Pope and other self-styled men of taste had been explicitly decrying for several years. To Clarke, who had pursued a successful political career in London before ostensibly retiring to Oxford, Brasenose's front quad would have appeared embarrassingly outmoded by 1727, especially in the context of the plans he was hatching with Nicholas Hawksmoor for the new Radcliffe Square. (At the same time Clarke was machinating for a complete rebuild of Brasenose College along grandiose neoclassical lines, incorporating a massive portico of columns facing the new square.) His choice of the Samson statue was very much of the moment. We know the piece was bought at a 'London statuary' – which would have been one of the

fashionable yards clustered around Hyde Park Corner at that time – and transported to Oxford by barge. Lord Burlington, that great arbiter of garden taste, had a copy of this statue in his celebrated neo-Palladian garden at Chiswick House, and another can still be seen today in the garden at Chatsworth, in Derbyshire. There were various others to be found in modish landscape gardens of the period dotted around the country. The original had been in London since the mid 17th century and was well known to the cognoscenti.

The statue remained in Old Quad until 1881 and several photographs of it *in situ* exist. It also cuts a stark figure in J. M. W. Turner's 1805 watercolour of Old Quad. Comparison with the Chatsworth version – and they would have been identical – suggests that at some point the right arm of the Brasenose statue was repaired. Predictably enough, Samson had proved to be an irresistible focus for college pranks, especially in the 19th century, when the college was known, perhaps even more than Christ Church and Trinity, for welcoming men

from the less intellectual reaches of the English Shires gentry. Brasenose's archivist ruefully reports that Samson was dressed up or painted over on many occasions. It turns out there is a reference in the college accounts to a plasterers' bill of 1825 for the manufacture of a new horse's jawbone (Samson's weapon) in lead, and the soldering on of a new arm. That is why, in the end, Samson's death blow to the Philistine was underarm rather than overarm (not quite cricket, perhaps). Clarke's dramatic choice of subject matter may have been a knowing reference to his college's reputation for toughness and a readiness to commit violence in the medieval period – all of course in the name of 'just war' against marauding townspeople or the undergraduates of other colleges. From the evidence of the college annals, it does seem to be the case that Brasenose men got into a lot of fights. These took place in the streets and fields, sometimes supported by squads of supporting servants; if they were caught, the college had a sliding scale of fines to impose on undergraduates, according to the level

of violence and any weaponry used. This sort of energy, at Brasenose as elsewhere, was eventually channelled into sports such as rugby and rowing.

As for the statue, it was melted down for scrap. The Philistine had triumphed. Perhaps Brasenose ought to consider reinstating its statue?

The character of Brasenose was tested in the 1730s and 1740s as James Gibbs's magnificent domed Radcliffe Camera took shape in its own large square right in front of the college. This project necessitated the demolition of School Street – including several old halls which Brasenose had been using for accommodation – and the various tenements and gardens that had made this area into something of a medieval warren. The college was able to expand in other directions to compensate, but the atmosphere of this part of Oxford was decisively altered, and the result is that today Brasenose's early-16th-century frontage has an attractively old-fashioned air, the door into the entrance lodge perhaps the most speakeasy-like and intriguing of all the colleges. The Radcliffe Camera is from a wholly different architectural tradition but it has become one of the college's finest adornments – the upwards view towards it from the west side of Old Quad is well known as one of the best in Oxford. This vista also encompasses St Mary's spire just to the south, as well as Brasenose's own tower above the entrance lodge, pleasingly diminutive in this company. The architectural contrasts are striking, surprising and delightful.

Who would have thought that Brasenose has a Deer Park? That is the name rather mischievously given to its tiny second quadrangle, which was added to the south of Old Quad in the 1660s, though it would probably be of more use as a hamster park than a deer park. As with the Brasenose name itself, the derivation of the Deer Park nickname is unclear. Perhaps it has something to do with a historical account printed in the *Gentleman's Magazine* in 1820 of a stag hunt where the quarry was hunted from Blenheim Park to Oxford. It 'proceeded up the High Street, as far as Brazenose College, when…the stag took refuge in the Chapel during divine service, where it was killed *sans cérémonie* by the eager hounds.' Today the Deer Park has the air of a through passage to New Quadrangle beyond, with a square of lawn surrounded by thickset mahonias, viburnums and other sturdy and easy-to-maintain flowering shrubs. It is overlooked by a cloistered library, though the cloisters themselves were enclosed and converted into rooms in the early 19th century. Perhaps the deer park nickname stuck in part because the space was formerly surrounded by a post-and-chain fence, giving it the appearance of a tiny paddock.

Brasenose has an interesting garden history but little by way of gardening today, so we shall respectfully bid it adieu and move on.

LEFT An exotic note is provided in the Deer Park by the contrasting leaves of banana (*Musa basjoo*) and phormium. Swirling around them are the intermingling flowers of purple *Verbena bonariensis* and white nicotiana.

ABOVE Pots and window boxes are a speciality at this college: here variegated ivy froths up beneath the prim blooms of polyanthus primulas and the tight blue flower spikes of muscari.

Christ Church

CHRIST CHURCH IS AN almost overwhelming architectural experience – chiefly because of its size. It is conceived on an entirely different scale to all other Oxford colleges. Its garden elements are very much set in-between and around-the-back, and will not be the main focus of any visit. Within the walls, the college's two great quadrangles are its main landscape interest. Without, there is the War Memorial Garden and the cold, magnificent and mysterious Christ Church Meadow, which extends southwards to the river.

The frontage of Christ Church can be found opposite Pembroke College, on the street known as St Aldate's, but touristic visitors – and there are now at least 400,000 of them each year – must enter via the unloved and unlovely mid-19th-century Meadow Buildings which overlook the meadow on the south side of the college. The only person of discernment who is recorded as liking the architecture of this range is the 19th-century art critic John Ruskin, who had his own motives (the style being a species of Venetian Gothic). The proper way in to college is of course directly through the great gateway topped by Christopher Wren's Tom Tower (1682), a gigantic soaring Gothic sugar-shaker (not pepper pot) which is pleasingly over-scaled even in the context of Great (or Tom) Quad beyond, the largest of all the university's quadrangles. But good luck to the stranger who tries to enter the college this way – Christ Church's bowler-hatted porters have long guarded this entrance with a kind of fanatical zeal, challenging

Japanese anemones in the War Memorial Garden, a cottage garden that occupies the land between St Aldate's and Christ Church Meadow, south of the cathedral and the main college site.

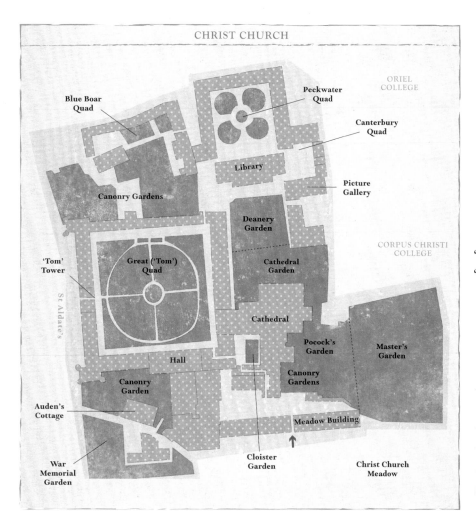

CHRIST CHURCH

anyone who dares step inside. The visitor will probably have to be content with gazing past them into the inner sanctum. No matter. The best views of the main architectural event, Tom Tower itself, are anyway obtained at greater distance – looking south down St Aldate's from the vantage point of busy Carfax, or from Pembroke Square.

Christ Church is different in all sorts of ways. To begin with, this most aristocratic of colleges – the alma mater of no fewer than 13 prime ministers (while the tally for the whole of Cambridge University is 15) – is first and foremost Oxford's cathedral and only secondarily a college. Hence the solecism of describing it as Christ Church College. Christ Church refers to itself as 'the Dean and Chapter' for brevity, or more colloquially, 'the House' (not mere arrogance but a reference to its name in Latin, *Aedes Christi*). It has no master, president, rector, provost or warden, but a clergyman who is dean of the cathedral, in charge of matters both religious and academic, supported by six canons who are academics as well. Uniquely, the fellows of the college are here known as students, and until the later 19th century they had very little say in the running of the college. So there is no fellows' garden, but an extremely private Deanery Garden, immortalised by its associations with Lewis Carroll's *Alice's Adventures in Wonderland* (1865) – Alice being a daughter

of the dean incumbent when Carroll was a 'student'. Then there are the seven private 'canonry gardens' tucked away to the north and east of Great Quad, the exclusive retreats of the canons and their families, who each have their own residence or place, which is known as a 'stall'. Christ Church even has two ranks of porters: the porters proper and the 'custodians', whose main job is touristic crowd control. All are bowler-hatted. There are complexities in the garden set-up at Christ Church, too, in that the college employs a head gardener and six gardeners, while the cathedral has its own gardener to cultivate its precincts.

Christ Church makes its own rules.

Great Quad, which is also known as Tom Quad after the ancient bell in the cathedral's belfry tower, is at the heart of the college and comprehensively upstages the cathedral itself, which seems to be tucked into its back pocket. It is testament to the scale of the architectural endeavour here that it is perfectly possible to come in to Christ Church and not even to register that it is also home to a cathedral. Great Quad is a vast, open and somewhat barren space which still has a slightly unfinished feel owing to the existence all around the walls of tracings which show where the cloister arches would have been, had the college's founder, Thomas Wolsey, been able to fulfil his vision. One doubts whether the insertion of a cloister in this space would have particularly relieved the relentless insistence of its scale, which is accentuated by the fact that its ranges are not particularly high, consisting of two low storeys. There are grass lawns in the four quarters and wide asphalt paths. Tom Tower is the saving grace of the space – it's as if Wren realised he had to create something outstanding in every way to counter the overbearing grandiloquence and over-proportion of the quadrangle below. Wren wrote that he designed Tom Tower to fit with Wolsey's Great Quad, a comment as much about scale as it is style. The pool in the centre of the recessed quad has since 1928 contained a copy of Giambologna's statue of Mercury, prancing above the waterlilies; it was placed there on a pedestal designed by Sir Edwin Lutyens, in a rare Oxford commission for him.

Christ Church suffered a false start to life and for a century and a half its main quadrangle was left palpably unfinished, lacking not only its cloister but also the entire western range. This caused its own problems, evidently, given an early-17th-century chapter order decreeing that 'no student, scholar, chaplain nor servant or any belonging to the House shall lodge any dogg except the porter to dryve out cattell and hogges.' It appears that grazing animals – and there were plenty of those in medieval Oxford's city centre – occasionally encroached on the noble quadrangle. The vision of a porter's dog driving out pigs from Great Quad seems a long way from the scene Cardinal Wolsey might have envisaged for his magnificent new educational institution.

Evidently to the glory of both God and himself, Wolsey founded the first incarnation of what became Christ Church as Cardinal College in 1525, and immediately set about building the main quadrangle. The old church of the suppressed Augustinian priory of St Frideswide's was requisitioned, with Wolsey overseeing the destruction of part of its nave and half of its cloister to make way for the quad. St Frideswide, the patron saint of Oxford, had established a nunnery on the site in the 8th century and the priory church dates to the 12th century, but Wolsey was a cardinal in a hurry and dreamed of an entirely new chapel across the north side of Great Quad – a chapel which was never built.

The magnificent new hall, which forms part of the south range of Great Quad and stands as one of the greatest rooms of the university, was the finest architectural addition of Wolsey's era. The airy staircase up to it, with delicately carved fan-vaulting, is perhaps even better, and serves as a transitional space which is neither indoors not outdoors.

The cardinal's vision for a cloister, on the other hand, was positively gargantuan – Great Quad is 80.5 metres/264 feet by 79.5 metres/261 feet – symbolic, perhaps, of the wholesale requisitioning of religious life for political ends at this period. There may also have been in Wolsey's mind the idea of

Peckwater Quad, designed by Dean Henry Aldrich in the first decade of the 18th century. Lawns now adorn the quad in a pattern inspired by an 18th-century engraving.

categorically trumping the cloister at Magdalen, the college where he was fellow and bursar until 1500. The notion that those who commission great buildings and gardens do so in order to show off, or to display their wealth and power, is one of the biggest clichés in architectural history, and is usually only part of the picture. In the case of Wolsey and Cardinal College, however, it seems true enough. His Great Quad is surely the Tudor equivalent of the modern plutocrat's shiny skyscraper – it's all about the size. The Tom Quad nickname is mainly associated with the college's great bell, but perhaps both are also related to Tom Wolsey, whose grand folly it must be accounted.

Wolsey's fall from grace occurred in 1529, at which point Henry VIII confiscated his property and relieved him of the offices of state; he died the following year. Cardinal College was suppressed and remained in limbo for a time, known as King Henry VIII's College. It was re-founded by the king as Christ Church in 1546, with the chapel converted to a cathedral and a new bishopric created (the city of Oxford having been up to that moment within the jurisdiction of Lincoln Cathedral). It was at this point that the college's peculiar form of governance was initiated, with the dean presiding over the canons and all of them presiding over everyone else at the college.

It sounds as if the king had finally ridden to the rescue of the stricken college, but that was not quite the case. One cannot help thinking it was something of an inherited project for him, and not exactly top of the agenda. Why, otherwise, did Henry – that great builder, responsible for the construction and refurbishment of so many palaces during his reign – take so long to do anything about the college, leaving the Great Quadrangle unfinished and plans for a fine new chapel unrealised? Perhaps Henry left the new cathedral in the misshapen and truncated form we find it today as a kind of memorial to Wolsey's whole career: a botched job. If a change of heart was in the offing by 1546, it was already too late – the king would be dead in a few months.

Christ Church cannot, therefore, claim that Henry VIII had an affectionate personal interest. And it has always struggled properly to memorialise the discredited Wolsey as its founder. As a result, an air of discomfiture surrounds

Christ Church's foundation, and perhaps this has in part moulded the college's character. The production of successful politicians notwithstanding, Christ Church is not a particularly democratic sort of a place, with little of the sociability and sentimentality of other colleges. It can be a difficult place to love, especially for those used to cosier set-ups. For Christ Church is a political and religious foundation, not the vision of an individual or small group. It was never going to be the king's personal project – he just sorted out what could have been a national embarrassment. Consequently it does not have the feel of a great house, secular or religious, benignly presided over by master or abbot, as the other colleges do. Christ Church is grander, almost regal in its feel, and one suspects it takes a long time to find (and understand) one's place here. But as those of 'the House' might say, cosiness and high achievement do not always go hand in hand. Perhaps what politicians and others gain from Christ Church is a sense both of the limits of democracy and the prerogatives of leadership.

A fine example of this in action can be found in the man who was perhaps Christ Church's greatest dean, John Fell, a tyrant who was universally despised but nevertheless got a number of things done. It was Dean Fell who instigated, finally, the completion of Great Quad in the 1660s, when the opportunity was taken to create two-storey residences for the canons in a new northern range. The associated canonry gardens ranked behind were realised in fashionable style as discrete compartments filled with geometric parterres. It is these gardens which can be seen on the 17th- and 18th-century engravings of the college (such as those by Loggan and Williams) and which impart to the northern part of the college the appearance of a complex miniature city. The layout – there are more compartments than there are canonries, and many are not directly attached to buildings – suggests that here, as at other colleges, the divisions between the gardens were in fact quite permeable. It is likely that until the turn of the 19th century at least, members of college were probably free to wander in them. Several of these garden spaces are still in existence, though the biggest one made way for modernist Blue Boar Quad in the 1960s. Archaeological research has

revealed the foundations of several of the formal paths and other features – three of the canonry gardens had fountains, for example – but today they have the character of modest domestic gardens and are never open to the public.

Blue Boar Quad itself is discovered down a pathway to the left of the wide passageway connecting Great Quad with Peckwater Quad in the north-eastern part of the college. Designed by Powell & Moya in elegant modernist fashion, this accommodation block is comprised of prismatic vertical buttresses of Portland stone that interrupt horizontal expanses of plate glass. The building is fronted by two raised platforms of mown grass, like twin daises – a simple but highly effective landscape component which allows the building to breathe freely and to express itself. It is a rare example of a late-20th- or 21st-century college building being given its own designed landscape setting. (The general lack of this is perhaps the greatest collective failing of modern work in the Oxford colleges as a body.)

Peckwater Quad, or Peck Quad, is Christ Church's second

great space and is just as monumental in its way as Great Quad, though perhaps it is more successful aesthetically. Until the early 18th century the building ranges of the old Peckwater Inn (which dated back to the 1260s) were retained as college accommodation, but in 1705 these were largely demolished to make way for the progressive neoclassical architecture of the then dean, Henry Aldrich. His three ranges are often accredited as the first example of Palladian architecture in England – that is, neoclassical design in the 'pure' spirit of the 16th-century Italian architect of the Veneto, Andrea Palladio. The result is not precisely Palladian, but that is not the point of the definition. Aldrich was certainly ahead of the game, politically, because he was a Tory and Palladian architecture was to become the house style of the Hanoverian regime, which was aggressively Whiggish as it turned out. But that was a few years ahead. (George I was crowned in 1714, the year Peck Quad was finished.) At the time, Aldrich's building was essentially a scholastic rather than political exercise. There

was an explicit political statement made at Christ Church at this time, nonetheless: the installation in 1706 of a statue of the reigning Queen Anne in a niche in Tom Tower. This was the gift of Robert Harley, Earl of Oxford, a leading Tory, and reflects the way the queen managed to play off Whig and Tory against each other, encouraging the loyalty of both sides.

Aldrich's experiment in architecture looks like three identical Palladian mansion facades conjoined, with massive triangular pediments surmounting rows of Ionic columns in facades consisting of 15 bays each. It was the first Oxford quad to be united across several of its ranges by one of the classical orders of architecture (in this case, Ionic) and it would have appeared novel at the time. Those who love Peck Quad are entranced by the rationality and idealism of the proportions; those of more baroque sensibility are appalled by what they see as an anaemic academic sterility. John Ruskin was in the latter camp, and he had to live there. 'At the moment I felt that, though dull, it was all

very grand,' he wrote, 'and that the architecture, though Renaissance, was bold, learned, well-proportioned, and variously didactic. In reality, I might just as well have been sent to the dungeon of Chillon.' What Ruskin could see from his window in Peck Quad was yet another monumental neoclassical edifice on its south side: the new college library, which was built between 1717 and 1772 on the site of the last remaining buildings of the old Peckwater Inn. Designed by George Clarke of All Souls, it was originally intended to be another accommodation block, but was redesignated the library partly to house Dean Aldrich's own magnificent collection of books, which he had bequeathed to the college. It is the sort of building you might expect to come across in Rome, an exceedingly muscular and very nearly charmless exercise, with imperious Corinthian columns, huge windows and a monumental cornice and balustrade. The arcades on the ground floor were originally open.

In 1978 the grass shapes of Peck Quad were installed to

an unexecuted pattern depicted in Williams's 1733 engraving. While better than bare gravel, these lawns hardly relieve the oppressive grandiosity of the space, however, which is leavened somewhat only during the Christmas period, when a giant, fairy-lit tree is placed at the centre and pleasingly adjusts the scale of the whole. One time-honoured undergraduate challenge is the attempt to chip a golf ball from the centre of Peck Quad into the Mercury Pool in Great Quad, a feat that has been achieved at least once. There is another story about an undergraduate who was sent down (expelled) for shooting – as one might a pheasant – a fridge which had been thrown off the roof of Peck Quad. But that tale is really too good to be true as a Bridesheadian caricature of aristocratic arrogance and indolence. Having said that, the official historian of Christ Church exhibits unusual candour, when, in an aside about the college in the 18th century, she remarks: 'Of course, there were the duffers, the social climbers, and the hunting brigade, who paid just to be at Oxford for the social scene and to fill in time before inheriting the family estates, but there

were also men of great learning and erudition. The same has applied to all generations!'

Canterbury Quad, to the east, is far smaller than Christ Church's other quadrangles and does not in fact feel like a quadrangle at all. It is used as a car park and is dominated by James Wyatt's great arch of 1778, Canterbury Gate, which serves as the college's back door. Though less spacious than the rooms in Peck Quad (where students get two large rooms apiece), the rooms in this quad feel set apart and were traditionally reserved for the most senior aristocrats who came up to the House. The hyper-proportioned flavour of the architecture here is of a piece with much of the rest of Christ Church, where the quadrangles feel like bombastic

LEFT May (hawthorn) blossom on the trees leaning across the River Cherwell in Christ Church Meadow, for centuries a popular country walk in the centre of the city.

BELOW The so-called Master's Garden, at the south-east perimeter of the college. The name is curious because Christ Church has no master – only a dean, at the head of both cathedral and college.

intellectual exercises rather than places in which to dwell. Most of the college's public spaces are large and open – almost lunar in feel – and the college often feels out of scale with itself. The visitor who exits from here into Oriel Square, with its quaint Georgian and earlier houses, will feel as if they have been transported, like Jonathan Swift's Gulliver, from Brobdingnag to Lilliput (or from Wonderland back to the real world – the Alice echoes multiply the more time one spends in this surreally expansive environment). Canterbury Quad also houses the entrance to Christ Church Picture Gallery – another fine piece of 1960s design by Powell & Moya – containing the bequest of General Guise, one of the greatest 18th-century collectors of pictures and drawings.

Hidden on the other side of the library is the deanery and its garden, which was a floriferous wonderland in the days when Alice played there with her siblings, overlooked by the maths tutor Charles Dodgson (pen name: Lewis Carroll) who was a sub-librarian, spending many days in the library. When he was invited into the Deanery Garden he invented a game called Croquet Castles which was published in 1863. Closed to the public, nowadays the Deanery Garden is a large grassy expanse with shrub borders that is used for cocktail parties and other events, the great library providing a distinguished backdrop, its glazed ground-floor arcades creating the appearance of an orangery. Still standing, though propped up, is the old chestnut tree which is reputedly the one where the grinning Cheshire Cat sat, at least in Lewis Carroll's imagination. The size of the garden has been significantly reduced following the encroachment of the picture gallery, but recently a wildflower meadow and a vegetable garden have been added. A high wall atop a low terrace running east to west divides the Deanery Garden from the 'garden' surrounding the cathedral itself, which is left laid to grass in conventional ecclesiastical fashion, though the wall is lined with somewhat overgrown shrub plantings (mahonia, euonymus and so on). There is a suggestion that this terrace was formerly the site of a Tudor bowling alley. It is a rather strange and vacant space which feels entirely separate to the college proper, though it was previously categorised as one of the canonry gardens.

Over by the entrance to the cathedral, the half-cloister which was left over from Wolsey's 16th-century modernisations has been subject to several redesigns in recent years. The garden historian Mavis Batey created a complex historical design in 1985, but this was replaced in 2008 by a symbolic garden featuring an olive and a bubbling spring, each set in inscribed lead containers. These are fronted by formalist Mediterranean plantings of lavender and sage in what is a busy tourist thoroughfare. This garden adds some interest but it does not really solve the half-a-cloister problem.

Far quieter are the two gardens which can be seen through the gates looking out on to Christ Church Meadow at the south-eastern corner of the college. The first of these is a large lawned area that was laid out in 1926 partly on land reclaimed from Merton Field (which belongs to Christ Church) and partly on the site of the old Deanery Orchard. It is named the Master's Garden, a very odd appellation, given that Christ Church has no master, and one is likely to be told off for saying so. But then again it could not be called a fellows' garden, either, because Christ Church has no fellows. There are well-maintained, multicoloured herbaceous borders (alstroemerias, eremurus, heleniums) running down both sides of this garden, which is used by Christ Church undergraduates in summer for croquet and the general lounging about that is the prerogative of students at 'normal' colleges not also designated cathedrals. There is a fine cornus on the western border and a splendid sycamore near the entrance, but with very few trees and no other structural interest to relieve the lawn, Christ Church's Master's Garden does seem a little bare. Perhaps it is the horticultural analogy to the architecture of Great Quad. The fact that there is no named designer associated with this garden – only Orpington Nurseries, who executed the first planting beds – explains why it feels curiously under-designed today. In fact the best views of it are not from Christ Church at all but downwards from the terrace walk in Corpus Christi's Fellows' Garden. College tradition has it that this garden was laid out anew in the 1920s, but in fact there is a historical precedent. Several old maps show that this area was enclosed as a garden – for example William Williams's 'new and accurate' city map of 1733 shows a geometrically arranged garden of beds and paths (possibly a kitchen garden as well as an orchard), and there is

even more detail on William Faden's 1789 map, which shows eight decorative plats. It appears on maps up until 1818.

Pocock's Garden, immediately to the west, is more successful. Until the 1980s this area existed as a canonry garden which was kept determinedly private, but it was taken into general use by the college thereafter. It has been renamed in honour of the magnificent oriental plane tree that was reputedly planted in 1636 by the celebrated oriental scholar of that name, who returned to Christ Church after his journeyings in the Middle East, whence he obtained seed of this tree. Edward Pocock's plane is surely one of the finest trees in all Oxford, its trunk and multifarious mottled branches twisting every which way and giving an uncanny impression of movement and life. This tree is now propped up by metal struts, but it does not look as if it is going to fall down any time soon. Pocock also brought back the seed of a fig tree which still grows against the back wall of Tom Quad in one of the private canonry gardens, the South West Lodging. The northern end of Pocock's Garden, against the dramatic bastion which terminates the terrace walk in Corpus Christi, has been redesigned most effectively by head gardener John James, with swirling pathways, a seating platform and exotic plantings – bananas (*Musa basjoo*), foxglove trees (*Paulownia tomentosa*), tetrapanax, cordylines, bamboo, skimmia and euphorbia. Elsewhere in this garden is an immensely ugly modern sundial which was the result of a competition; it is surely evidence that there is still a schism between the arts and the sciences, whatever C. P. Snow's detractors might say.

Nearly all visitors to Christ Church reach the Meadow Buildings entrance by going down St Aldate's and turning left along a path which eventually reaches the Broad Walk running west-east along the northern edge of Christ Church Meadow. One benefit of this detour is that everyone can enjoy the War Memorial Garden, designed by John and Paul Coleridge in 1925–26 (with plantings again by Orpington Nurseries) in commemoration of those who had died in the First World War. Our first glimpse of it comes, tantalisingly, through the jet-black railings which front St Aldate's – a truly romantic English cottage-garden moment. For that is the theme of the garden's borders, which are raised up on drystone walls as in some Cotswolds hamlet, with burgeoning herbaceous flowers including white phlox, rudbeckia, geraniums, agapanthus,

verbascums, kniphofias and acanthus. The domestic feel is enhanced by the presence of the gable end of the cottage-like building in the canonry garden of the South West Lodging, which forms a backdrop at the eastern end of the space. This is still known as Auden's Cottage; it was where W. H. Auden lived – in customary disarray – when he was Professor of Poetry at the university. Visitors cannot actually enter the War Memorial Garden proper, but progress through a grand gilded iron gateway along a straight flagstoned pathway lined with lavender, with a row of limes and a lawn to the right, and a weeping willow at the far end. The sense that the War Memorial Garden is out of reach only adds to its romance, and also a realisation that it was the preservation of just this sort of classical English rural idyll, and its associated way of life, that many soldiers were fighting for (or thought they were). Next comes a bridge across the Trill Mill Stream – the mill used to stand just here – and then on the right the visitor discovers a small enclosed garden, almost circular, with abundant plantings including yellow nasturtiums and red wallflowers, and a pool in middle. It has a slightly municipal air and is none the worse for that, because these gardens were intended to be enjoyed by the public freely.

Finally we come to the meadow, which remains the private property of the college, though it is generally treated as a public park. 'Municipal' it is not. Like Port Meadow, on the other side of Oxford, Christ Church Meadow is a mysterious and semi-wild space very close to the city centre, prone to flooding and icing-over and in fact railed off so that the visitor never actually walks on the meadow itself, but progresses around its perimeter. The meadow is tenanted, and a herd of longhorn cattle graze there in the warmer months, while the grass is cut and baled in the autumn – but still it does not have the air of agricultural land. The meadow is not particularly large, at about 400 metres/437 yards across, but nevertheless creates a feeling of space and of countryside. It was part of Christ Church's demesne from the beginning and is marked on Ralph Agas's 1578 map as 'Christ Church Medows and Walkes' – an extremely early example of a designed walk at this scale. There are records of planting (though we know not what) in the meadow in the Christ Church records for 1624, railings having been put up in 1606. The most celebrated section was for a long period the Broad Walk, which appears

to have been created in the mid 17th century as it is labelled as 'New Walks' on the Loggan map of 1675. In the Victorian period the Broad Walk was overhung by immense elm trees and was a popular venue for perambulation for the 'quality' of Oxford and a must-see for tourists. But it is currently rather denuded and open, despite the attempted replacement of the elms with oriental plane trees. There are admirable plans to reinstate elms along here, with four supposedly disease-resistant varieties currently being trialled (and Mr James says that one of them looks promising). The other main thoroughfare in the meadow is the Poplar Walk, first laid out in the 1870s, which runs directly south to the river, the chilly dawn route of bicycling rowers who are heading down towards the boathouses. The visitor can then trace the edge of the meadow where it follows the line of the river (the Thames, which is here called Isis), with wild columbines and tulips in spring. From here one can enjoy the classic distant view of Oxford, with the towers of Merton and Christ Church and

the dome of the Radcliffe Camera, before heading north again along the line of the tributary known as the Cherwell, popular with punters, which in a few minutes flows past the Botanic Garden and under Magdalen Bridge.

The idea that permission was very nearly granted in the 1960s to allow a sunk road to be cut diagonally across the middle of Christ Church Meadow, supposedly to relieve traffic in the city centre, now seems like a bad dream. It was this controversy which was one of the factors leading to the creation of the Garden History Society, an organisation which has played such a decisive part in the protection of our historic landscapes – so some good came of it. As for the traffic, instead of desecrating one of its finest open spaces, the city of Oxford instigated Britain's first park-and-ride system.

The north end of Pocock's Garden, looking across the Master's Garden and into the meadow beyond. The best views of Christ Church's private gardens can be obtained from the terrace and bastion in neighbouring Corpus Christi College.

59

Corpus Christi College

ORPUS – AS CORPUS Christi College is familiarly known – is renowned for its diminutive size, relatively low number of students and intense academic atmosphere. The hole-in-the-wall quality of its entrance is exaggerated by the long sweep of Merton Street, which makes one wonder whether Lewis Carroll at neighbouring Christ Church may have gained the inspiration, while walking down here, for the corridor with a tiny door in which Alice finds herself on the way to Wonderland. The college's own rather stubby gatehouse tower is overshadowed by Merton's taller and more elegant tower just beyond, and of course the college wakes each morning to find itself hard by both Oriel and great Christ Church, too, whose back door, Canterbury Gate, is considerably more impressive than its own front door. (In fact, the elegantly proportioned Canterbury Gate is hugely oversized in this architectural context, which serves to augment the slightly surreal nature of this part of Oxford.)

This college does not feel especially small once the visitor is inside, however, and – like Pembroke over on the other side of Christ Church – it more than makes up for any perceived physical shortcomings by dint of its strong character. In Corpus's case this is immediately declared in Front Quad, which not only packs in hall, library, junior common room and chapel (just around a corner) into a small space – all overlooked by peeping dormer windows – but also boasts one of the most extraordinary ornaments extant at any college: the Pelican Sundial, erected in 1581.

Rose 'Constance Spry' growing against the walls of the Fellows' Building in the college garden.

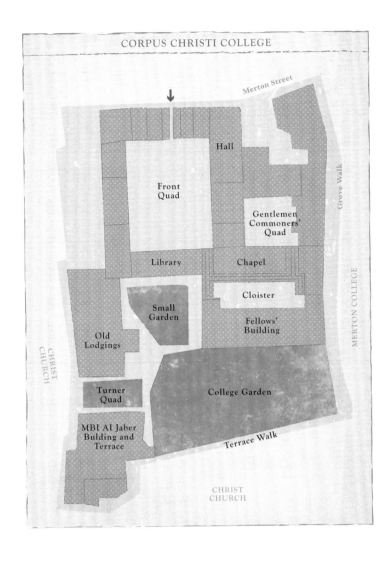

CORPUS CHRISTI COLLEGE

ABOVE The Pelican Sundial in Front Quad. This quadrangle is unusual in Oxford in that it is not grassed, as most quads were from the mid 19th century on.

RIGHT Remarkable horticulture in Front Quad, with yellow-leaved philadelphus, cow parsley, bamboo and lime-green euphorbia surging up from the base of the walls.

This tall column stands proud in the centre of the paved quad, with both the column itself and the lack of the usual grass creating an impressive aura of the antique. The pelican is plucking at its own breast, a reference to the ancient idea that this strange bird would selflessly feed its own blood to its chicks, as an allegory of the way Christ offered his body and blood to his followers. The motif is appropriate symbolically because Corpus Christi means 'body of Christ'.

The college's super-religious name is a reflection of the fact that its founder, Richard Foxe (or Fox), Bishop of Winchester, originally conceived of Corpus as a purely religious institution for the training of monks. But he was persuaded out of this early on and after its foundation in 1517 it became known as a centre of humanistic learning, with one feature of its statutes being the provision made for professors of Latin, Greek and theology who would lecture to the whole university. The visiting Erasmus, no less, commended the well-stocked library at Corpus as one of the finest ornaments of all England, and Catherine of Aragon stayed here for periods while Henry VIII was hunting in Woodstock park. Corpus is still a hotbed of classicists, with more students arriving to study that subject than any other. Perhaps this intellectual pedigree adds to the college's

generally rather refined air. In addition its small acreage demands a compactness and neatness to the layout which results in the abiding impression of a self-organising college with no fat on it, as it were. The entirety of Front Quad was complete by the time the college opened for business, and now it presents an orderly face to the world, with no Victorian additions or ill-matched ranges.

The sundial in Front Quad is an arresting enough sight, but in the past few decades Corpus's idiosyncratic air has been enhanced by the extraordinary horticulture practised by head gardener David Leake, who is an avuncular and popular if occasionally uncompromising presence around college. There is good gardening everywhere here – sometimes in places where you might not expect it – and one hopes that the fellows and student body are aware of what an asset it is. Mr Leake likes to relate, with barely concealed glee, his ongoing battles with certain college officials over the exuberance of his plantings and other interventions. There have been setbacks, but overall he appears to be winning the battle.

The opening salvo in Front Quad is both a surprise and a delight, with big plantings rocketing up from crevices in the base of the walls – verbascums, euphorbias, valerian, pink hollyhocks, yellow corydalis and grasses lending most weight. Bamboos of various kinds are a unifying theme, straining up to about 6 metres/20 feet in height, while a wide range of other plants chosen for their demonstrative foliage and exotic allure burst on to the scene as well. The first thing the visitor sees from the gatehouse is the south range of the quad, where the bamboos threaten to obscure the windows of the library on the first floor. Turn around and there is more to enjoy: another irrepressible border flanking the gatehouse, with white roses, huge yellow inula, spiky phormiums, a fatsia in a pot and even a eucalyptus. It's a wonderful Eton Mess of a border, with a little bit of everything – and all of it nice. Corpus's Front Quad is an exciting horticultural space which also raises a smile, not

just for its explosive vivacity but for little touches such as the common blackberry that has been allowed to curl around the passageway in the south-west corner.

That passage takes the visitor through to a space which is too modest to be called a quadrangle and is known within college, somewhat disarmingly, as the Small Garden. It's an odd-shaped space with forgettable architecture but Mr Leake has made the most of that, with a line of purple-flowered dahlias in six terracotta pots marching up the pathway and a variety of flowering shrubs scenting the air. To the left is a small greenhouse which is very much the head gardener's domain. It is filled with cacti, houseleeks and other tender or succulent plants, as well as all kinds of objects and artefacts gleaned from the natural world (fossils, stones, corals, dried seed heads, driftwood) and the man-made (a shop dummy, religious kitsch, Egyptian relics, jewellery, tiles, bird sculptures, a lobster creel). Mr Leake was recently compelled to tone the whole thing down because it was deemed to be looking more like an art installation than a working greenhouse.

There is another way in to the Small Garden which is perhaps more beguiling. If the visitor takes the left-hand (south-east) passage out of Front Quad, passing by the curiously truncated cloisters by the chapel, a sharp right turn will lead one into the Small Garden through a wooden door and down a straight, flagged pathway that is completely enveloped by foliage and flowers in hot colours, including fuchsias, heleniums and crocosmia. It's a secret-garden moment, and if you are lucky the bells of Oxford might toll as you enter.

A word about the cloisters at Corpus. At present this is a cloister, singular, with more the look and feel of a classical arcade, since it runs along just one side of the small quasi-quadrangle that gives on to the 18th-century Fellows' Building, and leads in to the chapel. The cloister was realised in its present form at the same time as the Fellows' Building. It is quite successful as an arcade in its own right, but the setting is too cramped. At one point there was a

real, four-sided covered cloister here, which appears to have been constructed in around 1515 with the rest of the early college. It is clearly shown on the earliest extant map of Oxford, dated 1578.

The Fellows' Garden at Corpus, at its southern boundary, is known simply as the college garden nowadays and has long been open to the whole college community – Corpus is too small to bother overmuch with the usual college-garden hierarchies and distinctions, and in any case that is not quite its way of doing things. It appears there has been a garden on this spot – or partially on it – for many hundreds of years, for the college was founded on a site packed with old academical halls and their adjacent gardens. The years 1480 to 1530 were dark ones for the university, with the city repeatedly hit by outbreaks of the plague and student numbers accordingly low. Many of the smaller established academical halls that had lodged students for a century or more were left empty and had fallen into disrepair or

FAR LEFT A great copper beech dominates the college garden, with shade-loving plants such as *Vinca major* growing beneath.

LEFT The Fellows' Building is perhaps the most underrated piece of architecture in Oxford. The exhuberant border in front is dominated by roses and wisteria, bolstered by cotoneaster, lavender and other demonstrative shrubs and perennials.

RIGHT J.M.W. Turner's watercolour of the college garden, published in the *Oxford Almanack* of 1811. It shows the gardeners at work with pots, some of them displayed on planks in the manner of a 'theatre'.

vacancy, which is why the buildings and gardens on this site could be acquired easily enough by Bishop Foxe. Five such halls made way for the new college – a late-15th-century survey map of the Corpus site marks them all clearly enough. The legal document regarding the acquisition of the land records 'a tenement now decayed wyth a Garden thereto belongynge called Cornerhall and another tenement now decayed with a Garden thereto belongynge called Nevylls Inne, and another Garden called Bachelers Garden'. There is also a record of St Christopher Hall having a 'College Garden'. It appears that portions of these gardens were in places retained for the new college – most particularly the fellows' garden. The 'Bachelers Garden' referred to above was at the time the fellows' garden of neighbouring Merton (and they were 'bachelor fellows' of course). The Warden of Merton controversially sold, amid much protest, this and all of its western landholdings to the nascent college in 1515, perhaps in part because of Merton's own policy of expansion eastwards at this time. (That might be a generous conclusion, for there is a darkling footnote in the 19th-century official college history of Merton: 'A not unmerited suspicion rests upon the Warden of having betrayed the interests of the College to his own profit herein.')

The garden remains today the largest single space on the college's ground plan and is overlooked on its northern side by the Fellows' Building, a supremely elegant edifice in neoclassical style designed by the college's then president and erected between 1706 and 1716. Conceived in the same pioneering spirit as Peckwater Quad in neighbouring Christ

Church, and slightly ahead of the invasion of Palladianism that accompanied the appearance of George I in 1714, this would have been innovative in its day. Today it is one of the most underrated buildings in Oxford. The bulk of the garden space is taken up by lawn, which is overshadowed by a vast copper beech tree growing out of an ancient mound that rises up to a surviving portion of city wall on the bounds of Christ Church property. Along here, three mature lime trees persist as the ghost of an avenue that once extended east-west, on top of a terrace raised in 1623. Charles I would probably have walked along this terrace during the English Civil War when he used Corpus as a conduit between his own lodgings in Christ Church and those of his queen in Merton. By the time of an engraving of 1728 the trees had gone and the terrace walk is lined with small urns. (The trees were back again by the time of another engraving 30 years later, which shows how quickly college gardens can change in appearance.) In the mid 18th century the Fellows' Garden was a formally organised space with four grass plats, each with a clipped topiary piece in a square tub, and a small labyrinth formed of hedges or small trees to the east. By the end of the century this formal scheme had been swept away: an unpublished watercolour in the British Library shows the Corpus Fellows' Garden as a level lawn surrounded by a dense shrubbery, with young plants growing against the base of the Fellows' Building and a gardener unloading potted plants from a wheelbarrow. There is a low table in the corner of the lawn on which four pots have been placed – each containing a different specimen – with others on the

A bed in the western part of the college garden displaying roses, osteospermums and honesty, with views to the cathedral tower behind.

ground, on the principle of the tiered 'theatre' for plants (notably auricula primulas) which had been fashionable earlier in the century. A gowned college fellow appears to be perusing the plants.

There was also formerly a small summer house in the south-west corner of the garden, on the wall, much in the spirit of the little corner garden pavilions for undergraduate use at Merton and Pembroke (styled 'summer common rooms'). Today that space is occupied by a pavilion of a different sort: the MBI al Jaber Building, erected in 2009 to the designs of Rick Mather (who also made Mr Leake's greenhouse). This glass-walled structure features a decked roof terrace with fan palms and easy chairs, a pleasingly incongruous contrast with the cathedral rising up behind. The roof and the city wall itself afford fine views across Christ Church's Master's Garden, Pocock's Garden and the expanse of Christ Church Meadow beyond. The cathedral's tower dominates the scene; the views south are perhaps even better than those from Merton, just to the east. The mound contains a fox's hole, which Mr Leake happily tolerates on the grounds that it was a Foxe who founded the college in the first place. It is claimed that Loggan's 1675 engraving of the college shows a fox cruelly chained up in a yard to the east of Front Quad, apparently kept in memory of the founder; closer inspection reveals this animal to be a dog.

Corpus's Fellows' Garden has an informal, naturalistic feel; there are no 'keep off the grass' signs. It is well used and much loved by fellows and students alike, the venue for outdoor tutorials in summer, and formerly for rather eccentric games of bowls on the uneven surface. (It's croquet if anything nowadays, as at most colleges.) One particularly tricky depression in the lawn was known as Abraham's Navel until the mid 20th century. The planting is shrubby, with a fair number of interesting species in among the ubiquitous and lovely roses, such as pineapple-scented *Philadelphus microphyllus*, the trumpet-flowered climber *Campsis radicans* and aromatic *Myrrhis odorata*. There are also some good trees, such as *Prunus serrula* with its peeling bark. In spring there are carpets of bulbous flowers including narcissi, hyacinths and thousands of snowdrops, while in summertime annuals add splashes of colour. (Scarlet poppies were a big hit in 2014.)

The Fellows' Garden is memorialised in a poem by the novelist Vikram Seth, who was a student at Corpus in the 1980s. In it he reflects on the way his memories of the college garden have eclipsed entirely those of his emotional upheavals at the time.

Fellows' Garden

Despite the blights and doubts of love,
The windswept copper beech above,
Incognizant of what and why,
Tattered the puzzle of the sky.

When, snivelling on my grieving knees,
I'd feed the College tortoise peas,
The torpid glutton, on the whole,
Poured balm on my afflicted soul.

And from my unrequited heart
All Angst and Weltschmerz would depart
As spiteful mallets clicked away
A Christ Church twilight of croquet.

O mighty loves and griefs long gone,
Why won't your details linger on?
Why should it be that I recall
Beech, beast and mallet – and that's all?

There are a couple of other gardened spaces to seek out in the college. Below the new glass building is L-shaped Turner Quad, where the Old President's Lodgings are, with more interesting potted specimens. And hidden away behind the chapel in the eastern part of the college is the tiny and delightfully named Gentlemen Commoners' Quadrangle. Here, Mr Leake has made a lot out of a little by creating a new border down the side of a recently installed disabled-access ramp, and by ranging modernist black pots filled with sculptural fossil fragments along the top of a wall.

Corpus is a college with several animal associations. There is the founder, a fox; the pelican in Front Quad; and the college tortoise. But the animal most closely associated with Corpus, historically, is the bee. This has arisen because of a remarkable passage in Bishop Foxe's statutes, describing 'a certain bee garden, which we have named the College of Corpus Christi, wherein scholars, like ingenious bees, are by day and night to make wax to the honor of God, and honey, dropping sweetness, to the profit of themselves and all Christians.' As a result various bee stories have attached themselves to the college and a hive is kept to this day.

The college's tortoise fair has been held each summer since 1974, with the college electing its own *Custos Testudinum* from the undergraduate body. On the day, tortoises from various colleges are 'raced' in Front Quad by being placed in the middle of a circle formed by lettuce leaves. The first tortoise to cross the lettuce line wins, with the result often featuring in the local and even national press. It is a highly competitive event. Corpus's own tortoise, Foxe, won in 2013, though it was reported that he blotted his copybook by afterwards urinating on a spectator. The following year Foxe's behaviour was even more egregious: he was disqualified for assault on another tortoise.

The antics of this tortoise should not be allowed to blacken the name of the garden at Corpus Christi. It ought to be on anyone's list of college gardens to visit. And rarely can a head gardener have had such a decisive and positive impact on the overall look of an Oxford college.

OPPOSITE Pale yellow *Rosa xanthina* thriving beside the Fellows' Building.

ABOVE LEFT A glimpse into the head gardener's greenhouse.

ABOVE RIGHT A rose-festooned corner of the college garden, which has for many years been open to fellows and undergraduates alike at all times, unlike the more segregated arrangements at some other colleges.

Exeter College

ANY APPRAISAL OF THE aesthetic quality of Exeter College depends on one's opinion of Gilbert Scott's chapel (1856–59), which dominates the northern (left) side of Front Quad, and visually overawes the college. The chapel is 25 metres/82 feet high, with the spire at the west end touching 45 metres/147 feet, making it an important component of the Oxford skyline. Some commentators have found it hard to forgive Scott for this intervention, since it upstages the college's earliest surviving feature, its 15th-century tower. It can be read either as a gloriously positive statement of religious intent in the context of mid-19th-century Tractarianism, or as overweening arrogance and a disregard for the past. (The old, medieval chapel was reportedly blown up with gunpowder.) The stakes are farther raised by the fact that Exeter is a small college and Front Quad is its only quadrangle, in the traditional sense. This is it.

But I like Exeter's soaring chapel, and I like the way it sets the tone for Front Quad and the college as a whole – for Scott added various other buildings at this time, including the Rector's Lodgings and the library in the Fellows' Garden, of which more in a moment. And of course there is the grass of the lawned quad, laid in a single piece, to offset it properly. Front Quad could not be described as an intimate space, but the beds skirting the college's ranges and especially those in the chapel's bays boast attractive and superabundant planting, with blue agapanthus bursting forth above echinaceas and eryngium, *Melianthus major* mixing with grasses for foliage

The view back to the Senior Common Room (straight ahead, obscured by the horse chestnut) and the college library (on the right) from the terrace walk in the Fellows' Garden.

EXETER COLLEGE

Broad Street

Margary Quad

Rector's Lodgings

Chapel

Rector's Garden

BODLEIAN LIBRARY AND DIVINITY SCHOOL

RADCLIFFE SQUARE

Library

Turl Street

Front Quad

Fellows' Garden

Terrace Walk

Brasenose Lane

BRASENOSE COLLEGE

RIGHT This path leads up to the Rector's Lodgings, which has its own large garden attached.

interest and strappy phormium contrasting with an attractive mess of lavender. The general theme of the south-facing chapel bays is Mediterranean.

But this is window dressing. The eye keeps being drawn back to the body of the chapel. All architectural commentators make mention of its vaulted interior and the way its un-aisled form echoes that of the Sainte-Chapelle in Paris, as well as certain other French examples, notably the 13th-century Chapelle Sainte-Marie at Chaalis. The Lady Chapel at Lichfield Cathedral in Staffordshire has also been referenced, but essentially Scott's new building is considered to be French-Gothic in inspiration. What seems curious is that no one appears to have made mention of the striking similarity of the chapel's exterior to that of Exeter Cathedral, the building which is in some ways the 'mother-church' of the college. The chapel's strong vertical emphasis, created by the pointed buttresses between the five bays, is surely an echo of the exterior form of the nave at Exeter Cathedral, where the buttresses and windows are similarly proportioned, and certainly have a comparable visual effect. There are distinct echoes of the cathedral's celebrated tracery, too. The interior of Scott's chapel is unusual for an English church in that it is completely vaulted. Is it coincidence that Exeter Cathedral has the longest uninterrupted vaulted ceiling in England? That question is rhetorical: this is Scott the ardent

experimenter, who was so adept and deliberate in his fusing of influences from diverse sources, the result of a great deal of study and travel. One last point to make is that the chapel is faced with traditional Bath stone and not made of brick, as several Victorian-Gothic chapels were at this time.

Perhaps this linkage with the cathedral has been overlooked because it seems too obvious a comparison to seek, but that does not take into account the ways in which colleges think. Exeter, true to its name, was from its foundation in 1314 right up until the 20th century intimately connected with the West Country, just as Wadham was at the first associated with Somerset, and Jesus is to this day 'the Welsh college'. Exeter College was founded by the Bishop of Exeter, Walter de Stapeldon, and was known as Stapeldon Hall in the first century of its existence. It was Stapeldon who also part-funded and oversaw the most important phase of construction of Exeter Cathedral. In this context, the use of the cathedral as a reference for the chapel seems particularly apposite.

If the visitor's spirits have by now soared too high, that can be rectified by the dullish Margary Quadrangle of 1964, cluttered with bicycle racks, cars and an unsightly bin store, and with no garden interest. It is as if the college has simply given up on this quadrangle. But no matter – one can now venture into Exeter's Fellows' Garden, situated directly behind (east of) Front Quad. This is one of the most interesting and unexpected of Oxford fellows' gardens, much enhanced by a remarkable high terrace walk along the south and east walls that provides close-up views of the circular Radcliffe Camera, which is part of the Bodleian Library and itself one of Oxford's great landmarks. The garden is rectangular in shape, and almost the whole of it can be seen in one glance, which augments the reassuring sense of enclosure. A great chestnut

RIGHT The Fellows' Garden as depicted in the *Oxford Almanack* for 1786. Note the youth of the plantings, gardeners using a ladder and, in front of the old library, two scholars discoursing on figs or philology (or both).

CENTRE RIGHT The library by George Gilbert Scott is perfectly scaled within the Fellows' Garden, and is clothed with wisteria and a mixture of perennials and shrubs on its lower storey.

FAR RIGHT the chapel in Front Quad, also designed by Scott in the mid 19th century. It echoes the form of the Sainte-Chapelle in Paris but also pays architectural homage to the college's 'mother church' of Exeter Cathedral.

BELOW This straight path runs the length of the Fellows' Garden towards the wall-top terrace walk. On the left is the main herbaceous border, somewhat denuded at this season.

shades one corner; a row of limes lends dignity to the south side. The library on the north (left) side, achieved in the approved ecclesiastical manner of Victorian Oxford, has not been allowed to bust into the centre of the Fellows' Garden to straddle and curtail the space, as did the library Scott built for University College. As a result the great herbaceous border against the south wall is well balanced by the library building, which is itself considerably planted around its base, as well as by the Divinity School of the Bodleian Library, which continues the garden's northern boundary. The main border is achieved in classic English herbaceous style, with achillea, phlox, asters, crocosmia, anchusa and geraniums all jostling for attention in the sunshine. The Senior Common Room (SCR) presides over the garden like a private house at its western end, and for once in a fellows' garden, a visitor actually feels as if they are likely to disturb the peace of a reposing or roving academic, for the dons of Exeter can tumble out of the front door of their SCR and into their garden to regard this border, if they are so minded. There is a huge and famous fig against this range, known among college members as 'Dr Kennicott's Fig' in honour of a distinguished 18th-century Hebrew scholar who apparently had a liking for figs – a reputation which may have been enough to put him off figs altogether. It is also salutary to know that one's scholarly work may be forgotten while one's penchant for fruit may be remembered – a warning from history for the fellows? The planting continues around the library and also on to the terrace itself, with ferns, clumps of daylilies and some fine hydrangeas. The lawn plays host to a good display of bulbous flowers in spring.

Although it is not shown on David Loggan's 1675 engraving of the college, it is likely that the terrace walk was in place by the early 17th century. William Williams's engraving of 1733 delineates the garden as three formal parterres with a raised terrace at the far end, while an engraving in the *Oxford Almanack* of 1786 depicts a lawned space with a broken avenue of young trees leading east, presumably towards the terrace. Nineteenth-century engravings, such as that in *The Oxford Visitor* (1822), show the Fellows' Garden as densely planted to the point of being overgrown, clearly appreciated for its atmosphere of antiquity as well as for the best views towards the Radcliffe Camera and Divinity School. The terrace walk is depicted as an attractively embowered and romantic space in *Views of the Most Picturesque Colleges* of 1852.

The visitor to Exeter may also notice, near the library and Fellows' Garden, a sweet little gardened passageway with a path behind a white gate marked 'private' and a rose-arch above, which leads to the Rector's Lodgings. It creates a frisson, at least, of privacy for the rector and family – and who would begrudge that, in this academic hothouse set cheek by jowl among other hothouses? The Rector's Garden is almost a mirror image of the Fellows' Garden, in terms of size, on the other side of the library. It consists of an attractive lawn with herbaceous borders and mature trees, and is perfectly private.

In 2009 the college was responsible for an exciting addition to the Oxford streetscape, when it purchased Antony Gormley's typically anthropomorphic sculpture *Another Time XI* and had it placed on top of Blackwell's Art Bookshop overlooking Broad Street. It is one of the finest settings of contemporary sculpture in the city, and a refreshing change from the usual policy of simply plonking a piece down in the middle of a lawn or paved modern quad. Known colloquially as the iron man, the 2-metre/7-foot tall human figure, set at a diagonal, stares out impassively in the general direction of Balliol, the spire of Exeter's chapel rising up behind to complete the dramatic tableau.

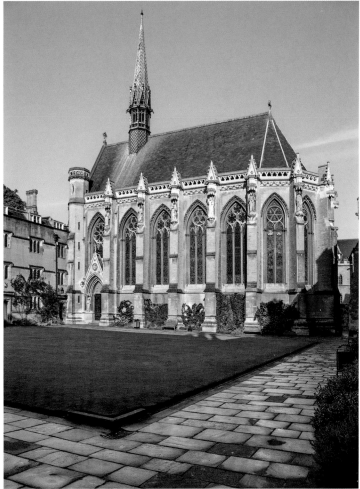

Green Templeton College

I T'S SUCH A CLICHÉ, but this truly is a gem hidden away in the heart of Oxford. I am not referring to Green Templeton College itself here (excellent though its gardens are) but to the Radcliffe Observatory which was built in 1773 on land that became the college's gardens only after its foundation as Green College in 1979. The observatory originally functioned as an outsized garden building set in its very own designed landscape, vestiges of which survive to this day – though alas not the pocket park and entrance drive that originally graced it. Many observatories are built on hills, which makes open terrain less of an issue; in this case landscape design was decisively influenced by astronomical requirements. One of the reasons for the observatory's splendid isolation – and its open, park-like setting – was the necessity of as clear a view as close to the horizon as practicable, to allow for the widest possible scope of observation.

The observatory itself is a remarkable building, consisting of an octagonal 'Temple of the Winds' sitting atop a large 'drum' (in fact a semicircular structure) with a pair of protruding wings. There's nothing else quite like it. Of course there were Temples of the Winds erected at other 18th-century landscape parks – Shugborough, West Wycombe, Mount Stewart and Castle Howard, most notably – and all of them were loosely based on the classical Athenian original, which was to be illustrated in James Stuart's influential architectural treatise *The Antiquities of Athens* (1762). But none was conceived at the scale of the Radcliffe Observatory. How strange it seems

The Radcliffe Observatory was designed in 1773 as a 'Temple of the Winds' by James Wyatt. The Observatory and the former Observer's Garden are now in the domain of Green Templeton College.

GREEN TEMPLETON COLLEGE

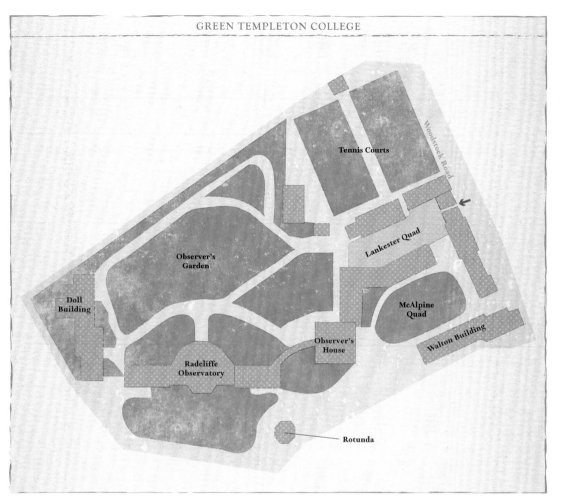

Tennis Courts

Woodstock Road

Observer's
Garden

Lankester Quad

Doll
Building

McAlpine
Quad

Observer's
House

Walton Building

Radcliffe
Observatory

Rotunda

presence of mind in 1768 to petition the Radcliffe Trustees to use part of the pot of money that had already enabled the construction of James Gibbs's Radcliffe Camera as an extension of the Bodleian Library. Matters moved apace, and in 1771 it was resolved that an observatory would be constructed on land near the infirmary in north Oxford, land which had been leased for this purpose the year before by the 4th Duke of Marlborough, who was as it happens an enthusiastic amateur astronomer.

that this extraordinary building should remain so obscure, hidden away off the Woodstock Road in the grounds of what is, to be fair, one of the lesser-known Oxford colleges. That distinctive silhouette is visible from various places in Oxford (there are good views from Somerville and from Walton Street) but effort has to be made – and has always had to be made – to appreciate at close quarters what is perhaps the finest example of scientific architecture in Britain.

Oxford has a long pedigree when it comes to astronomy: the university has had a Savilian Professor of Astronomy since 1619. The architect Christopher Wren held this post from 1661 until 1673, though he never entertained ambitions for a university observatory on anything like the scale of the one he had designed at Greenwich. In 1681 Wren wrote to the Dean of Christ Church suggesting that an observatory could be situated 'as well in a garden as a tower' and might easily be 'a little house of boards'. Modest indeed. The astronomer and mathematician Edmond Halley went on to confect just such a structure in 1705 on top of his residence in New College Lane, and this construction can still be seen. Another small observatory was built at Corpus Christi around this time, but the enterprising professor responsible for the great observatory which survives today was Thomas Hornsby, best known in star-gazing circles for first observing the transit of Venus from his room in a tower of the Bodleian Library. He had the

Henry Keene was initially appointed architect but was quickly dropped in favour of James Wyatt. There had been criticisms of Keene's design as too plain – the Rector of Lincoln College had gone into print calling it a 'heavy, sluggish heap', adding that it was a shame that the new observatory was so obscurely sited that it was unlikely anyone would ever see it. He had a good point on both counts. Wyatt's building, on the other hand, was an observatory that was itself intended to be observed. It comprises a semicircular core, which functions as an entrance hall, with a pair of side rooms for the Radcliffe Observer and his assistants. (The positions of Observer and Professor were separated at this time.) This new design certainly could not be dubbed too plain, with statues and other decorations adorning it, including a series of figures of the eight Winds personified, carved into the stone below the cornice, which have a strikingly modern appeal. The dome is surmounted by figures of Hercules and Atlas together struggling manfully to hold up the world. Slightly alarmingly, they appear to be losing the battle.

The cost of the observatory was, needless to say, astronomical: the final bill was £31,661, as opposed to the original estimate of £6,000 to £7,000.

The closest comparable building to this is not in fact one of the other 18th-century Temples of the Winds, but the celebrated Pineapple Building in the walled garden at Dunmore in Scotland – which is topped by a pineapple-shaped cupola over the drawing room – built just a decade before the Radcliffe Observatory. Comparison does not flatter the latter, which seems fussy and ungainly – but on the other hand, this was a building with a job to do. The main observing room on the upper floor, with a vertiginous metal gallery around the base of the dome, was filled with free-standing telescopes on stands, with globes and astrolabes scattered about for purposes of consultation.

One of the requirements for accurate meridian readings was a marker at some distance due south, within range of the observatory's telescopes, and a mark on a wall in Worcester College was duly made for this purpose. (The proximity of the observatory to Worcester can be seen in J. M. W. Turner's watercolour of the college – the observatory looming in the background, the view as yet unimpeded by buildings along Walton Street.) As long as the horizon was not overly compromised, it seems the authorities deemed it acceptable for the landscape setting of the new observatory to have some decorative appeal. The first trees and shrubs were planted in 1776 at a cost of £52, which represents a lot of plant material. Two thirds of the estate was taken up by pasture land to the west, and park to the south, while the area to the north of the observatory was described as the Observer's 'private garden'. There was stabling to the north-east, adjacent to St Giles'.

The southern parkland area gave the observatory a true landscape setting, as can be seen on a map of Oxford drawn by Robert Hoggar in 1850, which clearly shows the layout of the grounds. A drive led directly off St Giles' and took carriages due west along a lightly wooded drive following the southern perimeter of the observatory's demesne, with fine views opening up towards it across the lawns. A tree was cunningly positioned so that a full view of the observatory building could be obtained only when carriages were halfway along this entrance drive. Such controlled views were a core precept of 'Capability' Brown and other 18th-century landscape designers – and perhaps it is no coincidence that

it is also key to the experience engineered by Brown at Blenheim Palace, in nearby Woodstock, which was of course the principal seat of the Duke of Marlborough, on whose land the observatory had been built. The entrance drive formed a rough rectangle, bringing carriages around the front of the observatory and then either back to St Giles' or to the stables. This pocket park, and the pasture to the west, were lost to expansion of the hospital in the 1930s. There have been various other threats to the site over the years, with one 20th-century plan showing a road passing right through the middle of the observatory itself. So it is fortunate that the Observer's private garden has survived more or less unscathed. A 1797 map shows this area as laid to grass with two large, bracket-shaped planting beds taking up almost half the space. In the 1820s the nurseryman Robert Penson was engaged at the observatory; it was his father who had overseen the replanting and landscaping of the grove at St John's College in the 1770s. By 1850 the landscape look had been transmuted into a more domestic 'gardenesque' scheme – that is, winding paths around specimen trees and shrubs, and lozenge planting beds. The first edition Ordnance Survey map of 1876 shows that the planting scheme was farther elaborated, with more

formal groupings of trees and shrubs in what has remained an essentially amorphous design to this day. The gardener from around 1840 until 1874, William Quarterman, was highly praised by successive Observers. In 1862 the astronomical incumbent reported that 'the grounds have become famed for their picturesque beauty', and during this period of horticultural enthusiasm one Observer paid for a greenhouse out of his own pocket. A contemporary watercolour would imply that there was serious floriculture going on in the private garden at this time, though it must be stressed that the observatory was nothing like as open to casual visitors as the college gardens at this period; it was necessary to write to make an appointment with the Observer to gain entrance. By the 1870s the original trees were more than a century old and the Observer was moved to comment: 'The observatory is so surrounded with trees that it frequently happens that they are in the way of an object near the horizon, as seen from a position on the same level with the ground.' This could not be countenanced, of course, and many trees were removed, lopped or topped. Among the garden's other appurtenances of this period were the stable yard, which later became the site of Lankester Quad at the entrance to Green College, and a kitchen garden to the north-east that is now the site of the college's tennis courts.

By the end of the 19th century, the private garden was essentially a spacious lawn with flower beds and winding paths, and that remains its basic form today. A surveyor's report of 1926 described the area south of the observatory as 'laid out as a small park', indicating that something of its character was retained right up until the moment of its destruction. Oxford's Radcliffe Observatory became redundant as a scientific institution in 1934, when a new observatory was built in Pretoria, South Africa (partly because of Britain's polluted skies). The observatory and its land was then bought by Lord Nuffield (the Oxford car-manufacturer William Morris) who donated it to the university for the purposes of medical research. Over the next 35 years it served as the headquarters of several institutions before being subsumed into the new Green College in 1979. This graduate institution was established by Dr Cecil H. Green, founder of

Texas Instruments, and has always had a bias towards medical research. In 2008, in an unprecedented move for Oxford, two colleges merged to form Green Templeton College, and it is this institution which can now boast an 18th-century observatory in its back garden.

Under head gardener Michael Pirie (who also teaches garden history in the university's Department of Continuing Education), the gardens at Green Templeton College have built up an excellent reputation. There is some horticultural interest in the college's two small-scale quadrangles (burgeoning shrubs against the walls, including oak-leaved *Hydrangea quercifolia*), and the hard landscaping of Lankester Quad is refreshingly clever, with a variety of paving materials creating interest and pointing the way. But the main focus here has to be the garden around the base of the observatory, formerly the Observer's private garden. It still has a private feel today, despite its relatively large size.

Gravelled paths lead the visitor around a variety of mature planting beds stocked with a good range of shrubs and perennials. An island bed containing an aspiring group of *Sequoiadendron giganteum* (wellingtonia), *Calocedrus decurrens* (incense cedar) and *Betula utilis* (Himalayan birch) has been planted to counterbalance the height and mass of the observatory itself. The three-quarter span greenhouse functions mainly as a winter garden for tender plants and a propagation house for summer flowers; its glass is curved on the leading edge to take rainwater away from the timbers. Numerous specimen plants – a cotinus here, a eucalypt there – and a labelled bed devoted to medicinal plants give it something of the air of a botanic garden, which is appropriate considering the scientific heritage of the site. In this spirit, too, a fenced-off space in the lawn in front of the observatory contains the instruments of the Radcliffe Meteorological Station. Daily readings are made here for the Met Office's weather monitoring and forecasting service, a legacy of the days when the observatory was fully operational.

Hertford College

ERTFORD IS KNOWN AS one of the more modern colleges – it was founded in 1874 – but it actually has a haphazard history that stretches back to the late 13th century and Hart Hall, which first occupied the college site on Catte Street opposite the Bodleian. This was the institution attended by the poet and priest John Donne between the ages of 12 and 15. There have in fact been two Hertford Colleges, though a veil is usually drawn over the first, which was founded with a fanfare in 1740 to replace Hart Hall but was dissolved in 1805 in financial disarray. Hertford's website today grimly refers to it as 'a failed 18th-century college', as if it were an embarrassing family member. In 1820 the old medieval facade of the defunct college collapsed into Catte Street one morning. This could be described as a low point in Hertford's history.

Another academical hall, Magdalen Hall, promptly moved in to the vacated buildings and it was this foundation that was to become Hertford College (Mark II) in 1874. The new college set about erecting buildings to finish off the quadrangle's existing buildings, which included an experimental range known as Dr Newton's Angle after an early-18th-century reforming Master of Hart Hall. Since the angle was a single range, one supposes that the angle in question was 180 degrees. A 19th-century illustration of Dr Newton's Angle shows a fenced enclosure, open to the adjacent New College Lane, with a lawn and a few trees and a shrub border – more of a

Old Buildings Quad is a pleasing mishmash of architectural styles, with the chapel in the background and the main range, by Sir Thomas Jackson, clad in wisteria, Virginia creeper and other climbing shrubs.

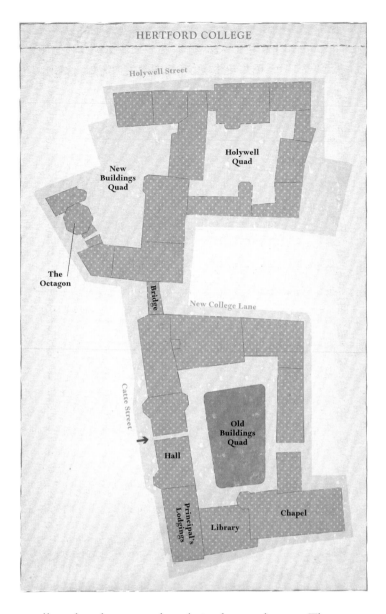

HERTFORD COLLEGE

Holywell Street

Holywell Quad

New Buildings Quad

The Octagon

Bridge

New College Lane

Catte Street

Old Buildings Quad

Hall

Principal's Lodgings

Library

Chapel

style was nicknamed 'Anglo-Jackson' because of its singularity. It has a curiously recessive and underwhelming impact, however, perhaps because it is an over-respectful amalgam – neither one thing nor the other.

Hertford's Old Buildings Quadrangle, or OB Quad, contains two important buildings by Jackson: the chapel (1908) and the dining hall (1887). The former is best described as an acquired taste, squeezed into the corner with its narrow tower and cupola, while the new dining hall is dignified by a dramatic twisting staircase tower, in the spirit of the one at Blois chateau. The other buildings are covered in ivy, wisteria and other climbers, while the lawn as ever helps to hold the divergent architectural ensemble together. An *Oxford Almanack* engraving of 1892 shows flower beds in each corner of the lawn, in the shape of a quarter-circle, an innovation that was not repeated anywhere else, it seems. Today there are climbing roses around doorways, red geraniums in window boxes and hellebores in shady parts. The overall feel is quite homely in its way. The mature tulip tree in one corner of the lawn helps to make this space into more of a garden than a quadrangle, with wood pigeons cooing from the eaves.

But such quietude is easily disrupted. It was in this quadrangle that Sebastian Flyte vomited into an open ground-floor window in *Brideshead Revisited*. (Evelyn Waugh was an undergraduate at Hertford in the 1920s.)

It's true to say that Hertford's Palladian facade is eminently forgettable, like a provincial bank, then its Bridge of Sighs spanning New College Lane is the college's great scenographic contribution to the urban landscape of Oxford. Yes, it's a bit of a 20th-century imposture, but the bridge is well executed and superbly positioned, adding even more drama to what is already an exceptionally interesting part of Oxford: the Bodleian Library is across the road; the Radcliffe Camera is around one corner; the Sheldonian Theatre around the next. The bridge plays a notable part in this ensemble of remarkable structures and has become a must-see for the thousands of tourists who naturally gravitate to this part of town.

Hertford's members will never refer to their most celebrated adornment as anything other than simply 'the

small garden than a quadrangle in the usual sense. There was even a walled kitchen garden within the college at one point, though any open space would be built on as time progressed, since the entire site – on this side of New College Lane – covers barely an acre (0.4 hectares). Hertford's gardens were rarely described or illustrated in guidebooks, but there is an engraving in J. and H. S. Storer's *The Oxford Visitor* of 1822, which shows the college quadrangle with a thick shrubbery on the western side and a wooden fence enclosing another area of garden. (There is also drama in this view, for it looks as if a pointing college fellow has discovered two small boys scrumping – they are holding a sheet filled with what looks suspiciously like a hoard of apples.)

Hertford's new buildings – and the college's very own Bridge of Sighs (1913) – were all the work of Sir Thomas Jackson, who was responsible for a good deal of other work in the city, including the Examination Schools on the High Street and parts of Brasenose. He ploughed his own furrow, architecturally, essentially adding Renaissance or English-Jacobean detailing to a basic neoclassical form. The resultant

Bridge', doggedly decrying the term Bridge of Sighs as false. They will point out – quite fairly – that it is in no way modelled on Venice's celebrated bridge. In fact they will argue – again, on convincing grounds – that their supremely elegant bridge, with its fine Serlian (three-part) window divided by narrow pilasters and its perfectly proportioned arched windows, is architecturally superior to the Italian antecedent. But almost any small neoclassical bridge across any narrow thoroughfare is liable to be thus labelled – so perhaps Hertford ought to give up and embrace the reality that theirs truly is the Oxford Bridge of Sighs.

The argument for the erection of a bridge over New College Lane came about after 1899 when the college acquired the land on the other side of the road which was to become New Buildings Quad (NB Quad) and later still, in the 1970s, extend east to Holywell Quad. (Neither of these areas have anything of horticultural interest, and they are closed to the public anyway.) The master had hitherto rented

a building here as fellows' lodgings, obliging them to cross the street in order to gain access to the main college. It led to the undignified scene of a procession of dons trooping across the road each night, napkins in hand, after dinner in college hall. This would never do. It only took 13 years for Hertford to overcome fierce objections from New College and secure permission for the bridge (which seems a little rich, given that New College already had its own bridge over the same lane). And in the event, most college members have always preferred to move about at ground level, meaning that the Bridge of Sighs functions more as an architectural caprice than a practical thoroughfare – which is precisely what the objectors had argued. It seems that common sense did not win out in this case, and the bridge went ahead. Visitors to Oxford today can be grateful for that.

Jesus College

J ESUS IS A GOOD example of a city-centre college with limited space – no groves or riverside walks here, just a market over the wall – which has nevertheless made the most of its horticultural capabilities by means of excellent gardening. The whole college seems to be blessed with a sunny aura, and that can be attributed in part to the care and flair evident in its horticultural dimension.

This is the only Oxford college to have been founded during Queen Elizabeth I's reign, and it was the great queen herself who was the founder and principal benefactress in 1571. Records show that the queen offered timber from Oxfordshire woodlands held by the Crown, and that this royal wood was used in the early years of the college's construction. The fact that this detail remains important in the college tradition is an indication of the symbolic power of timber in British history.

The college's early years followed a familiar pattern of development among the less well-endowed Oxford colleges: there was some new building immediately, but otherwise the college gathered itself around one or more medieval academical halls – lodging houses, essentially (at Jesus it was White Hall) – which were eventually subsumed into the college proper, gradually forming itself into quadrangles across the course of a century and more. The earliest college buildings at Jesus are in First Quad and now form Staircases 1, 2, 3 and part of 4, across two ranges, with the rest of the quad going up over a period of about 50 years.

The great strength of Jesus's First Quad lies in the fact

Orange dahlias and perennial helianthus light up First Quad, which is distinguished by a central pathway that curves delightfully, creating lawn portions of different sizes and shapes.

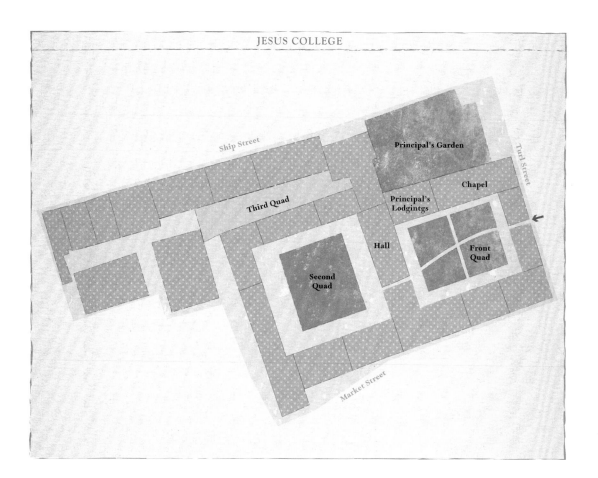

JESUS COLLEGE

Ship Street

Principal's Garden

Chapel

Turl Street

Third Quad

Principal's
Lodgintgs

Hall

Front
Quad

Second
Quad

Market Street

that there is no obvious architectural hierarchy among its elements – no strident chapel, for example – and the result is that the four ranges gel together with naturalness and ease, a benevolent sense of harmony arising despite quite considerable variation. Many Oxford quadrangles seem a little too big, or a little too small, or somehow out of kilter. Then again, if they are 'correctly' scaled and perhaps built all in one go, they can come across as over-severe or even a little dull. First Quad manages to be both interesting and perfectly proportioned. A curving pathway cuts across the lawned quad from the lodge and only adds to this discreet charm; it was never going to be a symmetrical design, anyway. The finely carved shell hood poised above the entrance to the Principal's Lodgings, in the north (right) range next to the chapel, is one of the great architectural details of the city. There are dahlias, roses and other bright plants all around, but the most attractive planting is in this corner, by the Principal's Lodgings, with wisteria hanging above cottage plants and some attractive window boxes stocked for foliage interest – grasses, heuchera and euonymus in the mix.

The strong character of Jesus as a college is considerably enhanced by its horticultural elements. This is perhaps most in evidence in Second Quad, which was completed in 1713, the year before Queen Anne's death, with considerably bigger dimensions than First Quad. It is reached via a perfectly delightful wood-panelled passage that leads past the hall, serving as a fine palate cleanser between the quadrangles.

Second Quad is topped by a row of rather dinky Dutch gables that continue in an unbroken line as inexorably as the waves breaking in the sea. There is a single plat of grass in the quad, which makes this feel like a 'sitting quad' as opposed to the 'walking quad' that the visitor will have just passed through. Unusually for a principal college quadrangle in Oxford, much is made of pots, with each corner of the quad boasting an interesting array in terracotta and wood, their contents clearly subject to regular titivation and refreshment. Charmingly, herbs such as rosemary or curly parsley, or even wild strawberries, are as likely to be used as a tender shrub such as phygelius or a colourful annual. Again there are window boxes which gratifyingly transcend the prevailing cliché of red pelargoniums or purple petunias, with purple-leaved heucheras mixing with ferns, small euphorbias and even dwarf conifers. The planting beds around the quad are generously stocked, especially against the west range, with hydrangeas, alliums, hollyhocks and other cottage flowers featuring, and white nicotiana used as a signature plant to create a sense of rhythm. Because these beds and boxes are carefully tended, there is none of the slightly dusty feel one encounters in other college quadrangles. It's almost as if each staircase has its own front garden, a feeling you also get at Corpus Christi and Pembroke. These and other colleges are proof that exciting gardening can convey a strong impression of liveliness and success in an educational institution.

The modern Third Quad, cobbled and paved, is something

of a let-down after all this, though it does contain some good trees including a *Magnolia* x *loebneri* which lights up the space and is well framed by the doorway from Second Quad. One part of it was built in 1907 as a great wonder: the college's own three-storey laboratory. This impressive amenity lasted just 40 years, when it was converted into a library and student rooms, with the college bar in the basement. Even more of a let-down visually is the Fellows' Garden, which must be the most denuded in all Oxford – a thin paved passageway squeezed in behind the western range of Second Quad, and not very inviting. To be fair to the college, this was always a narrow space (just 3 metres/10 feet wide at one point, and never wider than 6 metres/20 feet), but it was at least open in aspect for much of its existence; it is more recent building that has overshadowed it. The Fellows' Garden was begun in 1683 when the college accounts record a bill for 'Making a garden behind ye Comon Room'. A record from the year before, of payment to one 'Ellis for making an Arbour', could

have been the very start of this garden, which was extended from 30 metres/100 feet to a length of 52 metres/170 feet in 1735 and by the early 19th century had turned into a small grove for the fellows, its mature trees visible over the wall on to Market Street (as can be seen in an engraving of the 1830s). At this end of the garden was the fellows' privy, a common enough addition to such spaces. There were apple, pear and plum trees at this time, and more precise records of planting in 1821 reveal that fashionable Victorian shrubbery plants were used such as cypresses, laurels, lilacs, box trees, arbutus, jasmine, honeysuckle and a great deal of ivy for the walls. In 1846, flowering plants including phlox, fuchsias and currants were added. But the light was lost as new buildings went up, and the garden gradually became lost as well.

There was another garden at Jesus, earlier on, and it is still there, in altered form, behind the north range of First Quad in the north-east corner of college, a rectangular space with walls against Turl Street and Ship Street. Few would guess it

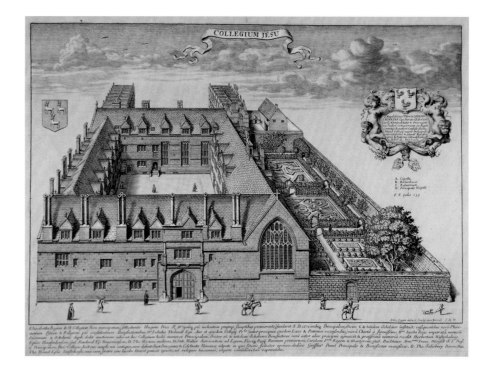

COLLEGIUM JESU

RIGHT David Loggan's 1675 engraving shows the college's tripartite garden in some detail; this space is today the Principal's Garden. The building at top right is the indoor ball court or *sphaeristerium* (long gone).

CENTRE RIGHT Magnolia blossom in Third Quad.

FAR RIGHT An entrance to one of the staircases in Second Quad, guarded by the foliage of a sentry coleus.

BELOW The view from Third Quad back in to Second Quad. Such moments of sudden transition are among the scenograhic delights of the Oxford colleges.

is there, however, because it is now the private and entirely enclosed Principal's Garden, invisible to all but invited guests. David Loggan's engraving of the college of 1675 shows this garden in considerable detail: three areas enclosed by low box hedges, with gravelled walks between planted beds, some of which may have been given over to vegetables. There is also espaliered fruit shown against the south-facing wall parallel to Ship Street. At the western end of the garden, behind a wall, was the building containing the college's ball (tennis or fives) court, though this is long gone. It appears that this garden was created in the 1620s, at the same time as the Principal's Lodgings. It does not seem to have been delineated as reserved for either principal, fellows or undergraduates – the likelihood is that all college members used it, given the restrictions on space at the college site. My own feeling is that Loggan's depiction is likely to have been extremely accurate, because there are relatively few instances of him going in to quite such detail in his engravings. (Brasenose's parterre is another example.) By the time of William Faden's map of Oxford of 1789, the Principal's Garden is shown as two formal compartments, one plain and one quartered.

The old scheme was swept away in 1826 by a principal with a novel idea – why not create a grand carriage entrance to the lodgings? A new gate was built on the corner of Ship and Turl Street, wide enough to accommodate such conveyances, and a sweep of gravelled drive was laid leading up to the Principal's Lodgings. The garden itself was made over into an informal arrangement, with elms, chestnuts, lawns and gravel paths – its basic form today. As with the Fellows' Garden, there are records of planting in the first half of the 19th century:

lilacs, laurels, box, arbutus and even a rhododendron in 1826, and 20 years later a huge amount of new planting including hundreds of bulbs (crocus, snowdrops, aconites) and numerous shrubs like pyracantha, berberis, aucuba, mezereon, acacia and sumach, as well as a great deal of privet and box. It seems there was also a well-stocked formal rose bed. The guest arriving at the Principal's Lodgings in the mid 19th century would have gained a delightful impression of *rus in urbe*, and some of that atmosphere is retained today.

The college archives contain some interesting detail on the use of gravel in the Jesus College quads. The idea put about by some, that every Oxford college quadrangle once contained a delightful formal parterre garden, which was subsequently swept away (usually by those dastardly Victorians) and replaced with grass, is erroneous. Decorative gardening of that kind was generally (but not exclusively) reserved not for the quads but for the master's, fellows' and commoners' gardens (though most colleges did not quite stretch to the third of those). The majority of quads and courts were left quite plain, either compacted dirt or – to be frank – mud in wet weather, up until the late 17th or early 18th centuries. To combat the quagmire effect, it is likely that colleges started to lay down gravel or paved paths in their quadrangles from an early period, with paving reserved for the newer parts of a college. The paths in the fellows' gardens would generally have been gravelled. Many of these paths are shown in Loggan's engravings of the colleges of 1675 and also in those by Williams published in 1733; it should be recognised that the non-path areas of quadrangles at this time were not grass but dirt. Lawns began to proliferate in the early to mid 19th century, though some

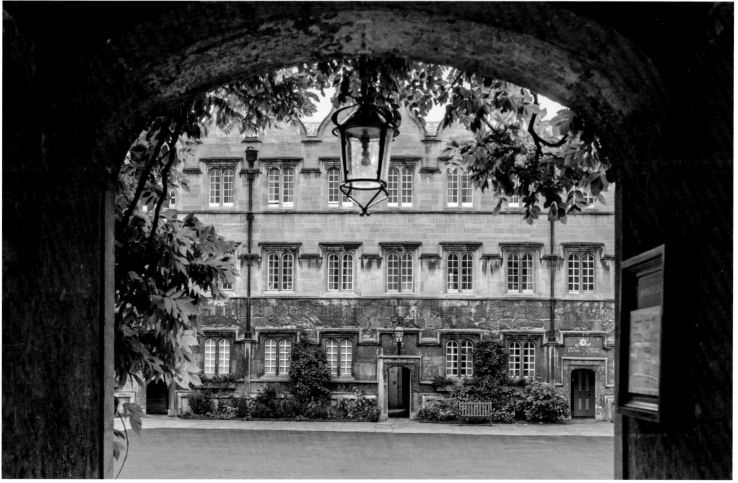

colleges – New College and All Souls for example – had one laid in their best quad by the mid to late 18th century.

At Jesus College the records show that First Quad was gravelled for the first time in 1662, with Second Quad from 1695. The gravel was replenished on an approximately annual basis, and casual labour was regularly employed to turn the gravel to keep it spruce and fit for purpose. An interesting note is that red gravel was tried at Jesus in the 1840s (though we know not where) in line with fashion in formal parterre gardening. A lawn was laid in Second Quad in 1859, while First Quad was grassed and paved as late as 1896. It seems that many colleges clung to the old formality of a gravelled front quad for a long time – even into the 20th century in some cases. It was considered more appropriate to have lawned areas in the more relaxed second quadrangle and beyond.

Jesus is still known as the Welsh college in Oxford. Today, for some reason, it occasionally tries to play down its historic Welshness, making much of its international intake. But the fact is, for the first 500 years of its existence nearly everyone involved with the college was Welsh or of Welsh descent – from the principals to the fellows to the undergraduates to the college servants. Today there are bilingual signs in the college and an annual Welsh-language service is conducted in the chapel. There is no escaping the fact that the college was founded by an English queen, but the principal is careful to point out that it was 'at the request' of a Welsh clergyman. It is not compulsory to be Welsh at Jesus, of course, and today most students are not, but this national identification is a strong part of the college's character. Yet one cannot argue that it is expressed in its architecture or gardens in any way. Perhaps, for the future, horticulture is the answer – should the college start to develop a national collection of narcissus, for example?

LEFT The elegant form of *Magnolia x loebneri* in Third Quad, with narcissi beneath.

ABOVE Deep pink chaenomeles (Japanese quince) contributes to spring in Second Quad.

Keble College

R ADICAL RED-BRICK KEBLE IS a college on a mission and it always has been. The exultant certainties of the High Anglicanism it was established to propound are reflected in the extrovert idealism of its architecture. This is evangelism made solid.

For some: too, too solid. Along with modernist St Catherine's, Keble has the most consistently realised architectural style of all the Oxford colleges. When it was built the focus, understandably enough, was not on planting but almost entirely on the novel style of William Butterfield's chromatically hyperactive buildings. The architect did not show any planting at all on his plans. Chapel, dining hall, library, warden's lodgings and the ranges of the two quadrangles were all constructed in short order across a span of just a few years in the 1870s – almost as if the college's benefactors were worried that the university might suddenly withdraw permission for such a radical development. It was not so much the nature of the multicoloured kaleidoscope of decoration which proved controversial, more Butterfield's choice of mere brick as his main building material. Hitherto associated with railway stations, factories, schools and public lavatories, it was not considered, by some, to be august enough for a new Oxford college, in this city of honeyed Cotswold limestone, so dignified and restrained.

As it happens, red brick and green grass offset each other to magnificent effect at this scale, as proved by the momentous scene that greets the visitor who first comes in to Liddon

William Butterfield's vaunting polychrome chapel may be the proverbial 'hard act to follow' but there are good Mediterranean-themed plantings in several of its bays. The slightly sunken lawn adds to the sublime drama of Liddon Quad.

KEBLE COLLEGE

subsp. *wulfenii*, and on the left by burgeoning *Verbena bonariensis* and a purple hibiscus, lit up by the vivid presence of yellow oenothera. The hot theme continues along this north wall with agapanthus amid *Stipa tenuissima*, rosemary, white roses and buddleia. But it is the green lawn which has the horticultural mastery here, successfully counterbalancing any perceived architectural overstatement. The steep banks down into it prevent Liddon Quad from appearing 'bald', while also creating a little drama of their own.

There is still a good case for trees in this quadrangle, however – a suggestion that might gain more supporters if the college's frontage on Parks Road is taken into account. A line of plane trees planted on the other side of the road offsets the college facade magnificently – the deep red of the brickwork and the bright green of the leaves, and even the grey bark of the tree trunks, simply seem made for each other.

The Fellows' Garden originally occupied the ground to the west of Liddon Quad which is now taken up by Newman Quad, containing the environmentally friendly Arco Building (1995) by Rick Mather. Formerly there was a long double border leading to a platform with a seat at the western end of the space, with a curving path following the college boundary southwards. All that remains of this decorative horticulture is a charming little sunken formal garden to the right, tucked behind the end of the chapel range as one enters the quad, with red salvias, mahonia and acanthus in the mix, creating a Victorian savour. There is a good border against the Butterfield range on the east side of the quad, with penstemons and roses in many colours giving way to ferns and shrubs. The theme of the sunken lawn continues here, too, giving the visitor the pleasant sensation of perambulation along a terrace walk, as if one is taking a stroll in the garden of some gigantic vicarage.

This walk brings the visitor into Hayward Quad and its strikingly modern buildings, which once again scandalised Oxford's good-taste mongers when they were opened in 1979. The highlight of Ahrends, Burton and Koralek's contribution

Quad, which was conceived on a scale to vie with Great Quad (Tom Quad) at Christ Church. The chapel erupts on the far (north) side, its chequerboard decoration more complex than anything else in the college, the impression of its height increased by the expedient of a sunken lawn. Perhaps the relative lowness and gloom of the entrance lodge lulls one into an expectation of monastic quietude – when what is really coming around the corner, like that proverbial freight-train, is an architectural thrill-ride. The whole quad seems to be yelling 'Alleluia!' Intense, idealistic and founded in the midst of Oxford's Tractarian convulsions, when elements of Catholic ritual and liturgy were reintegrated into Anglican worship, Keble has nothing to hide, nothing to excuse, nothing to obscure. There was apparently no requirement for horticultural fripperies to tone down its architecture.

Having said all that, Keble has changed – calmed down a bit, perhaps – and there is now some noteworthy planting in Liddon Quad, chiefly against the chapel. The wide recesses between the buttresses provide opportunities for shrubs such as honeysuckle and small trees, with the alcove nearest to the chapel door pursuing a Mediterranean theme – eryngiums, lavender and sedum growing attractively and well in gravel. The chapel door itself is flanked to the right by a large specimen of *Melianthus major*, backed by *Euphorbia characias*

is the snaking glass bar, which still causes excitement. Hayward Quad was once the site of an orchard and the presence of the two remaining apple trees in meadow-length grass creates an echo of this former identity.

From here the visitor can drift back round into Pusey Quad, which is Keble's second quadrangle, immediately to the left (south) of the entrance lodge, realised in the same exuberant brick manner. This has an airier and more relaxed feel than the showpiece Liddon Quad, with the library on the northern side and the Warden's Lodgings to the south. The quad has an unbuttoned feel because Butterfield deliberately chose not to enclose the space completely in the traditional Oxford manner, instead creating a sense of flow and unity between all his buildings, which were of course realised all of a piece. The sense of calm in Pusey Quad is enhanced by the presence of a fine old copper beech, underplanted with an ivy lawn and cyclamen, crocus and bluebells in spring. In addition there is an exceedingly handsome walnut tree on the eastern side.

For many years this quadrangle boasted a double herbaceous border, which seemed slightly stranded in the middle of the lawn, in the Victorian way. This has now gone and there is horticultural interest, instead, over by the library in the form of a dramatic group of eight evergreen magnolias set in unpainted Versailles tubs, underplanted with red geraniums and other bedding plants. This is a striking and unusual interpolation in a college quadrangle, and looks most effective. Finally, a predominantly white and green planting adds verve to the end of the southern (hall) range, opposite the entrance lodge, with hydrangeas and variegated euonymus. The visitor has now come full circle on the architectural-evangelical merry-go-round that is Keble College.

ABOVE LEFT The gateway into Newman Quad, looking back towards the perennial borders skirting the north range of Liddon Quad, by the chapel. Green has proved to be a good complement to the predominantly red-brick aesthetic.

ABOVE RIGHT An Indian bean tree (*Catalpa bignonioides*) in a corner of Hayward Quad.

Lady Margaret Hall

LADY MARGARET HALL, OR LMH as it is universally known, was in 1878 the first women's college to be established in Oxford, as a High Church scion of Keble College. It is not to be found, as the other former women's colleges Somerville, St Anne's and St Hugh's are, adjacent to the Banbury or Woodstock Roads, the city's main northern arteries. LMH is instead situated at one remove, deep in the Victorian garden suburb which is north Oxford. It can be found at the farthest end of Norham Gardens, 400 metres/440 yards east of the Banbury Road, hard by the northern perimeter of the University Parks. The college has to be sought out, therefore, so has a rather distant feel to many who dwell in the city centre. This also has its advantages, of course.

Chief of these is space, and LMH has always made the most of what it has. In a way we have St John's to thank for this, for that Croesus of a college owned the lands of Norham Manor and in 1894 compelled the college to buy up all the land in this area when it expressed an interest in expansion. This included the water meadows which run eastwards down to the River Cherwell, ground that cannot be built upon because it is prone to flooding. The college's acquisition of the 'useless' water meadow was additional to the viable piece of land that it really wanted, situated directly behind the existing college premises: the original white-brick Gothic villa that housed the first nine students, and a red-brick extension built in a slightly flustered Queen Anne style by Basil Champneys. (These original college buildings on Norham Gardens are

Romantic plantings – here including phlox in white and purple – are the order of the day at LMH (as the college is invariably known).

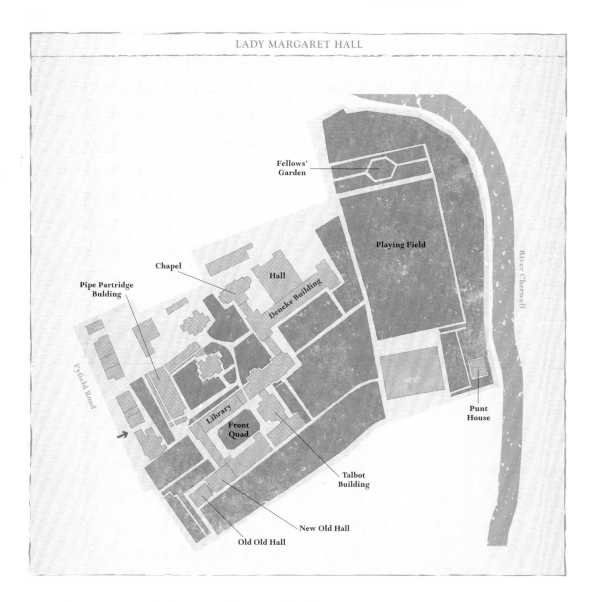

LADY MARGARET HALL

Fellows' Garden

Playing Field

River Cherwell

Chapel

Hall

Deneke Building

Pipe Partridge Bulding

Fyfield Road

Library

Front Quad

Punt House

Talbot Building

New Old Hall

Old Old Hall

BELOW RIGHT The River Cherwell seen through the willow and sycamore foliage at the college garden's eastern edge.

somewhat eccentrically known today as Old Old Hall and New Old Hall.) It may not have been part of Plan A, but the sense of spaciousness and ease created by the presence of the water meadow is the key to LMH's success as a garden college.

The architect Reginald Blomfield was engaged to design a series of new college buildings, on the understanding that these would have to be built one at a time, as funds became available, and that the scheme would possibly remain unfinished. In the event much of what Blomfield envisaged was completed, and it is his vision of austerely elegant red-brick buildings with a vaguely French feel that sets the college's tone to this day. His Talbot Building, with its domed porch, ornate pediment and cupola, is the first thing the visitor sees, straight ahead, on entering Front Quad, and it makes for a striking beginning. This is the nearest thing to a conventional quadrangle in any of the former women's colleges.

Blomfield was the author of *The Formal Garden in England* (1892) and styled himself as a garden architect as well as a buildings architect, causing a 'furious row' in the press with the Irish 'wild gardener' William Robinson – which was in fact a self-serving publicity exercise for them both and will

not be re-rehearsed here. Blomfield's interest in the landscape did mean that he naturally thought about the garden setting of the college, as can be seen from his plan for the new college buildings (in the LMH archive), which includes some ideas for the garden. The most decorative element was a formal parterre behind the Talbot Building, but this was never pursued. Next in importance was a double herbaceous border of considerable length, which was created and was probably the focus of activity for that Oxford novelty, an undergraduates' gardening club. The LMH garden club was set up in 1897 and according to that year's *Brown Book* (the college's magazine): 'the members…have displayed considerable energy and have cultivated a part of the garden with great success. A new border has been lately assigned to them.' Aside from 'Dig for Victory' efforts in the Second World War, this is one of only two instances of organised gardening activity among undergraduates I have come across (the other being a vegetable-gardening club at Worcester in the 2000s). But after just a few years this border was erased to make way for Blomfield's own lodge building on the south side of Front Quad – which was only completely enclosed with the addition of Raymond Erith's sympathetic additions in the 1960s.

Blomfield's specific garden ideas may have been sidelined, but the basic layout and proportion he proposed for the college site was adopted, and this was the important thing. It was Blomfield who established the idea that the college buildings would overlook garden areas which apparently stretch for some considerable distance south and east, when in reality the site is constrained by the river and the boundary with University Parks. The college buildings are large to the point of being oversized, but the landscape setting was considered intelligently and they sit proportionately within the space.

Blomfield is generally considered a 'formalist', for understandable reasons, but he was by no means preoccupied with parterres, statuary, balustrades, straight vistas and such formalist paraphernalia. His design sensibility was subtle and his understanding of space – including the value of 'empty' space – was sure, as can be seen at country houses such as Godinton, in Kent. There, as at Lady Margaret Hall, the garden spaces are allowed to breathe, to work in conjunction with the buildings in a natural manner which does not seek to constrain or privilege either element. He was happy for the lawned areas at the college simply to gather themselves around the buildings, with quite large expanses seemingly left to their own devices, so that the garden extending eastwards at LMH seems pleasantly rambling and unorganised. In reality this apparent lack of design intervention imparts its own dynamism and balance. If one wants the point proved, a comparative visit to any one of Oxford's many unplanned landscapes ought to do the trick: the western side of St Hugh's, Balliol's garden quad, the southern lawn at St Hilda's, New College's Holywell Quad...the list goes on. Even at LMH there are examples of a lack of landscape sensibility and planning – in the quasi-quadrangles formed in the spaces near the chapel (a wonderful Byzantine-influenced building by Giles Gilbert Scott) and in the sterile and oddly shaped grass court overlooked by the new neoclassical Pipe Partridge Building by John Simpson. It's hard to know what the gardeners can do.

The visitor to LMH today reaches the main garden by turning right (south) out of Front Quad, through an imposing gateway passage framed by Tuscan columns, with the black-ironwork Centenary Gate (1978) on its far side. There is an interesting ensemble gathered on the steps leading down into the garden: sculptural driftwood pieces, and scented-leaved pelargoniums and fuchsias in terracotta pots. This is one of those moments of idiosyncrasy which are so welcome in the college gardens.

From here the college gardens burst in upon the visitor's sensibility. There are big borders against the college buildings – roses, cardoons, lavender, geraniums, euphorbias, grasses and a host of other herbaceous perennials – and clusters of mature trees to the west, in the area that was originally the back garden of Old Old Hall and New Old Hall. These areas have a genuinely sequestered feel today and must be a great boon to the students. Directly opposite the Wordsworth Building in this east-west range is a balustraded sunken garden which has

been planted with a range of grasses and naturalistic subjects such as verbascums, lavender and *Centranthus ruber*. The visitor wanders on and around the corner where the gardens open up even more behind Blomfield's Talbot Building. There are mature trees in the lawn, including a fine *Cedrus atlantica* 'Glauca', large clipped yews and lozenge-shaped planting beds. A second, larger sunken garden, conceived as an Italianate feature, has also been given the naturalistic treatment. The monumental facade of the Talbot Building is superbly complemented by flanking *Hydrangea aspera* and an exuberant border fronting the lawns containing *Miscanthus sinensis* 'Zebrinus', white dahlias, honesty, crocosmia, foxgloves, white phlox, bergenia, allium, eupatorium, persicaria, geraniums, hemerocallis and asters. The fine horticulture (including

Different mowing regimes have been essayed in some parts of the grounds, in autumn creating patterns with fallen leaves – for example, close to the southern range of building (**ABOVE**) and around a larch (**LEFT**) in the copse at the edge of the Fellows' Garden.

the bright spikes of kniphofia and verbascum) continues against the Deneke Building, which extends east towards the river. (Helena Deneke did much to establish the quality and reputation of LMH's garden when she was a fellow in the early to mid 20th century.)

The visitor can foray farther, turning left (north) at the end of Deneke to discover the unusual Fellows' Garden. Before one reaches it, one passes the college's own playing field and then there is the pleasure of a vegetable garden arrayed like a border, with immaculate veg in raised beds and the colours and scents of sweet peas, nasturtiums, cardoons and asters.

The Fellows' Garden is an intriguing place, a double enclosure formed by castellated yew hedging, with specimen prunus trees planted in small gravel panels decorated with box balls. The second (eastern) garden is more relaxed, with clusters of box balls and a wooden summer house. It's a rather surreal space.

Finally, LMH loses itself in its own riverside walk next to the winding Cherwell. It is just a short distance along this walk, from the Fellows' Garden in the north to the college's large red-brick punt house to the south, but it is eminently refreshing nevertheless. LMH's gardens must be a real haven and escape for tutors and students alike, addled and wearied by the sheer intensity of Oxford academic life.

ABOVE LEFT A collection of sculptural driftwood and pots – most of them planted with pelargoniums and fuchsias – has been gathered at the Centenary Gate, which divides Front Quad from the college garden.

ABOVE RIGHT The curious Fellows' Garden features specimen trees including prunus planted in small gravel panels decorated with box balls, the whole enclosed by castellated yew hedging.

RIGHT The gnarled trunk of an old yew, with cyclamen at the base.

Lincoln College

THREE LITTLE QUADS, SQUARE-ISH, all about the same size. Front Quad, Chapel Quad and the Grove behind – the last somewhat optimistically named, given the modesty of its proportions. Lincoln is not the smallest college, physically, but perhaps there is a miniature feel about it for the first-time visitor, its ground plan apparently a simplified version of the classic college formula.

First impressions can deceive. Secreted beyond these three 'public' quadrangles is as much garden space again, given over to the Fellows' and Rector's Gardens, and an old graveyard connected to the church which has latterly become a magnificent home for the college library. All of this is squeezed into a triangular space bounded by Brasenose Lane to the north, Brasenose College to the east, the High Street to the south and Turl Street – with the entrance lodge – to the west.

Lincoln College was founded in 1427 by Richard Fleming, Bishop of Lincoln, with the express purpose of training up priests who would combat the heresy of John Wycliffe and the Lollards. Dynamic beginnings, then, but Lincoln was to settle down into a middle-of-the-road, almost somnolent, sometimes poverty-stricken existence over the ensuing centuries, attracting few of the aristocracy (unlike its neighbour, Brasenose) but becoming instead a comfortable berth for the sons of the rural Tory gentry. There was a moment of excitement when the Anglican divine John Wesley became a fellow in the 18th century, but that soon passed and the college immediately slumped back into its metaphorical leather club

Two-tone Virginia creeper making its presence felt in Front Quad. Lincoln is one of the few Oxford colleges still tolerant of foliar hirsuteness of this magnitude in its quadrangles.

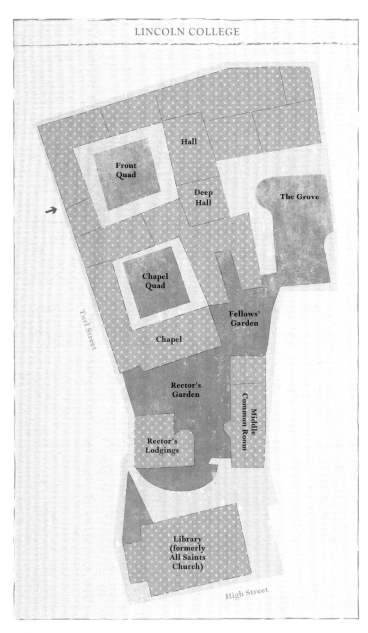

LINCOLN COLLEGE

Hall

Front
Quad

Deep
Hall

The Grove

Chapel
Quad

Fellows'
Garden

Chapel

Turl Street

Rector's
Garden

Middle Common Room

Rector's
Lodgings

Library
(formerly
All Saints
Church)

High Street

into 'the cook's garden' at this time. Just south of it was Deep Hall, an example of an old academical hall being remembered in a modern college's fabric: today it is the name of Lincoln's college bar. Perhaps the name stuck simply because the bar is 'deep' – in the old wine cellar below the hall.

Two distinct garden areas developed at Lincoln. First there was the Grove, which began as the kitchen garden behind Front Quad (completed by 1480) and was later extended farther south – which is the portion that survives today. Then there was the area known as the college garden, to the south and east of Chapel Quad (completed 1631). David Loggan's engraving of the college of 1675 shows only the Grove, as a modest rectangular knot garden with mature trees and a wooden bench. There is no sign of the 'college garden' behind the new chapel, which was possibly a much more modest affair. (The Loggan engraving does have one particularly unusual detail: a stand-off between a rook and a dog in Front Quad.) We know from references specifically to 'the Rector's garden' in the accounts, that by the early 1600s the 'college garden' was split into two, the southern section being given over to the fellows and the northern to the rector (who formerly had a small garden with a wicket gate and grapevine across the road in a college property on Turl Street). This portioning was reversed in 1930, when the new Rector's Lodgings were built in the south-west corner of the Fellows' Garden – which duly became the Rector's Garden. Nor is there in the Loggan engraving any sign of the tennis court which the college boasted until the 1660s – the accounts for 1566 show that a man was paid for 'setting certaine stoups on the Back-side of the colledge, with railes in the tennys-court and gardains'. Nearly a century later in 1654 one John Curteyne was punished 'for misbehaviour to the Rector in the ball-court and in the quadrangle'. (Curteyne became a fellow but was later expelled.) There was also a bowling alley recorded, but this was apparently destroyed to make way for the chapel.

The Lincoln College accounts contain sporadic references to its gardening activities and aspirations, mostly describing work in the Grove. It appears that the Grove, like most early college gardens, was considered to be simultaneously a productive and a recreational space, the preserve of the cook as much as the fellows and students. The first reference is remarkably early

chair. Lincoln is probably one of the most agreeable of the Oxford colleges for both students and fellows – but perhaps its members should not expect too much action.

As was the case with several other Oxford colleges, Lincoln was established on a plot of land that was in multiple ownership, a complex jigsaw of more than a dozen neighbouring plots. Most of these were the sorry remnants of the academical halls which had thrived during much of the 14th century but were now in several cases derelict, the 'waste' land on which they stood used instead as gardens. That was the case with Brend Hall and Saucer Hall, on which Front Quad was built. Oliphant Hall, occupying the site of the garden that was to become the college grove, was bought from University College in 1463, already described some 30 years earlier as 'quite ruinated and turned into a garden'. In many cases the gardens of the halls – or the halls which had become gardens – were built over by colleges, but at Lincoln there appears to have been no change of use with Oliphant Hall, at least, as it was made and records a payment for 'onyon seeds' in 1487. There was no college gardener early on, with piecemeal payments for garden labour recorded in 1517, and one 'father Sage', no less, paid for tending the college's apple trees in 1530. (There was an 'appil-house' among the outbuildings behind the kitchen.) The first reference to decorative gardening comes in 1548, when sixpence was paid 'for mending the seat under the bay-tree', which implies that the garden was definitely intended for relaxation (while the cook used the bay leaves). Rose bushes were paid for in 1568, and in 1575 there are bills 'for herbs to sett our knots' and 'for making 2 stampes to make the garden allys even and levell', which creates a vision of a low-hedged knot garden (privet is mentioned) interplanted with roses and other flowers and laid out with gravel paths. The garden may have become more elaborate over time, with a payment in 1576 'to father Harper, for him and his servand about the arbor in the garden, 20d.; for a burden of woodbinde [honeysuckle] to go about yt, at the same tyme, 10d.' The garden was clearly kept in good order: in 1584 a payment was made 'to Daniell for a daye's work about the seates in the garden, 12d.; for bordes for settles in the garden, 2s. 4d.' And there are references to presumably mature trees being cut down, including an ash.

All this time the college had relied on casual labour for its horticultural maintenance, possibly supplemented with help from servitors (students who paid their way through college by working as part-time servants, usually waiting at table in hall). There had certainly been a tradition of gardening by students at Oxford's academical halls. The college may have been formalising this kind of arrangement when in 1633 a 'serv. hortulanus' was appointed, a 39-year-old man who was the son of a Leicestershire clergyman (and was therefore likely to be educated to some degree). If this is the case, I have not come across any other reference to a servitor being formally employed as a college gardener.

The creation of Chapel Quad led to the laying out of the Rector's and Fellows' Gardens behind, and from here on it is not always clear which garden is being referred to in the accounts. There is no doubt with regard to one reference

in 1677 to payment 'to the carpenter for making seats in the garden, £2 8s 6d.; for colouring the seats in the Fellows garden, 5s. 0d.' It may have been this garden which was the recipient of ten loads of gravel and three loads of 'pebbles for a path into the garden' in 1661, while the 'poles, woodbines and trees about the summer-house' of 1680 could have been used to adorn either Grove, Fellows' or Rector's Garden. Given that Loggan shows only the Grove in his engraving, it is most likely that the summer house, arbour, honeysuckles and so on were put into the Grove, as the college's showpiece garden. In William Williams's engraving of Lincoln in *Oxonia Depicta* (1733), the Grove garden is shown as formalised in more contemporary fashion, an irregular rectangle with a central broderie (cut turf) figure surrounded by plinths for urns – though we cannot know that this was executed. The Grove was severely truncated in 1739 by the erection of the first Grove Building across its northern end. There were plans for an even grander formal garden to suit the new building, to

judge by an engraving in the *Oxford Almanack* for 1743, which shows a rectangular lawn lined with elaborate topiaries and centred on a single tree clipped into a saucer shape. But there is no evidence this was ever attempted. William Faden's map of Oxford of 1789 shows the Grove as a simple square plat with what looks like a pedestal for an urn at the centre. Today the Grove is not especially grove-like, just a simple grass lawn of amorphous shape and rather too much paving elsewhere – notwithstanding one gigantic sycamore tree at its south end. It is now an overspill area for the college bar in Deep Hall and a place for students to lounge without censure in summer. (The lawns in the other quads are kept strictly out of bounds.)

Front Quad has a delightfully old-fashioned feel, partly because Lincoln is one college where the habit of allowing climbing plants to festoon the buildings has been continued. Virginia creeper covers most of the quad, its scarlet autumn foliage contrasting with the green of the lawn, which is laid all in one piece and kept in good order. The tradition of

climbing plants in Lincoln's quadrangles goes back several centuries; an unpublished watercolour in the British Library of about 1790 shows at least three different climbers trained up the walls of Front Quad, with potted plants placed in the open ground-floor sash windows. One 19th-century college fellow relates how he knew several Lincoln men who had been up in the 1830s and who remembered conducting running races around Front Quad after dinner in hall 'to warm the feet well' before a presumably cold bed.

Chapel Quad has recently been cleared of its ivy and other climbers, which were threatening to completely overwhelm it. The old (possibly very old) college vines have been left and are being trained up smart new metal wires, while a pair of evergreen magnolias adorns the north front of the chapel itself. Now that the climbers have gone it is possible to appreciate that the chapel's four windows, which are distinctively wide and shallow-arched with just three lights (vertical panes) apiece, bear a strong similarity

to those at the east end of Lincoln Cathedral. There are some differences in the detail of the tracery, but it appears to be the case that Lincoln's Jacobean-Gothic chapel pays homage, architecturally, to its medieval mother church. I believe the same is true at Exeter College, with reference to Exeter Cathedral. Both colleges were founded by the bishops of their respective cathedrals, so such a homage would have been natural enough. It is perhaps curious this visual link has not been noted before – or perhaps more accurately, has been forgotten – but Oxford can be an inward-looking place.

OPPOSITE Sash windows in Front Quad illumined by jolly yellow primulas, in stark contrast with the dark and twisted stems of Virginia creeper. There have been window boxes in Lincoln's Front Quad since the 18th century – at which time they were certainly not the norm.

ABOVE Prima donna tulips burst above the polyanthus primulas clustered below: simple, repeated plantings can be highly effective in front quads, which tend towards order and symmetry.

The Fellows' Garden and the Rector's Garden at Lincoln were undergoing significant change at the time of writing, as the new Middle Common Room building was being finished in the southern section of the Fellows' Garden. The remaining part of this garden is a small trapezoid of lawn with a *Sophora japonica* tree and a tree fern in the corner. The Rector's Garden is an attractive space with considerable potential, the four bays on the south side of the chapel an excellent horticultural opportunity, and the gently sloping lawn an unusual characteristic in a city-centre college. The plan is to screen off the Fellows' Garden with a specimen *Cercidiphyllum* (katsura tree). In the 19th century, when it was the Fellows' Garden, it was made into an attractive spot to judge by *The Oxford Visitor* guidebook of 1822, in which an engraving depicts a college fellow playing with a dog while a gardener pulls the roller across a lawn that is surrounded by young plantings. The text states: 'Several houses, adjoining the College, were taken down a few years since; and a garden, for the use of the members, has since been made on their site.'

From the southernmost corner of the Rector's Garden a gate takes one up a flight of five steps and into the graveyard of All Saints Church, which has been the college library since 1975. It is a marvellous surprise to have a building of this magnitude suddenly pop up out of the back end of little Lincoln College. There is a historical link, too, because All Saints Church was one of three taken in hand by Lincoln at its very foundation, with one of the two college chaplains made responsible for it. This building, completed in 1720, is thought to have been designed by Henry Aldrich, the architectural Dean of Christ Church; and it does display the purity of line and proportion (if one is a fan of Palladianism) or the insipid predictability (if one is more sympathetic to the baroque) that is associated with his *oeuvre*. The old graveyard behind the church is now a hummocked lawn edged with little clipped box cones and set about with shrubs including skimmias and magnolias.

There is one more story of horticultural import concerning Lincoln College: the ivy ale tradition. Every Ascension Day (in May) a tiny passageway, normally kept locked, is opened up to allow Brasenose students to come in to Lincoln at noon. They are then given a special kind of beer which has been steeped overnight with ground ivy, *Glechoma hederacea* – not true ivy (which is poisonous) but an aromatic relative of mint that grows in woodland. The beer is apparently drinkable if a little strange-tasting, and the occasion is enthusiastically attended. This hospitality – slightly odd hospitality – is reputedly a form of penance for an occasion lost in the mists of time when a mixed group of Brasenose and Lincoln students were being chased down Turl Street by a crazed mob of townspeople. (In university stories the townsfolk are generally drunk and violent.) It is said that the porter at Lincoln only admitted the Lincoln students and that as a result one Brasenose man was caught by the mob and lynched. This is a colourful story but does not exactly have the ring of truth about it. Perhaps more believable is the explanation offered in the college history of 1898, which states that the tradition descends from the ritual of the beating of the bounds, when parishioners symbolically beat parish boundaries with sticks in order to reassert ancient territorial rights. Lincoln was built across two parishes, All Saints and St Michael's (on Cornmarket), and parishioners from both were invited into the college to perform the beating-the-bounds ritual every Ascension Day. The people from All Saints were given lunch in the hall and those from St Michael's were entertained in the buttery, each within their respective parishes. The college prepared the ivy ale for both groups. It is conceivable that this tradition stretches right back to around the time of the foundation of the college in the early 15th century, because herbs such as ground ivy, yarrow, sweet gale, mugwort and horehound were commonly used to flavour beer at times and in places where hops were unavailable. This form of beer was known as gruit or grut, and it is possible that Lincoln's ivy ale is a rare survivor of that tradition. The college might even consider marketing this drink commercially, given that several microbreweries around the world are now selling beers flavoured with herbs, in a conscious revival of the gruit tradition.

The passageway between Front Quad and the Grove. Such semi-open spaces are neither outdoors nor fully indoors and help to create the sense of a seamless spatial whole at several colleges.

Magdalen College

OR MANY VISITORS TO Oxford, it is the quintessential college: tranquil cloister, proud bell tower, chanting choristers, splendid neoclassical architecture, picturesque deer park, floriferous riverside walks. It sounds dreamy, and it certainly is, but not many of these elements are typical of Oxbridge colleges and nowhere else has them all at the same time. What visitors respond to at Magdalen is the sheer atmosphere of the place in all its varied phases and moods. (Its name is pronounced 'mawdlin', to avoid what is perhaps the worst of the university's solecisms.) When I first went into this college as an undergraduate, I have to confess that I did disloyally think for a moment: 'Why didn't I apply here?' And I know I am far from alone in this. Magdalen's delights are piled one on top of the other in quick succession; everything seems to be beautiful. Additionally, one unique quality at Magdalen, which occurred completely by accident, is that the college begins quietly and works up to a crescendo, as the entranced visitor progresses from open quad, to dark passageway, to enclosed medieval cloister, to open Georgian parkland, to tree-canopied riverside. It's an ascending sequence that appears deliberately planned, something one rarely comes across in collegiate design, which is generally haphazard. And amid all of this there is never a moment of sudden let-down, which can be the experience at other colleges, where the visitor might exit some dignified quadrangle only to be presented suddenly with a suite of overflowing wheelie bins, a rain-

The college's great plane tree, planted in 1801, towers above the daffodils in front of the New Buildings, which were finished in 1733 and originally conceived as one range of a new quadrangle.

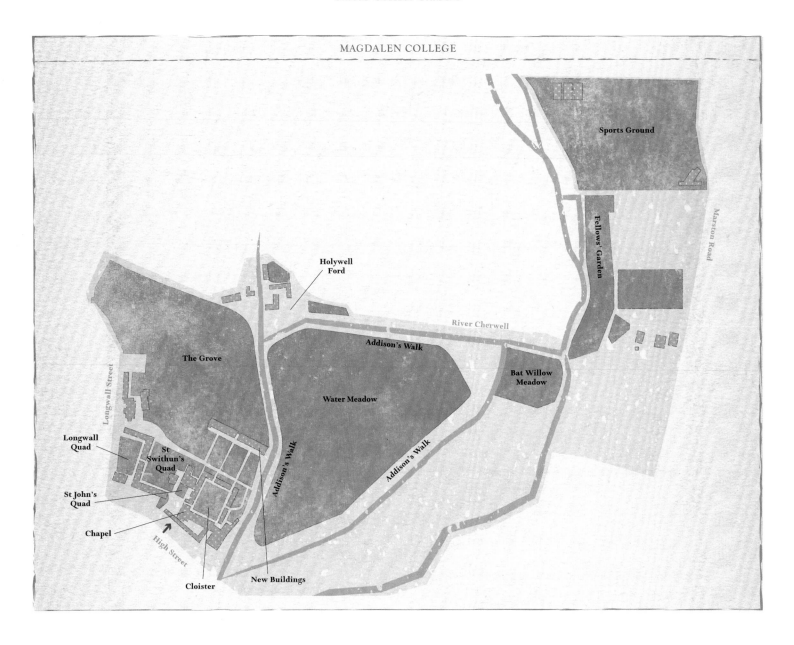

MAGDALEN COLLEGE

sodden municipal park bench or an unkempt and ill-advised concrete accommodation block.

Even Magdalen has one or two less-than-marvellous moments, however, and its least impressive aspect comes first, in that the entrance arrangements leave something to be desired. The blame for this can hardly be lain at the door of the college or its architects, however. It is the traffic which is the problem. Since the late 19th century Magdalen's entrance lodge has given directly on to the eastern extremity of the High Street at the point where cars career up and over Magdalen Bridge at speed. Safety has been slightly improved by the addition of a pedestrian island, but still the character of the area around Magdalen's lodge gives this venerable institution something of the air of a motorway service station. Better progress quickly inside, then.

Magdalen's entrance quad is surprisingly open and rangy for a 'front quad', which are usually enclosed and intimate. Despite the fact that there are numerous Oxford quadrangles

smaller than this, the space often goes unmarked on maps. Its name is St John's Quadrangle. This was part of the land enclosed in the 1460s by the wall that defined the college's boundaries, but it was in fact never intended to be Magdalen's front quad. Its character is elusive because of the diversity of its use and the semi-independent nature of its competing constituent parts. This section of the college was for centuries the domain of Magdalen Hall, the academical hall out of which Magdalen sprang (initially with premises on the High Street), and which largely burned down in 1821. It was also the first address of Magdalen Grammar School before it moved over the road and across the bridge, and became Magdalen College School. (The delightfully quirky 15th-century Grammar Hall survives, now used as offices.) The quad was named for St John because it was formerly the site of the Hospital of St John; the stone pulpit of the hospital's 13th-century chapel can be seen in the south-east corner. And today, the late-19th-century President's

Lodgings occupy the northern section. Something of a curate's egg of a non-quad, then.

Before the late 19th century, the arch beneath the Founder's Tower, just north of the chapel, was where the college really started, with the cloisters beyond conceived as the college's first act and highlight. At that time, there was a much more satisfactory approach to the college, via Nicholas Stone's grand arched entrance facing west on Longwall Street, which was installed in 1635 at about the same time as the Botanic Garden's arch. This entrance was approached along a pleasantly bucolic route named Gravel Walk, running parallel to but separated from the High Street by a line of elms and post railings. It ran east from the corner of Longwall Street, where the college's wall is today. The short route from this western gate to the Founder's Tower would have created the sensation for visitors that they were penetrating the college's outer precincts to its heart.

There is no such logic to the entrance lodge today, which deposits the visitor into this rather confusing mélange of a space, a diverse selection of buildings randomly arranged around paved areas and a lawn dotted with unremarkable trees. The college has been permanently disorientated by the change of the college entrance and expansion westwards. The best that can be said of St John's Quad today is that it functions as a kind of vestibule before the visitor progresses on towards the 'real' architectural action. One handsome adornment, however, in addition to the west front of the chapel, is the imposing Victorian-Gothic gatehouse which announces St Swithun's Quadrangle, to the west. It looks like the entrance to a whole new college, and was designed by G. F. Bodley and Thomas Garner in 1880–84, though only two sides of the architects' proposed three-sided quad were completed. (It was finally finished by Giles Gilbert Scott in the 1920s, who also extended farther west to create Longwall Quad.) There is some good horticulture in this part of the college, notably around the St Swithun's gatehouse, where

PREVIOUS PAGE *Anemone blanda* on a bank in the Fellows' Garden, in the farthest reaches of the water walks. The minaret and dome of the university's Centre for Islamic Studies lends a pleasingly incongruous frisson to the scene.

LEFT The cloister, with *Hydrangea arborescens* 'Annabelle' and wisteria.

RIGHT The design of Magdalen's cloister was innovative in the late 15th century, in that accommodation was inserted on the first floor above the roof of the covered walkway.

grasses, bergenias, viburnum and a purple-leaved plum partially screen off the quadrangle itself, and in large tubs flanking the entrance lodge (big ferns) and against the chapel (crocosmia, hydrangeas and persicaria).

Christopher Hussey in his 1932 *Country Life* guide to Oxford, captions a photograph of the Founder's Tower and the west front of the chapel as 'The Western Facade' of the college. Perhaps the entrance lodge at Magdalen ought to be thought of more in the way of a gatehouse situated at the end of the entrance drive to a house: it delineates the start of the property but is not exactly the threshold. (Trinity's gatehouse has a similar function.)

It is the cloisters which most people have come to see. An atmospheric passageway takes the visitor under the Founder's Tower, past the entrance to the chapel and into the wide cloister itself. This has been the beating heart of the college since its foundation in 1458 by William of Waynflete, that remarkable man who was successively Master of Winchester School, Provost of Eton, Bishop of Winchester and Lord Chancellor to Henry VI. Magdalen's core was completed in the years 1473 to 1510 (the celebrated gargoyles came last) and no other college in either Oxford or Cambridge is structured in quite the same way, with chapel and hall physically conjoined with the cloister. It does put religious life front and centre in the college's personality. There is a reference in the archives to a dispute in the mid 16th century when some junior fellows took to shaving their hair short to make mockery of colleagues who chose to wear the monastic tonsure; the jokers were made to don nightcaps until their hair

grew back. (The nasty Oxford practice of 'tucking', or forcible head-shaving, perhaps stems from such tonsure troubles.)

A cloister is an architectural element, in that it is a covered space, and dry – a valued characteristic until relatively recently, given the numbers of people who have died from chills of one sort or another over the centuries. It is also an element of landscape design, as it is partially open and necessarily creates a space or garden in the middle. It produces a completely different atmosphere to a conventional quadrangle, in that the walker feels safe and cocooned, licensed to walk quietly alone or to chat with friends; there is no self-conscious sense of exposure, of hidden eyes watching you, which is how a quad can make you feel on a bad day. Magdalen's cloister is also a functional space. It was never simply a desirable add-on, as it was at places like Wadham or would have been at Christ Church, if the cloister had ever been built. Nor is it a dead end – albeit an atmospheric dead end – as at New College. Each of the four sides or walks to Magdalen's cloisters is an important thoroughfare in its own right.

The college accounts for 1483 make mention of '*lavacrum in medio claustri*', which makes it sound as if the lavatory was set in pride of place in the middle of the cloister, where the customary cruciform of paths would have met. *Lavacrum* can also mean bath, which is a quaint idea but unlikely – though there are several medieval illuminated manuscripts that illustrate communal bathing in a garden setting. The word here is probably used to denote a hand-washing place, convenient for hall and chapel. (A central water source in a cloister was not an unusual arrangement in monasteries

and convents.) Today the *lavacrum* is situated elsewhere in college and the centre of the cloister now a perfectly kept lawn, mown in stripes. All around its perimeter is a planting of *Hydrangea arborescens* 'Annabelle', a rather one-note effect but nevertheless an inspired choice, exaggerating as it does the impression of infinity created by the identical cloister ranges.

By now we have seen as much as we would expect to see at any other college. Perhaps we will also have heard the E major chime from the belfry of the exceptionally beautiful 15th-century tower. But there is so much more to come. A door in the middle of the north range of the cloister leads the visitor out to face the New Buildings (1733), a perfect vision of Georgian complacency, splendidly isolated like an architectural quotation set against abundant parkland. Who could have imagined an Elysium on this scale could exist almost immediately behind a busy city's High Street? Indeed, the transition between the tightness of the cloister

and the openness of the lawns in front of New Buildings has as great an impact as anything built in the college (a point overlooked in all architectural guides, including Nikolaus Pevsner's classic *Oxfordshire* in the *Buildings of England* series). Similarly exhilarating transitions can be enjoyed at St John's and Wadham, for example, but the surprise that awaits visitors to Magdalen is perhaps the most dramatic.

The New Building sits serenely, its triangular pediment benignly presiding over two storeys of tall sash windows and a dignified open ground-floor loggia. With pasture in front and a big sky behind, it forms a satisfying contrast with the intimate medieval flavour of the cloisters and the later Victorian-Gothic work within the college. Emerging from the quiet cloister into the exuberance of nature, it's as if one has finally reached the sunny uplands; and perhaps there was in the 18th century a desire for a sense of release from the 'Dark Ages' of old Magdalen, into the dazzling bright Enlightenment clarity of the building which must for ever declare itself as 'New'.

In her book about Oxford, travel writer Jan Morris noted the contrast between 'regal' Christ Church and the more 'matriarchal' Magdalen – which she pictures as the abode of a pearl-wearing chatelaine with a rose garden and a cook. This part of the college is indeed a little like a deconstructed country house. Despite the presence of the grove to the west and the water walks to the east, the overall tone is domestic, with the grass in front of the New Buildings closely mown as in a garden as opposed to pasture-length as it would be in a landscape park. (Some of the most evocative shadows in England are cast across those striped lawns.) The chief horticultural element is the great herbaceous border running south to north along the line of the Holywell Mill Stream that divides Magdalen from its water walks. This border does not develop either randomly (as most do) or thematically, but is wholly dependent on rhythm and the repetition of a specific palette of plants. Yellow rudbeckias alternate with blue cranesbill geraniums and salvias, bushy pink

eupatorium, massed hostas and heleniums, white phlox, purple astrantia, miscanthus grass, white persicaria and firework kniphofias – all set against a marvellous backdrop of plane and chestnut trees.

The college's most venerable plant, an enormous London plane tree, still ferociously healthy, can be found in the south-west corner of the lawn in front of New Buildings. It was planted in 1801, a scion of the specimen raised in the Botanic Garden in 1666. Just south of here is the garden of the President's Lodgings, which was quite celebrated in the late 19th century. An engraving in the *Oxford Almanack* for 1876 shows a glasshouse, specimen trees and some island beds, while another from 1890 depicts a typical late-Victorian shrubbery with ladies taking tea on the lawn, seated in court chairs. The college accounts make mention of a president's, vice-president's and kitchen garden in this area to the north

Gates to the mulchy and fecund water meadow. In his poetic paean to Magdalen's walks, Oscar Wilde referred to its scents as much as its visual delights.

of the cloisters, but these were gone by the early 18th century. The earliest map of the town of Oxford, dated to 1578, shows Magdalen as a cloister with tower and 'gardens', 'pasture', 'orchardes' and 'walkes' marked in subdivided sections stretching some distance north. This is the area that was to become known in its entirety as the Grove; indeed, Magdalen can probably lay claim to being the first college with its own grove, an amenity to which most colleges in due course aspired. It began life as a place in which to walk or ride, and only since the 1720s has it become a deer park. As a result the term grove is something of a misnomer, since ordinarily deer are found only in parks.

The herd of fallow deer in Magdalen's Grove is one of the most magical treasures in all of Oxford. These regal beasts seem somehow of another era altogether, and a glimpse of them at dusk may transport the imaginative visitor away from the dull quotidian reality of 21st-century life. One Magdalen story relates how in the 1830s an ancient don fell dead from his window one night and when his body was discovered the next morning at the foot of the New Buildings, it was encircled by deer. Venison from the herd is consumed at college feasts.

The accounts for 1637 show considerable expenditure on improving the walks in the Grove – there was also a large private bowling green made for college use – while some 200 trees are recorded to have been planted after 1660. The Earl of Dover mustered and encamped the Royalist university regiment – 630 men – here in 1644. An idea of the potential extent of Magdalen's formal gardens in the 17th and early 18th century can be gleaned from the map of Oxford appended to William Williams's *Oxonia Depicta* of 1733, which shows a large number of small compartmented gardens in the Grove area – including six square, decorated parterres, in identical pairings – with the bowling green at the northern end. By 1747 it appears that most of this had gone, for *The Gentleman and Lady's Pocket Companion for Oxford* remarks:

> What they call the Grove was once a charming Solitude, but most of the Trees are cut down, except those that stand upon the Walks, which consist of lofty Elms;

but the Walks are too narrow. Since the Trees have been cut down, they have converted the Grove into a Paddock, which feeds about twenty Head of Deer, and there is a very fine Bowling-Green to one Side of it.

Today the Grove has far fewer mature trees than in the past, and it is no longer a place in which to rove (or to present arms). The ancient elms whose distinctive jagged silhouette was once so common have been replaced by softer-edged oak, hornbeam and lime. The Grove extends north to the Holywell Ford site, also owned by the college, though to the visitor these acres may appear to march on for miles. We know that deer are not the only animals to have roamed these plains: a mammoth's tusk and teeth were discovered in the 1920s and displayed in the small museum which was once housed in New Buildings. What an excellent talking point a dish of mammoth would have made at high table.

The fact that New Buildings today stands like a country house in its own parkland setting is purely accidental – it was originally part of a much grander plan. As a college Magdalen developed a habit of hyperactive architectural tinkering in the 18th and 19th centuries, though in the event not much of its tinkering came to anything. In fact the college probably amounts to one of the most annoying clients in architectural history, as it repeatedly commissioned the best architects to produce conjectural designs, many of which were original and interesting, but in the end either went for the safest option, did nothing, or else made a disastrous decision (such as the demolition of the north range of the cloister – which was rapidly rebuilt, thankfully). Howard Colvin devoted an entire chapter to what he called the college's 'epic of architectural mismanagement' in his book *Unbuilt Oxford*, commenting that between 1720 and 1844 at least 20 different architects were engaged by the college, with only a small handful managing to see their idea through in some form.

In the case of New Buildings, the original idea was that it would be the north range of a huge neoclassical Great Quadrangle, with new ranges to east and west and the existing cloisters to the south. (This was just one of a large number of ambitious ideas mooted for this part of the college; James

Wyatt and John Nash were among those asked to come up with plans for a quad.) But the money simply ran out and New Buildings was left beached in its ocean of meadow – which was, aesthetically speaking, the best thing that could have ever happened to it. Even so, the college managed to interfere to the detriment of the ensemble in the 1820s, using the wrong coloured stone for its terminating extensions, after it had it finally become obvious that the Great Quadrangle was never going to happen. Only one engraving, published in a guidebook of 1794, shows the truth of the New Buildings' appearance for nearly a century – that the ends of the range were left obviously unfinished, with bare and raw blocks left protruding, as if awaiting workmen who were to appear 'tomorrow' (like all workmen). But of course they never came. This vexed history explains the strange pluralisation of the term New Buildings, which after all refers to just one building. The college was evidently unable to come to terms with the fact that this was a building, singular, as opposed to buildings,

plural, and so just powered on through, insisting that it was the first element in a suite. And it – or they – remain the New Buildings still. At Magdalen, singular becomes plural by means of sheer collective academic will.

The water walks, which follow the perimeter of Magdalen's own triangular water meadow, are now known as Addison's Walk, in honour of Joseph Addison, the early-18th-century essayist, playwright and poet who was a fellow at Magdalen in his twenties, before going off on a Grand Tour of Europe and then on to London, his magazine the *Spectator* and doctrinaire Whiggish politics. Addison is commemorated in this way because he championed the naturalistic approach to landscape design – the kinds of pleasures offered by the water walks – which was to become the dominant force in landscape aesthetics through the 18th century, and arguably up until the present day. It may also be a reference to the tree-canopied walk at Addison's own estate, at Bilton in Warwickshire, which likewise came to be known as Addison's Walk. This is not the place to venture into a disquisition on Addison, the influence of Locke and Newton and the pleasures of the imagination (the title of his most famous essay, written in draft while he was still at Magdalen); suffice to say the agricultural fields, mill and other light industry that would have been visible from Magdalen's water walks in his day, would have played into Addison's idea of a desirable fusion of aesthetic pleasure with practical, profitable business – a very Whiggish cocktail, of course.

Addison's Walk is reached via a gateway and a little bridge across the river, whence one is immediately plunged into another time and place altogether, where clocks become unimportant – notwithstanding the incessant tolling of Oxford's bells. The pleasure is of walking along a raised path under mature trees – ash, beech, yew, chestnut, hornbeam, sycamore – next to a little river as it winds its course on one side, and the grassy expanse of the meadow on the other, where the deer graze for part of the year. The college's site

was reputedly chosen by Waynflete because of a great oak tree which grew close to the entrance to the water walks on the east side of the river. Already about 50 years old in 1458, it became known as the founder's oak. This was a huge tree that the natural historian Dr Plot – author of a 1677 *Natural History of Oxfordshire* – reckoned could shelter 256 horses or 3,456 men under the shadow of its spreading boughs (an admirably exact calculation – one wonders where he found all the horses). It finally fell in 1789. The most celebrated plants at Magdalen today must be the population of snake's head fritillaries (*Fritillaria meleagris*) which flower in the meadow to marvellous effect, usually in the second week of April, best viewed from the eastern side of the meadow. One of Oscar Wilde's earliest poems, a sub-Keatsian effort published in 1878, was entitled 'Magdalen Walks' and it reflects his appreciation of

LEFT Snake's head fritillaries usually flower in around the second week of April.

BELOW Sorbus (whitebeam) trees and daffodils in a small garden area adjacent to the High Street – the chapel in St John's Quad is just visible through the railings on the left. The sorbus are in full blossom during May Day celebrations.

the flora and bird-life of his college. In the poem Wilde notes, in this order: daffodils, larches, the odour of leaves, grass and earth, birds, briar rosebuds, crocuses, plane trees, pine trees, elms, doves, larks, kingfishers, lilies and chestnut trees. There is no mention of lobsters. (Wilde reputedly kept one in college as a pet and took it for walks in the cloister.) Or swans: the college maintained its own swannery on the Cherwell in its early days.

At the north-eastern extent of Addison's Walk is the Fellows' Garden, surely the most romantic in all Oxford. Through a gate and across a little bridge, one discovers a quiet riverside spot and a veritable small arboretum with numerous interesting trees including a pendulous silver lime, Lombardy poplar, copper beech, two giant redwoods and a variegated sycamore, and hundreds of narcissi in spring. But I suspect few visitors will be ticking off these plants, because this place is a destination for 'courting couples', or even for nervous souls looking to propose marriage (perhaps gay marriage, given the Wilde connection).

It could all have been very different here, because in 1801 Humphry Repton was invited by the college to come up with ideas for the fabled new quadrangle and how it might relate to Magdalen as a whole. To illustrate his plans Repton made one of his celebrated Red Books, comprising 'before and after' images of the college with flaps that fold out to reveal his intentions. Repton had a revolutionary scheme, which would have been spectacular if implemented. He noted in his text that:

In the various plans which have been suggested by architects only, there seems to have been a total disregard to these local circumstances and advantages which are possessed by Magdalen, over every other College in either of our Universities…in every design which I have seen for Magdalen, the Command of Property seems to have been neglected and no advantage taken of the adjacent Meadow, and trees or the River Charwell which flows through the premises.

Repton proposed creating an artificial lake out of the river in the southern part of Addison's Walk, submerging the meadow completely but thereby creating a succession of noble views across water back to a Great Quadrangle which he envisaged as Gothic. Finally, a portico or covered garden seat dedicated to Addison would be placed at the point of the widest view.

Whatever. In the event, Magdalen's fatal indecision also extended to landscape design and Repton's plans were never seriously considered. Perhaps this college, with its groves and gardens, its fritillaries and fawns, is best thought of as a place in which to dream.

LEFT A gateway marks the formal entrance into Addison's Walk. For spellbound visitors, it is a portal into another world.

ABOVE Horse chestnuts are among the trees to be found along the banked-up pathway that is Addison's Walk. Ash, beech, yew, hornbeam and sycamore contribute to this symphony of greens.

Merton College

S EVERAL COLLEGES PRESENT TWO different fronts to the world, but Merton is the only one which could truly be called Janus-faced. Its Merton Street facade to the north is classic Oxford Gothic, modest and private, though varied at its eastern end by the buildings of St Alban Hall, a medieval academical hall that was eventually absorbed into the college proper, and at the western end by the college chapel. Merton's southern face, which can be seen to best advantage from Christ Church Meadow, is quite different in tone. Its multi-gabled and chimneyed facade presents to the world a grand vision of some medieval palace high on its bastion, presided over by its own fine four-square tower, with the spires, towers and domes of a fabled city looming all around. From this vantage point, Merton manages to convey the impression that it somehow *is* Oxford, with all the other elements in view subservient to it. These two faces seem to reflect something of Merton's complex character – on the one hand it is quietly and unassumingly studious, in recent decades generally vying with St John's for the title of most academically successful college; on the other hand, it is sublimely and securely confident about its place in the pecking order of Oxford. Walter de Merton granted the college its statutes in 1264 and as a result it is usually accounted among the three oldest colleges, alongside University and Balliol. (The arguments as to which is the oldest will probably never be resolved.)

Like many Oxford colleges, Merton was established on land formerly occupied by a number of academical halls (ten

Autumn-flowering colchicums in the Fellows' Garden, where J.R.R. Tolkein lounged and T.S. Eliot paced.

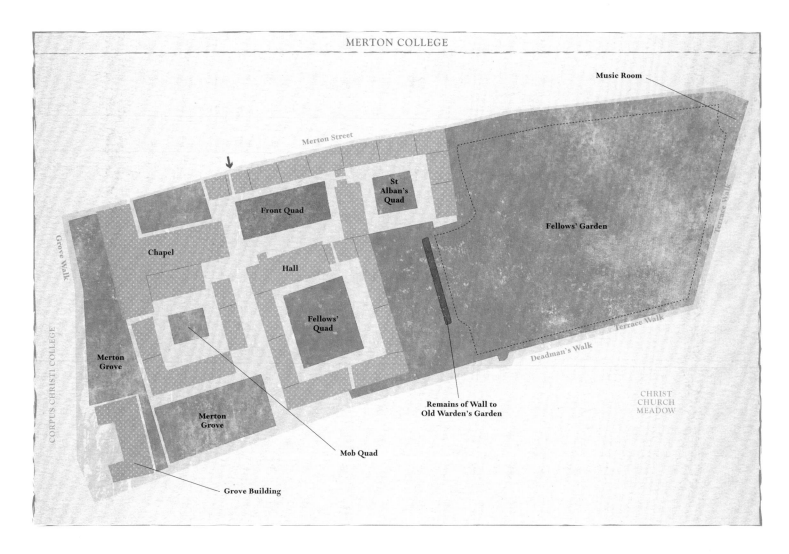

MERTON COLLEGE

Music Room

Merton Street

Front Quad

St Alban's Quad

Fellows' Garden

Chapel

Hall

Terrace Walk

Grove Walk

Fellows' Quad

Terrace Walk

Merton Grove

Deadman's Walk

CORPUS CHRISTI COLLEGE

Remains of Wall to Old Warden's Garden

CHRIST CHURCH MEADOW

Merton Grove

Mob Quad

Grove Building

in all), several of which had their own gardens. Merton's Front Quadrangle – its hall, chapel and the original Warden's Hall – had been built by 1300, while Mob Quad, indisputably the university's oldest, was begun in 1288 and finished a century later. (Neither today have much horticultural appeal, though it is interesting that Mob Quad was grassed over as late as 1930.) In 1320 a piece of land to the west of the college was purchased and accorded the title 'Bachelors' Garden', a reference to the bachelor-fellows of the college and possibly to nearby Mob Quad, also known as Bachelors' Quad. There are no records of what form this garden took or how the fellows may have used it, though the fact it was termed the bachelors' garden does imply that it was used for more than just growing vegetables and fruit for the kitchen. (It is likely that early college gardens such as this one had a dual role, as places for walking and retirement as well as for production.) In 1515 this garden was sold by the warden to Corpus Christi College, next door, in controversial circumstances (see the chapter on Corpus). By that time the college had anyway acquired more land to its east, a rectangle south of St Alban Hall which was initially delineated as the Warden's Garden. This remained a separate entity until the 1850s, when the dividing wall was lowered. More academical halls were taken

over as the college extended eastwards, and by the mid 16th century the extent of the present Fellows' Garden had been established, south and east to the city's rough walls.

In the 17th century the Warden's Garden was laid out in formal baroque fashion, with compartmented parterres. The Fellows' Garden itself was more informally arrayed, with the emphasis on trees. Fine sycamores are mentioned in the 1680s, and there are three good, old sycamores still, one of them planted in 1705 and associated with J. R. R. Tolkien, who apparently used to like to sit beneath it when he was a fellow of the college. The formal layout of the Fellows' Garden is shown on William Williams's 1733 engraving of the college, which is marked with the *Hortus Custodis* (Warden's Garden) of three enclosed plats and east of it the much larger *Hortus Sociorum* (Fellows' Garden), depicted with trees. The Fellows' Garden was described by a fellow of New College in 1723 as 'large and pleasant, being encompass'd on the East and South side thereof with two noble Terrass walks, and shaded in the midst'. This quality of variety, of the progression from light to shade, from sombre enclosure to bright and open vista, was intrinsic to the early-18th-century garden aesthetic and persisted through the 19th century. One hopes it may develop again in time, as the current crop of Merton's trees grow older.

Engravings made later in the 18th century indicate that those files of trees grew up to become almost a woodland, which is perhaps why the term Merton Grove came to be used for this part of the garden as well as for the area around the chapel.

The Fellows' Garden is discovered by penetrating east from Front Quad and through St Alban's Quad – reconstructed in 1904–10 by Basil Champneys, the south range left unbuilt so the quad now looks out to the garden through a wrought-iron screen. This route bypasses Fellows' Quadrangle to the south, which has considerable architectural but no horticultural interest. Some of the delight at finding the Fellows' Garden, which opens up in front of you in unexpected fashion as you pass through the gate from St Alban's Quad, is derived from the pleasure of contrast, the transition between the evident antiquity and somewhat cramped feel of the old college areas, and the openness and naturalism of the mead-like Fellows' Garden. These characteristics are cherished and nourished by head gardener Lucille Savin, who at the time of writing is

one of just three female head gardeners at Oxford's colleges.

The chief recommendation of the Fellows' Garden at Merton has long been its terrace walk, created in 1706–07, and the refreshment offered by its open views where it follows the college's southern boundary overlooking Christ Church Meadow. This terrace walk was planted with a lime avenue in the 18th century that was afterwards accorded high praise by visitors. The avenue has recently been replaced with different varieties of acer (such as *A. griseum* and *A. pensylvanicum*), while numerous other specimen trees are dotted about the lawns, including a Hungarian and a Turkish oak, varieties of cornus and variegated hollies. A gilded sundial and armillary sphere were installed here in 1830. The terrace walk, which is reached via an elegant flight of steps, has also recently been transformed by the addition of a border of irises along its entire length, with tall bearded 'Black Knight' listed as a favourite. There are numerous shrubs on the eastern terrace walk, including fragrant, yellow-flowered *Edgeworthia chrysantha*

and several of the larger hebes. Merton College was used as a base by Queen Henrietta Maria during the English Civil War, its walls fortified and cannons ranged along the terrace. It is said that one of the Royalist soldiers then garrisoned in Oxford was executed (shot) on the eastern terrace for cowardice or desertion. This walk is itself terminated at its northern end by an elegant summer house of 1706, built as a summer common room for the fellows and now used as a music room (its basement a well-appointed toolshed for the garden team).

This was not the first summer house to be raised in Merton's Fellows' Garden. The antiquary and historian of Oxford, Anthony Wood, a Merton man, wrote scathingly about an expensive new accoutrement which was the vanity project in the 1660s of a hated warden, Thomas Clayton, and – what was evidently worse – of his wife. Many Merton fellows were outraged by the decision to install a married man as the head of their house; 'the Lady Clayton' was unpopular and accused of extravagance. Wood caustically noted:

New trees planted, arbours made, rootes of choice flowers bought, etc. All which tho unnecessary, yet the poore college man must pay for them and all this to please a woman. Not content with these matters, there must be a new summer-house built at the south end of the warden's garden, wherein her ladyship and her gossips may take their pleasure, and any eaves-dropper of the family may harken what any of the fellows should accidentally talk of in the passage to their owne garden. And this the warden told the society that it would not cost the college above £20 yet when it was finished there was £100 paid for it by the bursar.

The summer house can be seen on Loggan's 1675 view of the college, an elegant little room reached by a narrow stairway of 16 steps, on top of the city wall at the foot of the Warden's Garden. Clayton was, by Wood's account at least, a bully, driving one fellow and the college gardener to suicide.

The gardener had been made to kneel down before the warden and beg forgiveness of him after he had said some intemperate words in frustration at not having enough money to maintain the garden. He was apparently buried 'stark naked' in the garden he had tended. The college's human-resources director would have something to say about that today, no doubt.

The northern part of the Fellows' Garden is today dignified by a fine and interesting double herbaceous and shrub border, one side against the college wall – its buttresses forming discrete garden zones – and the other along the top of the low terrace running east to west through the garden. Among the interesting shrubs and climbing plants here are *Rhamnus alaternus* 'Argenteovariegata', *Kolkwitzia amabilis*, *Actinidia* and *Indigofera*, as well as a wide variety of flowering herbaceous perennials. Everything is carefully labelled, a unique trait among Oxford's college gardens today.

From the western end of the terrace walk it is possible to reach the part of the garden which abuts Corpus Christi, known as Merton Grove, via a narrow path running behind the south range of Fellows' Quad. This passage is also densely planted, with *Viburnum carlesii*, *Azara microphylla*, a huge *Melianthus major* and thrusting echiums – the last a signature planting here and in other parts of the garden.

What is termed Grove Walk today denotes a public path within railings that leads from Merton Street along the western edge of the college and out into Christ Church Meadow. But the Grove actually extends all the way round the south and west sides of Merton's chapel. The area to the south of the chapel originally belonged to Goter (or Gutter) Hall, but by the 1420s it had gone and the Grove grew up here and eventually to the west of the chapel, too. Only eventually, because that area first served as a small outdoor tennis court, which is shown being used on the 1675 Loggan engraving. In case any more proof were needed, three ancient tennis balls were discovered during restoration work on the chapel, lodged in various crevices in the stonework. The college still has a ball court, over the road.

The character of Merton Grove was compromised farther by the addition of the Grove Building, constructed in 1864 to provide more accommodation within college. The architect was William Butterfield (the designer of Keble), whose characteristic polychrome brickwork proved so unpopular that the building was finally refaced more conventionally in 1930. Today the Grove has the character of a wildflower meadow adorned with small trees such as acers and cherries, with croquet played on the lawn in summer. Formerly it was populated with mature trees – mainly elm, chestnut, sycamore and ash – and this tree density was perhaps a contributing factor in a period of Merton's history which caused some discomfiture at the time.

The Oxford colleges were generally open to the public before the mid 19th century, and several of the larger gardens – those of St John's, Trinity and Magdalen, for example – became favoured resorts for university and town alike, especially on Sunday evenings in the warmer months. This was obviously a prime opportunity for 'innocent' flirtation between the sexes, but there were times when the atmosphere was differently tinged. Prostitution had been a fact of life in Oxford ever since young men had started to come to study in the city, and college fellows had begun taking their vows of chastity; and sex work (as we would now call it) was a well-established way for women, who were often married, to augment their incomes. Magpie Lane, formerly Grove Lane, connects Merton Street with the High Street to the north, and this was perhaps the centre of this activity in the city. As a result Grove Lane was also known as Grope Lane (and worse) – even on some official documents. Perhaps it was Merton's proximity to Grove Lane which led to Sunday-evening perambulations in the college's Grove and Fellows' Garden becoming notorious as an opportunity for licentious behaviour. A poem of 1717 entitled *Merton Walks or, the Oxford Beauties*, made humorous mention of the phenomenon:

In Merton Groves a nobler Strife is seen,
A claim more doubtful and a brighter Scene.
O! Merton cou'd I sing in equal lays,

Not These alone shou'd boast Eternal Praise,
Thy soft Recesses, and thy cool Retreats,
Of Albion's brighter Nymphs and blissful Seats.

A poetic response to this paean the next year entitled *Strephon's Revenge*, took a far dimmer view of Merton Grove's blissful seats and soft recesses, and noted approvingly the college's decision to close its grounds to the public:

Well, O! ye Sons of Merton, you exclude,
From your Recesses this licentious Brood:
No more by Day they haunt your crowded Groves.
Nor stain by Night with their unhallow'd Loves;
Henceforth some other publick Walk they seek.
To meet their blust'ring Coxcomb once a week.

In case we are in any doubt about his views, in the preface to this poem the author sternly remarks: 'I am not the only one that has taken notice of the almost universal corruption of our youth, which is to be imputed to nothing so much as to that multitude of Female Residentiaries who have of late infested our learned retirements and drawn off Numbers of unwary young persons from their studies.'

'Almost universal corruption'? It sounds as if Merton's undergraduates were almost to a man to be found wandering the Grove in search of corrupting diversions of a Sunday evening. And to think, they could have been glossing Horace's epodes instead... Perhaps it was this traumatic experience which caused the college ever after to keep its Fellows' Garden strictly private, reserved for use of college members and their guests only. Today, it is one of the last of the fellows' gardens which cannot be freely enjoyed by visitors.

But let us not leave Merton on a negative note. That celebrated clergyman and naturalist, Francis Kilvert, visiting in May 1876, recorded his visit somewhat breathlessly in his diary. In the process he summed up some of the timeless pleasures of an old Oxford college garden:

When service was over and the very small congregation had passed out we sauntered through the quadrangle till we came to the iron gate of the college gardens. It was open and we went in. I had never been in Merton Gardens before. They are very beautiful and the famous Terrace Walk upon the old city walls and the lime avenue are most delightful. The soft green sunny air was filled with the cooing of doves and the chiming of innumerable bells. It was a beautiful peaceful spot where abode an atmosphere of calm and happy security and the dewy garden was filled with a sweet green gloom as we loitered along the celebrated Terrace Walk, looking on one hand from the ancient city walls upon Merton Meadows and the Cathedral spire rising from the grey clustered buildings of Christ Church and the noble elms of the Broad Walk which hid from us the barges and the gay river, and delighting on the other side in the picturesque grey sharp gables of Merton College half veiled by the lime avenue rising from the green soft lawns and reposing in the silence and beauty and retirement of the shady happy garden.

TOP LEFT Salvias in profusion.

TOP RIGHT A decorative herm, surrounded by young *Verbena bonariensis*.

BELOW The armillary sundial with white cleome. Since 1971 the sundial has been the 2 a.m. start point for the college's 'time ceremony', when the student body progresses backwards around Fellows' Quad, while drinking port and in full academic dress, in order to maintain the integrity of the space-time continuum.

FOLLOWING PAGE The main border in the Fellows' Garden, with pink sedum and cranesbill geraniums in the foreground, and the orange dabs of tithonia behind.

New College

CHRIST CHURCH KNOWS ITSELF to be great; Magdalen knows itself to be beautiful; Merton is venerable, and knows it too.

New College – always New College, never just 'New' – is all of these things but, sitting quietly in the very centre of Oxford, it does not feel the need to declare itself. That is because almost everything at New College is self-evidently fine – not least its garden, remarkable for its scenography.

The college's main entrance, an addition by Gilbert Scott in the late 19th century, is at four storeys high one of the grandest collegiate frontages in Oxford. Yet it looks over not the busy High, sociable Broad or towny St Aldate's, but gentle Holywell Street, where it appears quite out of scale and tone with the surrounding quaint, pastel-painted houses. (It appears Scott had envisaged a three-storey building but several of the fellows insisted on a fourth.) So despite its grandiosity this is also, paradoxically, one of the quietest of college entrances, tucked away, somehow, behind everything else in the city centre.

The Holywell Street entrance is not, in any case, the most convenient way in to the college today, and now almost feels like a back entrance for goods vehicles. Fortunately for the college, the most used and most atmospheric entrance lodge is secreted down high-walled New College Lane, just by the dog-leg turn where it becomes Queen's Lane, at the point where the Oxford mason William Byrd's little bridge (late 1670s) crosses the street, leading to who knows where (of which more later).

The view to Garden Quadrangle and its grille. On the bank: *Narcissus* 'February Gold', *Tulipa praestans* 'Unicum' and lilac *Anemone blanda*.

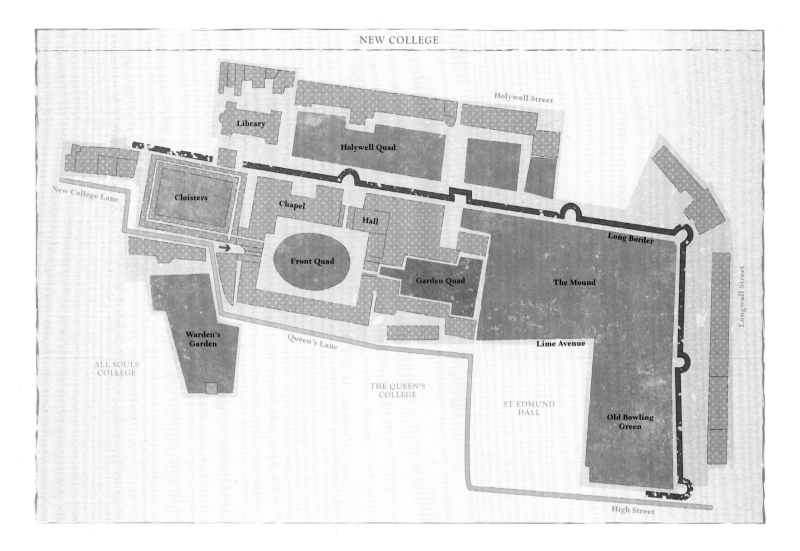

NEW COLLEGE

Known as the Old Lodge, this is a quiet entrance, too, but mysteriously and appropriately so, for by following this route, in just a few minutes the visitor to Oxford can be transported from the touristic maelstrom around the Bodleian Library into a palpably medieval milieu. The few steps from this gatehouse into the Great Quadrangle, with the Perpendicular chapel arising suddenly and majestically to one's left, constitute a marvellous Oxford moment.

All the buildings of the Great Quadrangle were completed in 1386, seven years after the college's foundation by William of Wykeham, so it can therefore lay claim to being the earliest enclosed quadrangle in all of Oxford. Also known as Old, Front or Founder's Quad, its medieval grandeur perhaps led the Victorian poet Robert Bridges to dub New College 'this gothic college', a term which fits colloquially as well as architecturally, since parts of it do feel pleasingly cobwebby even today. This quality must delight a new generation of visitors who come to New College because of its association with the Harry Potter films (having been used as a location for *Goblet of Fire*).

An impression of width is created by the relative dimensions of the lawn in the middle of the quad and the path around it, the latter being quite narrow. The sense of spaciousness means that the chapel appears almost as a cathedral in a meadow.

New College's founder was the Bishop of Winchester, after all. The simplicity of the lawn also nicely offsets the regularity of the large Georgian sash windows around two sides of the quad (the Old Buildings) and the crenellations which crown these ranges, topping the extra storey that had been added in the 18th century.

As befits such a venerable and architecturally strident set-piece quadrangle, planting is kept to a minimum – mainly in the bays between the chapel's buttresses, where some shrubs and trees were added only after 1920. The most notable is a large specimen of *Magnolia* x *soulangeana*.

This quad saw a revolution in 1789. A statue of Minerva was removed and a new lawn laid. Perhaps wise Minerva, so prominent in the visual life of the college, served as putative 'wife' to the fellows, much as nuns become the 'brides' of Jesus Christ. It would be another 80 years before fellows were allowed to marry. One hopes they bore up after being divorced from their goddess.

To the north-west are the cloisters, built just a decade after Great Quad and squeezed into the available space as an afterthought (at least according to the official college history). In their quietude and semi-darkness, the cloisters are cut off from both the college and the world beyond. Nowhere else in

Oxford seems quite as 'not in Oxford'. No matter that New College's are not the greatest example of medieval cloister architecture, given mistakes such as the even number of bays down each side, necessitating off-centre openings into the central garden; this sequestered space boasts an atmosphere which feels authentically monastic in a way that the cloisters at Magdalen, for example, do not. For those who seek it out, it is one of the most memorable places in all Oxford. As one's

footsteps echo on the flags in the always cool air, the memorials to New College's members across the centuries also pace out the life of the college.

The space in the middle of the cloister began as a burial ground but was probably at one time a garden filled with beautiful and useful plants. Today it is laid to grass (in poor condition) with a single massive ilex or evergreen oak in the far north-west corner. This tree dominates the space and could

now be removed, having surely run its course. At the time of writing it is cordoned off, with health-and-safety notices warning visitors about falling branches. A single variety of variegated weigela has been used around the perimeter of the cloister garden.

All of the above does not constitute what people generally think of as the 'gardens' at New College. These can be found to the east of Great Quad, approached via Garden Quadrangle.

The college's leaflet guide directs visitors at this point to 'circumambulate' the chapel to reach Garden Quadrangle. This is one of the 'newer' parts of the college, having been built between 1682 and 1707 to the designs of Byrd (he of the bridge) and William Townesend. The massive and muscular

PREVIOUS PAGE Fragrant *Rosa* 'Ispahan' in Holywell Quad.

ABOVE The long border by the old city wall, with a profusion of roses and a fringe of blue nepeta (catmint) at the front.

Purple asters, *Helianthus* 'Lemon Queen' and *Salvia involucrata* 'Bethellii' in the mixed borders designed by Robin Lane Fox.

style is somewhat reminiscent of John Vanbrugh's work, but lacking equivalent finesse. The quad is reached by means of the Middle Gateway, a deceptively modest archway beneath the Founder's Library which leads the circumambulating visitor into what is yet another architectural tour de force at this college. Garden Quadrangle consists of twin ranges each with three crenellated blocks of graduated scale, which open out on to the garden's lawns. The bonded gravel surface of the quad (why not real gravel?) creates something of a municipal car-park feel initially, but as one progresses inexorably towards the garden, this is soon left behind.

Before the creation of Garden Quadrangle there was a high wall between the college and its gardens, which were reached through a communicating door. But this 1.4-hectare/3.5-acre space, bounded by the 13th-century city walls to the north and east, has always been a special place in Oxford, and the focus of jealous regard by other colleges. After all it contains that unlikely survival, the Mount, the single most extraordinary garden feature in all Oxford, with the possible exception of the 18th-century observatory at Green Templeton College.

The earliest references to New College's gardens make it clear that they were seen primarily as a productive space, including a vineyard. The Mount is possibly first recorded in the bursar's rolls for 1529–30, when 500 wagonloads of rubbish or spoil were tipped into the garden, though the term used, '*bigati fumi*', could also mean manure. Then in 1594 the college gardener was given £3 'towards ye making of ye mount', which could refer to its ornamentation – the creation of the customary winding paths up to the top, where trees and a small pavilion might be added. Medieval mounts were built for a variety of purposes, the foremost being decorative, though they could also serve as vantage points for views across an estate or the countryside (which one assumes would have been the case at New College, by the old city walls), or to watch deer or coney (rabbit) hunts. Alas, there is no record of fellows hunting rabbits here. Mounts were fashionable features in the 16th century. Of Italian origin, they were often nicknamed Parnassus with reference to the sacred mountain that the ancient Greeks dedicated to poetry. New College's Parnassus (it is referred to in this way at least once) is recorded as having

been 'perfected' in 1649, which may have been the moment when a well-documented quartet of parterres, consisting of the arms of William of Wykeham and Charles I resplendent alongside a sundial parterre and a swirling knot, were added at the foot. These are recorded in David Loggan's engraving of 1675.

One interesting new theory concerning the Mount has a persuasive political context. It has been suggested that the 16th-century Mount was probably barely a Mount at all at that time, but was considerably built up in 1642 by the ardently Royalist warden, Robert Pinck, who could also have added the parterres incorporating the arms of the king. The argument is that Pinck was making reference to Henry VIII's famous Mount at Hampton Court, thereby demonstrating his allegiance to Charles I in the tense period just before civil war broke out. This would at least explain why such an old-fashioned feature was being created or enlarged – an anachronism usually explained away as an example of the stubbornly old-fashioned college fellows, which seems a stereotype too far, even for Oxford. During the Civil War, the cloisters at New College were used as an ammunition dump.

Given the long collective memories of colleges, especially on matters pertaining to 'the real world', it is a little surprising that this story, if true, has not survived at the college. It goes unmentioned by the perspicacious diarist Celia Fiennes, who visited the college in 1694 by dint of a family connection. She found the fellows rather geeky, but observed approvingly of the way they delighted in the scents of potted lemon and myrtle trees dispersed about the college precincts. She also noted, of the garden proper, 'gravell and grass walkes, some shady, and a great mount in the middle which is ascended by degrees in a round of green paths deffended by greens cutt low, and on the top is a Summer house, beyond these Gardens is a bowling-green'.

It always helps if those in charge of a college have a feeling for gardens, and Warden Pinck certainly did. The botanical author and New College man William Coles in 1657 remembered him as 'a very learned Man, and well versed in Physick, and truly he would rise very betimes in the morning even in his later dayes, when he was almost four-score years old, and going into his Garden, he would take a Mattock or Spade, digging there an houre or two, which he found very advantageous to his health.' This is a rare record of the head of a college actually doing some gardening.

The ancient parterres were kept in place almost until the end of the 18th century, by which time the landscape garden craze had swept the land. Some have expressed incredulity about the accuracy of William Williams's engraving of 1733, which shows the quartered parterre still intact below the Mount. But such 'old-fashioned' features were retained at many gardens at least until the 1750s and the ascent of 'Capability' Brown, while mounts in gardens were often seen by families as a badge of ancient association with a place – whether they were reforming Whigs or dyed-in-the-wool Tories. If this sounds at odds with the earlier theory about the creation of the college Mount for political purposes, it might be remembered that it is only the addition of a 'new old-fashioned' feature which surprises, not the retention of one that already exists. The evolution of most Oxford colleges can

be characterised as centuries of inertia punctuated by moments of extreme activity and fashionability, so it is not unlikely that New College simply maintained the Mount and parterres in the same form for years.

Perhaps it should not come as a surprise, then, that an undergraduate at Queen's, whose rooms overlooked the college grounds, should write to his aunt as late as 1742 of its 'fine Variety of Vistas, Shady Walks and Arbours', noting too the parterres and their precise themes, still just as described by earlier visitors. What might be more of a surprise is the identity of this student: William Gilpin, who later in life came to excoriate such garden formality. As a Surrey clergyman he would single-handedly pioneer the fashion for all things Picturesque by means of his vivid accounts of 'tours' to places such as the Wye Valley. (The Picturesque movement in garden and landscape appreciation, broadly between the 1780s and the 1820s, favoured naturalistic scenes that were thrilling and beautiful.) But for now a bevy of old-fashioned parterres were a pleasant distraction from Gilpin's window.

The parterres may have been retained in good order until as late as 1761, when the *Pocket Companion for Oxford* makes reference to them (though such books were often simply cobbled together using earlier sources and cannot be relied upon). By the end of the 18th century, the parterres were certainly gone and the Mount overgrown by yews and other evergreens, much as it is today. Despite some effort at replanting, the Mount now has a lumpishly dark if not brooding presence, when it ought to be the bright focus and triumph of the garden. Parnassus has fallen silent, its nymphs enchained, its Muses departed. It is occasionally suggested that the Mount has now become a 'Picturesque' feature. It has not. One sometimes has a feeling that this term is used too easily as a euphemism for overgrown.

The received idea is that Garden Quadrangle was built in order to make the most of views out across the garden towards the Mount. But it seems just as likely that the intention was to make use of what was seen as the old and purposeless Mount to provide a vantage point for a vista back towards the new architectural composition, the most nearly palatial of all the quadrangle ranges of Oxford. It is indeed a splendid sight. The different-sized sash windows for each of the three blocks is a particularly effective architectural detail: conventionally proportioned sashes for the outermost blocks, narrower and taller for the next, while the innermost blocks have only a single standard window for each floor, lending the square-ish little blocks an attractive stubbiness which gives them something of the air of twin entrance pavilions or gate-lodges at an estate. The Muniment Tower protruding above the north range unbalances the symmetry in a pleasing manner. In fact this is barely a quadrangle at all, as the buildings unfold themselves towards the garden, moving the focus outwards rather than inwards. Garden Quadrangle is really more of a

In late summer the colour continues (above and left) and dahlias come to the fore. The border is segmented by evergreen buttresses.

RIGHT Evergreen and shrub plantings on and around the Mount, which is today treated as an informal landscape feature – if not precisely 'Picturesque'.

OPPOSITE LEFT Morning glory (ipomoea) twining through the gilded gate into Garden Quad.

OPPOSITE RIGHT Dahlias in pale yellow and scarlet, with clematis and asters behind.

OPPOSITE BELOW Annuals including white cosmos and red zinnias by the screen against Garden Quad.

garden front in the 17th- and 18th-century country-house tradition, its twin ranges to be accounted as 'wings'. That impression is bolstered by the 'gate-lodges' together with the screen to the garden with its gilded gateway, which replaced the old wall in 1711.

This screen 40 metres/130 feet in length – black iron railings with a magnificently moulded central portion – is what bounds and heralds the college garden today, with shrub roses, anemones and other plants growing through it almost along its length. It was made by Thomas Robinson, who had worked alongside the French master Jean Tijou (responsible for the great screen in the Privy Garden at Hampton Court). The positioning of the screen – which is not in fact the original, but an excellent replica made in Oxford in 1894 – cleverly disguises an underlying asymmetry that allows for a straight vista from Old Lodge to the Mount. It is not aligned directly on the Middle Gateway, and nor is it dead centre in the context of the quadrangle; the elegant bulging of the screen near the gates helps obscure the discrepancy by means of distraction. The result is that, looking back towards college, the visitor has that unusual sensation in Oxford of a vista which takes the eye through multiple quads.

But the Mount is not all this garden has to offer. It has long been a place in which to wander as well as wonder. The Williams engraving of 1733 shows straight tree-lined avenues by the old city walls, while the Loggan illustration of 1675 reveals a walled bowling green in the far, south-east corner of the gardens. The crumbling city walls with their towers, to the left of the Mount as one looks from the 'viewing platform' of

Garden Quadrangle, are today just as arresting as the Mount and add to the general sense of New College as a place of ancient decorum. What is more, the northern range of this wall is fronted by the longest and most magnificent herbaceous border in Oxford, overseen in recent years by classics don Robin Lane Fox, who is well known for his long-running gardening column in the Saturday edition of the *Financial Times* newspaper.

Lane Fox is a critic of the naturalistic 'New Perennials' school of planting design, reliant as it is on repeated drifts of certain key perennials. Several leading protagonists hail from the Netherlands and Germany, so Lane Fox has dubbed it the 'waving Euro-grasses' phenomenon. It has to be admitted that there is a certain kinship between gardens realised in this style. For those steeped in the English garden tradition of plantsmanship, the new perennials look can be dull both visually and horticulturally, while it is also subject to accusations of relative sparseness until late August or September. Now is not the time to get into the minutiae of this argument (for that, see my book *The New English Garden*, 2013) but suffice to say, it is an ongoing debate in British gardening circles. As such, Lane Fox's border at New College is very much in the late-20th-century tradition of English planting design – a complex border which delights in combinations of colour and form to produce the sensation of an unfolding tapestry along its length, and across a long season. Flowering shrubs mingle and intertwine with herbaceous flowers and annuals in a constantly evolving, hedonistic display, which is 'big' enough to cope with the formidable

backdrop of the ancient city walls, including a turret about halfway along. The emphasis is on clumps of plants meeting and marrying, creating circular movements within the bed, rather than drifts that produce a linear movement along its length. Of course there will be changes every season, but among the key plants are clerodendrum, phygelius, jasmine, pink sedum, white nicotiana, penstemons, salvias, heleniums and, later in the season, bright and blowsy dahlias and daisy-formed asters. There are no grasses. The design emphasis is on contrasting flower forms as opposed to colour theming, which leads to some strident combinations that are, deliberately, not always carefully controlled. The great north border at New College has been a nexus of horticultural activity in Oxford for several centuries – it is shown as mature, broad and densely planted with a wide variety of trees and shrubs as early as 1822, in an engraving in *The Oxford Visitor* guidebook.

The curious visitor will explore behind the Mount, where a door in the wall opens on to the modernist Sacher Building of 1962, with Barbara Hepworth's bronze *Garden Sculpture (Model for Meridian)* in the foreground. This ought to be another highlight of the garden, but the sculpture is spoiled by a large black 'Private' sign placed beneath it.

In the south-eastern corner of the garden, very much tucked away, there is a depression in the rough grass indicating that this was formerly the site of the college's bowling green. Mature trees now encircle the area, including several large planes, and although they are not handsome individual specimens, there is a pleasantly cut-off atmosphere here, with just the wind in the trees for company. This grove is effectively a temple to the pleasures of susurration. It was in a corner here, where now stands a decrepit water pump, that 'there was some time', according to Anthony Wood, the 17th-century member of Merton, antiquary and diarist, 'an ancient custom belonging to New College Fellows [on Holy Thursday]…some of them going up to a well or spring in the grove, which was strewed with flowers round about for them, they sung a song of five parts.' Maybe not so ancient: the college's historian John Buxton states that this song was Thomas Morley's madrigal, 'Hard by a Crystal Fountain', published in 1601 and dedicated to Oriana the Bright (aka Queen Elizabeth I). Perhaps this

was a relict of a pagan ritual on this ground that predated the creation of the college, kept alive by the superstitious or sentimental fellows. It would be nice to see the custom revived, perhaps by the college choir.

A lovely line of lime trees adjoining the wall running east-west on this side of the garden perhaps produces something of the old sensation of walking here when the garden was in its early 18th-century form. The pleasures of walking under files of trees was one of the key sensual effects of the baroque garden, easily forgotten when we are used to thinking about them as barren exercises in formality. There are no ornate features typical of that period any more, but a gently undulating apron of sward nicely offsets the buildings of Garden Quadrangle up and beyond it.

Perhaps it is necessary to mention here the necessary, the fabulously capacious college lavatory, which John Pointer enumerated as one of the 'curiosities' of the college in his 1749 guidebook to Oxford, between remarks about a statue of the Virgin Mary and the cut of the college gowns: '8. Give me leave in this Place to mention a very necessary Edifice call'd, The Long-House, that has never been emptied since the Foundation of the College.'

Finally, we can return to that mysterious bridge over New College Lane. It leads to the warden's private garden, set apart from the main college and hardly ever open to the public (though in recent years there has been an opera evening in July, open to alumni and special guests). This is a charming place and surprisingly large – a lawn surrounded by shrub roses, lavender and other plantings, focused at its far end on an elegant little flat-roofed pavilion of about 1720, most likely the work of Townesend. Indeed, this little building could be a reference to the architecture Townesend was responsible for in the 'public' part of the college, since its proportions and fenestration make it look like a portmanteau version of several different elements of Garden Quad. If this is the case, it would be a rather academical-architectural joke – but if that's not appropriate here, then where?

The cloisters and bell tower, with variegated *Weigela* 'Florida Variegata' growing around the perimeter.

Nuffield College

SITUATED IN AN UNATTRACTIVE and car-blighted part of town, halfway between the railway station and the city centre, Nuffield is at least conveniently placed for those who wish to escape Oxford almost as soon as they have arrived. One suspects this is quite often the case at Nuffield, because since its creation in 1937 as a graduate institution, it has (uniquely for an Oxford college) formally specialised in one discipline above others: the social sciences. Given the left-leaning bias of many who have worked and studied here – including numerous journalists and trades unionists – and the fact that the college's non-academic visiting fellows often combine their tenure with 'day jobs' in London, proximity to the fast train to Paddington will presumably have been a considerable asset. If this is sometimes the case today, then it was not always so. In its early post-war days, the college was well known for offering a standard of accommodation and food which far outstripped what was on offer at more venerable colleges. Nuffield provided central heating, convenient bathrooms and excellent food, with students given sets of multiple rooms, as if they were the noblemen in Christ Church's Peckwater Quad.

The largesse flowed from the purse of the college's founder and sole funder, but the irony was that a college specialising in social sciences was not in any way the intention of Will Morris of Morris Motors, who as Lord Nuffield donated the land and all the money needed to establish the college. His original idea was that it would specialise in engineering and its application to business, a perfectly reasonable notion which

Verbena bonariensis in Lower Quad, characterised by architect Austen St Barbe Harrison's super-extended Cotswoldery.

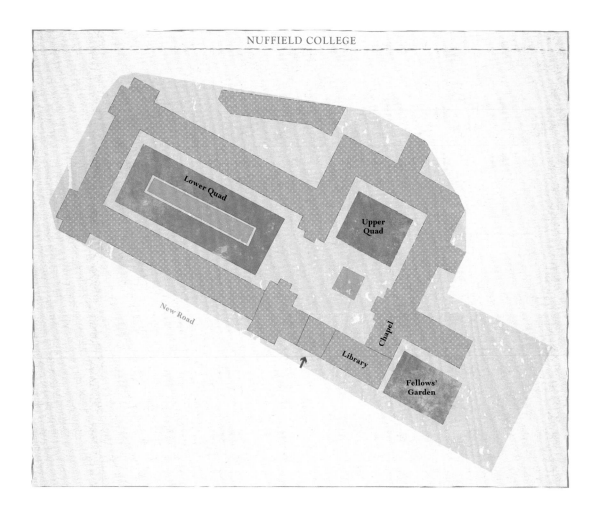

NUFFIELD COLLEGE

Lower Quad

Upper Quad

New Road

Chapel

Library

Fellows' Garden

RIGHT Peter Randall Page's *Flayed Stone IV* on the lawn in the Upper Quadrangle.

was perhaps rather ahead of its time, given the emphasis on exactly this within universities nowadays. But this man of working-class origins, who left school at 15 to set up a bicycle-repair business and went on to lead the car industry in Britain, was consistently ignored and condescended to by the Oxford establishment. He reluctantly agreed to the social-science option, but at the end of his life said he felt cheated by the university for setting up in his name the college tagged 'the Kremlin by the station'. Presumably he would have approved, however, of the way the college has managed its own endowment since this small and relatively young college is now the fourth richest in the university.

Architecturally, Nuffield has come in for a hard time from commentators, who appear reluctant to give it a second glance. The college's vexed design history has contributed to the impression that the place is a botched job, physically. But closer inspection reveals an interesting, effective and quietly subversive design. As with St Catherine's in the 1960s, the college was created in one go, all of a piece, with a single architect designing all the integral quadrangles or garden spaces – as opposed to the hodgepodge which is the history of the typical Oxford college. As a result Nuffield presents a pleasing homogeneity of design and an attractive and consistent sense of scale.

The choice of an architect was taken out of Lord Nuffield's

hands at the outset as was, apparently, any real say in the design. (Nuffield had professed a desire for a tall tower and traditional English architecture, neither of which he got in the first instance.) Leaving the donor out of the discussion was a major error on the part of the university, given the car magnate's obvious interest in the way his money would be spent and his reputation for forceful opinions. The architect selected by the panel was, in addition, a rather adventurous choice in the circumstances.

Austen St Barbe Harrison (1891–1976) was born into a middle-class, middle-of-the-road English family in Kent, his Christian name proudly reflecting the fact he was distantly related to the author of *Pride and Prejudice*. He trained as an architect in Canada and London before the First World War intervened. He saw action at Passchendaele in 1917 but became disillusioned by the carnage and attempted to resign his commission. In a compromise with his commanding officer, Harrison served out the war as a stretcher-bearer. Subsequently he pursued a long career almost entirely abroad (Nuffield College was to be his only major commission in Britain), living as a self-styled recluse. All of this is relevant because it helps one understand how and why Harrison came to design Nuffield in the way that he did. Harrison carved a niche for himself designing buildings for the British authorities in the Middle East, especially in Palestine during

the British Mandate. He also worked in Greece, and towards the end of his career created the masterplan for the University of Ghana. His longest stint was in Jerusalem, however, where he designed two buildings which have an important bearing on the designs for Nuffield College: the Rockefeller Museum (1930–38) – where he collaborated with the stone carver Eric Gill – and the British High Commissioner's Residence (1933). Both buildings reflect Harrison's specialism, which was monumental versions of local vernacular architecture that also reflect the neoclassicism of the British inheritance. This kind of fusion approach to architecture was known as Beaux Arts and was widely taught at the time – in the first couple of decades of the 20th century, before modernism changed everything. And both these buildings contain gardens as important elements of the design – most notably at the High Commissioner's Residence (which has been the United Nations headquarters since 1948), where the formal sunken garden is sheltered by walls and flanked by monumental

vaulted cloisters. There is something of the later work of Edwin Lutyens about Harrison's *oeuvre* – the monumental solidity of a Castle Drogo intermixed with the joyous decorative appeal of the Viceroy's Palace and garden in Delhi. And it transpires that Harrison in fact spent several months working in Lutyens' India office. His evident ambivalence about the late-imperial British establishment – perhaps a sense that he now belonged nowhere and everywhere – meant that Harrison was comfortable experimenting with vernacular styles from the eastern tradition, and mixing them up with European principles. This was the wellspring of his work at Oxford, too, where he applied exactly the same approach. The twist was that the local style he was plundering was not Arabic or Mediterranean, but English.

Harrison's first design for Nuffield College was accepted by the university's panel in 1939 but went down disastrously badly with Lord Nuffield himself, as it bore no relation to anything he had envisaged. This first design was an ambitious

Lower Quad, with the too-dominant library tower beyond, its arrow-slit
fenestration a stark counterpoint to the windows found in the rest of the college.

and imaginative medley of southern Mediterranean features,
all to be realised in stark white Portland stone. With tall,
flat-fronted, flat-roofed accommodation blocks featuring
narrow windows, a squat polygonal tower and a massive
aisled chapel like a Roman basilica, Harrison's conception for
Nuffield was both palatial and, to English eyes, palpably exotic,
owing much to the Arab-inflected architecture of Sicily and
southern Spain. There was to be no honeyed Cotswold stone,
no steeply pitched tile roofs, no villagey atmosphere, not even
a tall tower. It did not help that the large model Harrison
presented was made of brown clay. All of this was anathema
to Lord Nuffield, who was horrified, decrying the plans as 'un-
English and out of keeping with the best tradition of Oxford
architecture', and 'of an oriental type more suited to Cairo and
Baghdad'. All of which was true enough – if only someone had
told the architect what was wanted.

To his great credit, Harrison did not walk out on the
project at this point but instead went back to the drawing
board. In an interview recorded in 1970, Harrison recalled
that he and a colleague toured the Cotswolds by bicycle in
search of vernacular inspiration. His second design for the
college – and the one which was executed – is, on the face of
it, Cotswolds in inspiration, with Clipsham stone being used
together with self-consciously old-fashioned details such as
gable ends, tile roofs, tall chimneys and dormer windows.
As a result the main accommodation ranges look like super-
extended Cotswolds cottages, while the floral interest of
the beds in the college's two quadrangles, which intersect
at right angles at different levels, give the place more
than a soupçon of Nuffield's dream of an English country
idyll. These elements of Harrison's alternative composition

have led to it generally being considered as the second-
best option, the compromise, the unfortunate offspring of
Oxford's greatest architectural missed opportunity. In style
it is characterised as an outmoded Arts and Crafts solution,
what John Julius Norwich dubbed the 'cautious Cotswoldery
of the thirties'.

But I am not so sure about this characterisation. Harrison
retained certain architectural features redolent of the East –
most notably the Mozarabic doorway arches and the lantern
to the tower – and also made some interesting decisions when
it came to the garden, which does not feel fully 'English' if
one stops to think and feel. The long pool running most of
the length of the Lower Quadrangle might be considered a
species of Arts and Crafts feature – an Italian sunken garden
– were it not for its excessive length and narrowness. The
view down it from the Upper Quadrangle terminates in a
gable end and open archway, and there is close-mown lawn
all around. Harrison himself said: 'The pool in the main
quad was intended to be a reminder of the canal which was
there before.' Notwithstanding this, the scale is all wrong for
an English garden. In fact it bears more resemblance to a rill
in the Islamic garden tradition, more akin to the waterway
in the Generalife garden at the Alhambra in Spain, than
something to be found in Edwardian Surrey. Ditto the small
square pool in the Upper Quadrangle – its geometric design
is much more redolent of the Eastern tradition than the
Western, where a pool of this size (such as a dipping pool
in a walled garden) would generally be circular in shape.
The insistent, repetitive fenestration and the smallness of
the windows (almost arrow-slits) in the Upper Quadrangle
likewise have more of southern Europe about them than

southern England. The presence in the Upper Quadrangle of good abstract sculptures – *Flower Fountain* by Hubert Dalwood in the pool, and Peter Randall Page's *Flayed Stone IV* on the lawn – adds another layer of complexity without undue confusion. They seem at home here because as well as the Eastern influence there is a frisson of modernism to Harrison's design, which was very much of its time. Other architects of this period, such as Lutyens, Oliver Hill and Giles Gilbert Scott (who designed the New Bodleian Library), were influenced by modernist ideas in the later phases of their careers, and in Harrison's case this trend is evinced at Nuffield by the geometric chunkiness of his 'Cotswolds' blocks, which are far too well-proportioned and rational to be wholly vernacular in feel.

As a general conclusion one might suggest that Nuffield College was made in the image of its architect. That is: traditional, conventional England gone walkabout in the Middle East and Mediterranean.

All of this barely registers with the visitor, it is so subtly done. And evidently it did not register with Lord Nuffield, either, for building finally commenced in 1949 and continued for a decade, during which time his foundation also received its charter as a fully fledged constituent college of the university. But perhaps, after all, the compromise solution was better than the exuberant pastiche originally envisaged, and the college deserves a better reception, architecturally speaking. Having said that, one aspect of Nuffield's design where I do concur with received criticism concerns the tower, an ungainly beast which somehow manages to appear squat despite soaring 45 metres/150 feet into the air over nine storeys. Its broadness was the result of a late decision

to house the college library there, while details such as the bright green copper spire and the prissy orderliness of its rectangular windows give it an unfortunate municipal air.

The horticulture, which is of a good standard, veers more towards the English end of the spectrum than the Mediterranean in the Lower Quadrangle, with bright flower borders around the doorways (magnolias, viburnums, anenomes, phlomis, fuchsias, roses, vines, bergenias) and orderly topiary on the lawns – corner squares of box with clipped pyramids, and sentinel Irish yews guarding the wide steps that connect Upper and Lower Quadrangles. One good landscape-design decision – again, easy to take for granted – was not to formally divide the two quadrangles but to allow them to flow into each other; the change of level provides just enough of a sense of progression. The Upper Quadrangle has an interesting mixture of hard materials, including panels of pebbles, while the planting here is more Mediterranean in inspiration, including euphorbias, lavender, thyme and spiky purple cordyline, plus a bold strip of purple *Verbena bonariensis*. The mature garden really 'makes' Nuffield College.

To visit Nuffield as the shadows lengthen and the scents of the flowers become richer by the moment, one would never imagine its genesis was accompanied by hand-wringing and controversy. Were he alive today, it would be nice to think that Lord Nuffield might be content with it, after all.

Is there something of the Islamic rill tradition about the central canal in Lower Quad?

Oriel College

O RIEL CONTEMPLATES ITS OWN little square with all the serene complacency of a duomo overlooking its piazza. No other college has quite such a dignified urban setting, where the traffic seems to have stopped out of deference to this ancient place of learning. Founded in 1324, this was the first of the Oxford colleges to be cobbled together from multiple existing academical halls – lodging houses for university students – and the majority of later collegiate foundations followed its example.

Oriel began as a rather superior sort of an institution, since the university rector, Adam de Brome, obtained a licence from King Edward II for a college designated for senior scholars only. (Oriel began admitting undergraduates some 250 years later.) The royal link is tangible to this day, since the reigning monarch is always designated the official college visitor. As a result the college has been known, at some moments in its history, as King's College. But it also belongs to the Virgin Mary, as we shall see.

Its first properties were Tackley's Inn, on the south side of the High Street (which is still part of the college's fabric) and the wonderfully named Perilous Hall, north of Broad Street. The royal link was cemented in 1329 when the Crown, by that time representing Edward III, granted the college the lease of a large house on the site of what is now First Quad. This building, which faced south on to Merton Street, was known as La Oriole in recognition of the oriel window which was a prominent feature, hence the curious name adopted by the new

A 'quad man' at work in Back Quad, with James Wyatt's elegant library of 1791 in the background.

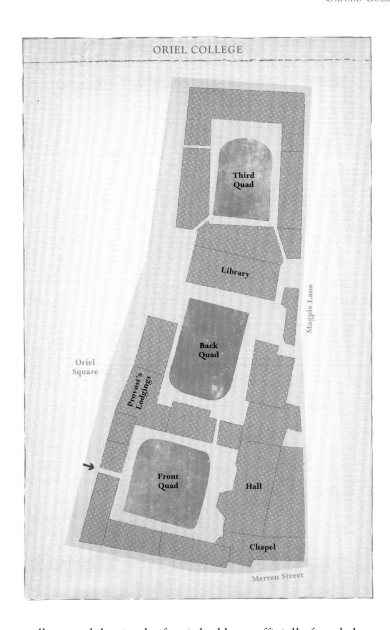

ORIEL COLLEGE

Third Quad

Library

Magpie Lane

Back Quad

Oriel Square

Provost's Lodgings

Front Quad

Hall

Chapel

Merton Street

The precise chronology of early building at Oriel is mysterious, but we know that two ranges of First Quad (not the present ones) had been completed by the end of the 14th century and that La Oriole itself was demolished to make way for this. Over the next several hundred years the college gradually gobbled up more academical halls, tenements and areas of open ground north of First Quad in its effort to unify the two core college sites. The earliest map of the city of Oxford, drawn by Ralph Agas in 1578, shows three ranges of First Quad forming an awkward, squashed rectangle bounded to the north by a cluster of old buildings. There is open ground farther towards the High Street, with a few more buildings dotted across it, including Bedel Hall which stood where the college library now is, and then St Mary Hall itself with a small enclosed garden of its own. Part of the open and partially unbounded area between Oriel's First Quad and St Mary Hall – the site of Back Quad today – was a property called St Frideswide's (after the Augustinian priory that originally owned it) which the college acquired in the early 15th century and which was then described as a garden. We know that the college employed a gardener whose duties were to tend it and the smaller garden of St Mary Hall.

This main garden space at Oriel was developed significantly in the late 16th century: an arbour, raised terrace walkway, seats, benches, several 'orchards' (one designated for the provost), flowers and a sundial were recorded. A small ball court, or *sphaeristerium*, was made in 1598 against the eastern wall, at one end of the raised terrace walk. New lodgings for the provost were constructed overlooking what was known as the 'inner garden' in 1613, though this building was to be demolished during the 18th-century development of Back Quad. The college garden came to be known as the Bachelors' Garden, a shortening of Bachelor Fellows' Garden (a term which crops up once or twice at other colleges). Up until the first decades of the 18th century the college garden provided both an amenity for undergraduates, provost and fellows, and a linking space between Oriel College and St Mary Hall. The raised walkway along the eastern wall would have been a relaxing diversion and a vantage point for admiring a garden

college, and despite the fact it had been officially founded as the Hall of the Blessed Mary at Oxford. (And what a shame it was not renamed Perilous College...) The Virgin Mary continued to be commemorated at Oriel since the largest and most important of the academical halls absorbed into it was St Mary Hall, which was situated like Tackley's Inn on the south side of the High Street, opposite the University Church of St Mary's, where the founding rector was based. It is clear that the links between the college and the university church, and indeed with the Virgin Mary, were extremely important to the college. St Mary Hall and Oriel College itself were for a long time deemed to be of equal status; St Mary Hall was the subject of its own engraving, alongside the established colleges, in David Loggan's *Oxonia Illustrata* of 1675, an indication of its rank. For centuries the hall functioned as an annexe to Oriel, with its principal a fellow of that college, though it was not until as late as 1902 that it was formally assimilated into the college. One of the last vestiges of its historical standing is the fact that the Vicar of St Mary's has dining rights at Oriel.

of knots and geometric paths below, probably divided into separate areas for the provost and the fellows (bachelors). The orchards would have been quincunxes (sets of five) or formal geometric arrangements and allées of fruit trees which would also have played a decorative role.

First Quad was completely rebuilt in Oxford Gothic style in two bursts, from 1620–22 and 1637–42, with strident Dutch gables crowned by pinnacles all the way around. It's a handsome quadrangle, with Merton's tower rising beyond and elaborate cartouches above the staircase doorways. The college hall and chapel take up the eastern range, and this is the first thing the visitor sees from the entrance lodge. It was a nice touch to add a pair of tall oriel windows at each end of the hall range, contrasting with the run of six Gothic windows that span its width, but the scale of First Quad cannot quite cope and the result is that it all looks a little over-compacted. The right-hand oriel window is in fact false, with a blank wall behind. The element which really commands the visitor's attention is the oversized porch and fanned staircase that leads

up to the dining hall, surmounted by a trio of statues in niches. It's a dramatic and slightly forbidding interpolation, with the letters *Regnante Carolo* (Charles is King – referring to Charles I) heavily picked out in the parapet above the porch, just in case one forgets this is the king's college. This was all restored in 1897. The influence of Wadham's Front Quad (1610–13) on other Oxford colleges is palpable at this time, setting a fashion for dramatic set-piece openers in colleges which advertise the status of benefactors – though it has to be said that Oriel's pair of kings topped by the Virgin Mary does rather trump Mr and Mrs Wadham from Somerset. The main horticultural incident in this conventionally lawned quad takes the form of a regiment of potted red pelargoniums set out in double rows which march up the granite hall steps like the Grand Old Duke of York's men. Red climbing roses against both hall and chapel, with lavenders below, add to the sense of drama, while planted in beds in front of the ranges are an orderly array of annual flowers, with red as the main colour theme, and more climbing roses in softer tones above.

An atmospheric flagstoned passage in the left (north) range takes the visitor into Back Quad, which was transformed in the 1720s when a pair of free-standing accommodation blocks were built facing each other across the garden, east to west. The Williams engraving of 1733 shows that these buildings, which are gabled in muscular fashion to echo First Quad, were intended to create the sense of an opening into the college garden, with a line of railings and a central gate linking the pair of buildings as if they were the wings of a country house fronted by a gravelled terrace. Both this and the Loggan engraving of 1675 illustrate the way the Bachelors' Garden itself had been much simplified by the late 17th century, with grass plats where the knots and orchards would have been, though the raised terrace running the length of the garden survived, with flights of steps at each end. This garden was described as pleasant indeed in the *Universal British Directory* of 1791:

The garden-court, which we enter by a passage in the same north side, receives an agreeable air from an elegant little garden which is formed in the midst of it, and fenced on this side with iron gates and pallisades, supported by a dwarf-wall and stone piers. The sides are two wings, in a stile correspondent to that of the quadrangle.

The next major intervention came in 1791 when James Wyatt's library was placed in the middle of the garden, facing south towards First Quad. It's a good building, with eight great Ionic columns dividing seven bays set with rectangular sash windows, and a confidently plain entablature above. But it did spell the end of Oriel's garden. Some tree and shrubbery planting was essayed around each end of the library during the early 19th century, but the character had changed from that of a garden to a quadrangle. The ball court and part of the raised terrace survived – the terrace can still be divined;

the ball court has gone – and today the small area around the library is known, slightly pathetically, as the Fellows' Lawn. The desired feeling of buildings set in a landscape was never going to work at this scale, and in many ways one can understand why the college in 1817–19 decided to join up the east and west ranges with the north range of First Quad. The joins are all too visible and this remains awkward as a space architectonically. But the wisteria-clad library is noble indeed, setting a quiet and sequestered tone, and there is an attractive west-facing flower border against the east building, dominated by yellows and oranges from hemerocallis, rudbeckias and other sunny plants.

Beyond Back Quad lies Third Quad, the domain of the venerable St Mary Hall and several of the other original academical halls, which still provide accommodation for students just as they did in the 14th century. Perhaps fittingly, there is little architectural unity. St Mary Hall dominates the quadrangle, rebuilt in 1743 in an olde worlde half-timbered

manner – an extremely unusual architectural style in an Oxford college context (although parts of Univ were also rebuilt in this way). St Mary Hall's old hall and chapel survive in the south-east corner, though they no longer serve their original function. The quadrangle itself is laid to lawn and features a distinctive border carved out of the lawn at its northern end, planted with red and white roses.

Architecturally as well as academically, Oxford colleges have a tendency to exhibit long periods of virtual stasis if not stagnation, punctuated by short bursts of frenetic activity. In Oriel's case this tendency was most dramatically exhibited from the 1830s and 1840s, when several of its fellows (Newman, Keble, Pusey) formed the beating intellectual heart of the Tractarian or Oxford Movement, which controversially sought to revive 'Catholic' rituals and values within the Anglican

Before the advent of the library and the twin accommodation ranges, facing each other across the lawn, in the 18th century, Back Quad was the site of a large garden featuring a terrace and raised walkway.

RIGHT The original, more grove-like form of the college garden can be appreciated in David Loggan's 1675 engraving.

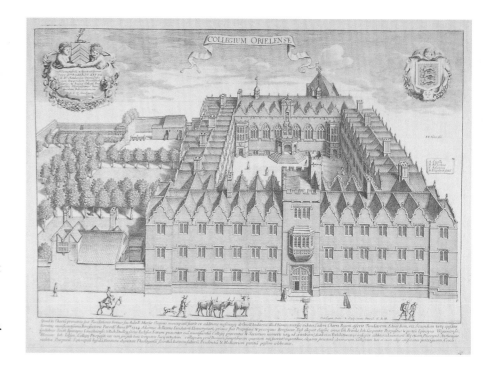

communion. (Its physical embodiment was to be Keble College and its chapel.) It is characteristic of Oriel that its provost at that time was vehemently opposed to the religious reforms being proposed by his colleagues.

Because Oriel likes to do things its own way. In the 1720s the Principal of St Mary Hall was a well-known Jacobite (when support for the Stuart cause was treasonous). More recently, the student body has periodically elected to secede from the official university students' union. And Oriel was notorious for a while as the last of the all-male colleges to resist opening its doors to female students (finally succumbing in 1985). It had been the undergraduates, rather than the fellows, who had voted to keep it that way; the same would be true, gender-reversed, at St Hilda's. Oriel is well known as a rowers' college, with a penchant for the ritual burning of its boats in celebration of success at Eights Week in its quads, with delirious boaties bounding through the flames as if to emphasise their invincibility. Other eccentricities abound. There used to be an extraordinary and rather macho custom in the cramped hall, it being acceptable for those dining with their backs to the wall, trapped in their places, to simply stand on the benches, clamber on to the dining table itself and walk across it in order to exit, regardless of whether anyone was still eating.

The greatest garden eccentricity nurtured by the college is a shell-encased denizen of the quadrangles who has traditionally been allowed to roam freely: the college tortoise, sometimes known respectfully by its genus name, Testudo. It is said that the first of Oriel's tortoises was introduced by a fellow in 1896, and the tradition has been kept up since with enthusiasm (and emulated by other colleges, including neighbouring Corpus Christi). In 1957 an old member sent a packing case to the college containing a giant Galapagos tortoise. An eye-witness recalled:

A gathering of dons and undergraduates, together with the Provost, watched in wonderment as this giant creature stepped out blinking. It just stood there looking at us all and its new surroundings…A signwriter/painter was sent for to paint the College arms on the creature's shell, as was always the tradition with Oriel tortoises. Some two or three days later the tortoise recovered from its jet lag, and during the night it must have felt very hungry. It ate every single plant growing in the second quad. It was a total demolition job, leaving only the stumps of the plants about three inches above the ground. The Provost was very upset, and sent for Mr Phillips, the Steward, to retrieve the packing case and repack the tortoise. I understand that it was sent straight back to the Galapagos.

If it survived the return journey, there would have been a tortoise wandering around the Galapagos Islands with the Oriel College arms painted on its shell.

On another occasion a group of undergraduates bought half a dozen baby tortoises from a pet shop in Oxford's covered market, which were purportedly chosen for their resemblances to different Oriel fellows. These were released in the gardens and the fellows apparently spent several pleasant hours chasing down the tortoises to ascertain which was their own doppelgänger.

There is a risk, admittedly, of too much information concerning the tortoise tradition at Oriel. But I shall persevere.

On his retirement in 1947, Provost Ross – who was known as an excessively taciturn and unsmiling person – gave an after-dinner speech in hall where he made reference to the college tortoise which was incumbent during his own tenure. He assured his audience that in 1938 the tortoise had laid an egg. This occurrence had happened during Eights Week, the university's rowing bonanza, during which college boats attempt to catch up with and 'bump' the boat ahead, thereby

taking its place one up in the rankings. On the first day, the provost recalled, the college bumped a boat and the tortoise laid one egg. On the second day the college bumped again and the tortoise laid two eggs. The college boat made no more bumps that week and the tortoise laid no more eggs. The provost commented drily that 'it was impossible to determine whether the series which the tortoise had begun would have continued in arithmetical or geometrical progression.'

The story does not end there. These happy events (the tortoise's progeny, not the two bumps in the rowing) were duly announced in *The Times* in the usual manner, which led to some slight confusion. The provost was contacted by an academic colleague from beyond the bounds of Oxford congratulating him on the news, commenting that he was unaware that the provost's daughter had married an Italian. The confusion was twofold. As anyone knows, only the provost's wife or daughter is permitted (officially) to give birth within Oriel's precincts. Knowledge of this fact led to the

correspondent assuming the baby was in human as opposed to tortoise form. Additionally, the name given in the newspaper announcement, Testudo, could easily be mistaken for an Italian surname. Hence the idea that the provost's daughter had married an Italian and given birth to a human baby. When in reality she had of course given birth to a tortoise.

I think I have dwelt on the tortoise theme because there is not in fact a huge amount to say about the gardens at Oriel College today. It sounds as if the old Bachelors' Garden was probably once rather fine, but pressures on space have led to most of the college's early garden being lost.

Have I mentioned the tortoise?

ABOVE The words *Regnante Carolo* (Charles is King – referring to Charles I) are inscribed in the parapet above the porch to the hall and chapel.

Oxford Botanic Garden

SITUATED IN A SWEET spot by the river, hard by the bridge and overlooked by Magdalen's tower, Oxford's own botanic garden demands to be on the itinerary of any horticulturally minded visitor to the city. No dreaming spire here, nor chapel, library or hall, but a noble entrance archway, ranks of glasshouses and planting beds arrayed in systematic order – as well as some rather fashionable new borders made in the 2010s. This is not one of those botanic gardens which shouts its eminence by means of magnificent palm houses, lakes and arboreta. At 1.8 hectares/4½ acres it is modestly sized, its edges always visible, so that the visitor feels they may even have a chance to see everything (for once). Victorian botanic gardens often seek to double up as landscape parks, but there is not the space here for that and as a result the scientific remit of the botanic garden looms large in the visitor's mind. For an hour or two, we can all become botanists and marvel afresh at the variation of nature while in intimate companionship with this botanical cornucopia. On the other hand, this is a public garden where visitors can lie down on the grass and relax in a way they simply cannot in most colleges.

Founded as a physic garden in 1621, Oxford Botanic Garden is the oldest in Britain. The land on which it was established had once been used as the city's Jewish cemetery. It has been presided over by a succession of eminent botanists and has long been used for teaching purposes in the university; the earliest published catalogue of plants dates back to 1648. The walled garden is home to the principal scientific collections.

A view back across the Merton Borders towards the walled garden, with Magdalen's tower beyond.

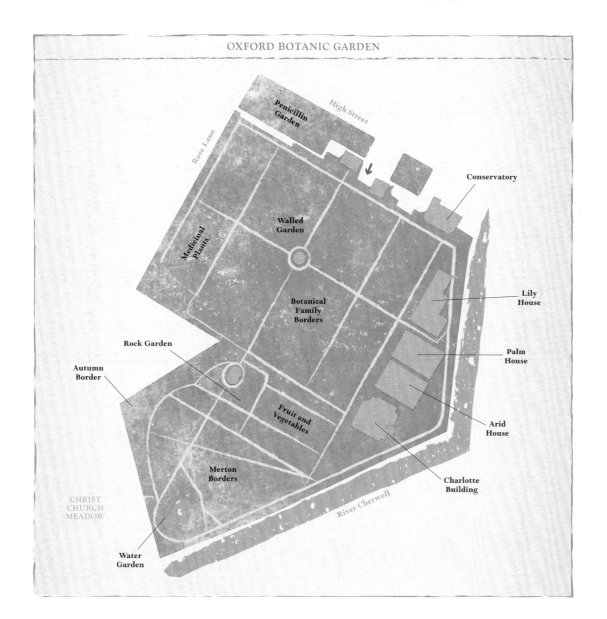

OXFORD BOTANIC GARDEN

Penicillin Garden

High Street

Rose Lane

Medicinal Plants

Walled Garden

Conservatory

Botanical Family Borders

Lily House

Rock Garden

Palm House

Autumn Border

Fruit and Vegetables

Arid House

Merton Borders

Charlotte Building

CHRIST CHURCH MEADOW

River Cherwell

Water Garden

RIGHT Snowdrops and *Crocus tommasinianus* 'Whitewell Purple' near the central pathway in the walled garden. Rising up behind is the imposing entrance arch of 1633.

These are arranged in borders by botanical family, to a plan 'perfected' in 1850, with the recent addition of a corner bed devoted to contemporary medicinal plants in honour of the 'physic' aspect of the early garden. The original walls of 1633 still stand and they provide a warm and sheltered microclimate for tender subjects. The site was significantly enlarged after the Second World War with the addition of the triangular Lower Garden to the south, which includes ornamentally themed zones such as the rock garden, herbaceous border, bog garden and autumn border. This land was formerly part of Christ Church Meadow, but having been used for the Dig for Victory campaign in the war, the college consented to its continuing cultivation as part of the botanic garden. (The Lower Garden is still therefore legally the property of Christ Church.)

The chunky and multi-pedimented entrance arch, completed in 1633 to a design by Nicholas Stone, creates a sense of drama and dignity, though as an architectural feature it does seem a little isolated and out of scale. Perhaps it was this slightly out-of-this-world quality which led the poet and gardener Alexander Pope to remark, on looking at the

'picture' of the botanic garden framed by the arch, that 'All gardening is landscape-painting. Just like a landscape hung up.' This was a foundational principle of the 18th-century English landscape school which eventually developed into the Picturesque movement itself. Since Joseph Addison, while a fellow at Magdalen just across the road, had already laid the foundations for the theories of aesthetic perception – derived from John Locke – which informed the early aesthetic of the landscape school, this little portion of Oxford can be said to have been something of a progenitor of the English landscape garden, sometimes described as England's major generic contribution to the visual arts. The arch itself is framed by niches containing statues of Charles I and II, while the main pediment features a bust of the 1st Earl of Danby, the ex-soldier and adventurer who had paid for the establishment of the botanic garden a decade earlier. Stone designed two other arched entrances for the garden, on the east and west sides; they are smaller and less ornamented but still add a great deal to the visitor's experience, along with several other antique artefacts one comes across.

Before entering the botanic garden, visitors may notice the large, labyrinth-like rose garden of box and yew hedges which sits in front of it, and a Georgian-styled accommodation block (both in fact the property of Magdalen College.) The garden was designed by Sylvia Crowe in 1953 to celebrate the development in Oxford of penicillin and, under the terms of the bequest that funded it, it was conceived as a rose garden. Along with Japanese 'Zen' gardens, rose gardens are notorious among designers as the biggest cliché in garden design – and difficult to design and maintain properly, to boot. But Crowe was clever as always and this is a diverting feature. There are stone seats and a line of pleached copper beeches, but the volume of traffic noise from the High Street above – the garden is set in a depression well below street level – makes it anything but a relaxing space nowadays.

It is slightly disappointing that visitors can no longer access the garden via the entrance arch itself, but must sneak in through a small visitor centre round to the side. No matter.

The overall impression of the botanic garden is of order and decorum, which is precisely as it should be. The 'family beds' in the main walled garden area are arrayed systematically on either side of a central path, and are quite narrow; they do look a little like beds in a dormitory. There is little attempt at ornamental gardening, which is again as it should be. The plants rather form little congregations and gardeners are reminded that there is a surprising amount of variation within individual plant families. The diversity of plant material on

ABOVE LEFT Orange-tinted kniphofia and red poppies provide vertical accents, while purple catmint (nepeta) mingles to good effect with yellow achillea and *Sisyrinchium striatum*.

ABOVE RIGHT In the foreground the white umbels of selinum nestle up to cranesbill geraniums, with yellow *Helianthus* 'Lemon Queen' singing out from the back row.

OPPOSITE PAGE The Merton Borders, recently redesigned with the assistance of James Hitchmough of Sheffield University: pink and yellow echinaceas (TOP); bright orange crocosmia and the grey-purple bobbles of eryngium (BELOW LEFT); and golden *Stipa gigantea* weaving among the flowers (BELOW RIGHT).

display also illustrates just how narrow the range of plants utilised in Oxford's college gardens is – something which can be said of most gardens, of course. Among the highlights is a national collection of euphorbia, including *E. stygiana*, which is verging on extinction in the wild. The 1648 border comprises some of the 1,400 plants mentioned in the botanic garden's first printed catalogue, including *Tradescantia virginiana* (Virginian spiderwort), asphodels, ferns and *Epimedium alpinum*.

The chief decorative aspect of the walled garden is provided by the mature trees peppering the lawns – again these are arranged in systematic fashion, but the maturity of the trees and their idiosyncratic growth patterns make them appear to be anything but museum specimens. Highlights include a grouping of beautiful mature parrotias, a Montpellier maple (*Acer monspessulanum*) with a twisted trunk, a *Sophora japonica* by the entrance arch and fine specimens of weeping larch, nootka cypress and *Ailanthus altissima*, alongside the more familiar *Magnolia* x *soulangeana* and the inevitable

ginkgo. The garden's celebrated black pine, planted in the late 18th century, finally had to be felled in 2014. The trees are probably among the least interesting aspects of the collection, in botanical terms, but they remain a vital component of the garden's overall impact.

The site is pleasingly open to the River Cherwell which forms its eastern boundary, so that the visitor might feel festively engaged with any watery shenanigans involving punts and other boats. This gives the garden a pleasantly unbounded and relaxed feel, as the visitor darts in and out of the palm house, fernery, arid house and the other glasshouses facing the river. There is an excellent border in front of the insectivorous house, with big and bold herbaceous plantings. The guidebook exhibits admirable candour in confessing that the botanic garden's original glasshouse was an abject failure because its windows were too small and the plants perished for lack of light.

Leaving the walled garden by its southern gate, opposite the entrance arch, the visitor discovers a small alpine garden

(1926) set around a pool, and then a series of themed areas including, on the left (east), the allotment-style fruit, vegetable and herb collection (conceived by Kim Wilkie Associates in 2005), and a herbaceous border set against the wall of the walled garden. But the highlight of the Lower Garden at the moment has to be the Merton Borders: deep plots – 11 metres/36 feet deep in places – arranged on either side of a diagonal pathway that runs for 75 metres/246 feet. These were redesigned in 2013 with the assistance of James Hitchmough of Sheffield University, who has pioneered public plantings which reflect the make-up of 'plant communities' found in the wild. The Sheffield School, led by Hitchmough and his colleague Nigel Dunnett, represents one extreme of the naturalistic turn in planting – or 'New Perennials' movement – which has occurred in British horticulture since the mid 1990s, with Dutch nurseryman Piet Oudolf considered the leading light.

Exclusively sown from seed, the Merton Borders really come into their own in late summer and early autumn, that new 'fifth season' in British gardening which is in many places coming to upstage even June as the high point of the horticultural year. The 'plant communities' used as inspiration for this scheme originate from the central to southern Great Plains of the USA; eastern South Africa; and from southern Europe across Asia to southern Siberia. This is a huge swathe of geography, so one wonders whether the plant-community rationale has any real meaning here. That will matter little to most visitors, however, who will be enchanted by naturalistic plantings that feature the classic New Perennials combinations of daisy plants (echinacea, gazania, erigeron), spire forms (eremurus, crocosmia, kniphofia), umbellifers (*Ferula communis* and

OPPOSITE One of Stone's 17th-century entrances into the walled garden, next to the lily house and a border of tender annuals and perennials, combining tithonia, persicaria and purple-leaved ricinus.

ABOVE Antique ornaments such as this urn with goat's-head handles are scattered through Oxford's botanic garden and greatly enhance its atmosphere.

other fancy cow parsleys) and grasses (stipa, miscanthus). The garden is organised to be drought-resistant (needing no irrigation), to need no staking or fertiliser, and relatively little maintenance. This last issue is a controversial topic, with some more traditional gardeners claiming that this style needs a higher level of attention than its cheerleaders admit. A less contentious critical remark might be that this approach does lead to a certain uniformity, given that the design sensibility of a human being is necessarily absent. But in smallish doses, as here, and in the right setting, the look can be beguiling. The Merton Borders are allowed to stand all winter, and are finally cut back only in spring.

The autumn border can be discovered at the western end of the Merton Borders. This was replanted in the 1990s by Nori and Sandra Pope, the Canadian couple who gardened at Hadspen in Somerset and were among the leading connoisseurs of garden colour-theming at that time. Orange and red dahlias are the stars of this border, offset by variegated grasses, cannas

and good shrubs including *Euphorbia mellifera*. There is a water garden at the far (southern) end of the Lower Garden, focused round a pool at the apex of the garden's triangle. James Ingram, in his *Memorials of Oxford* (1837), mentions 'a Salicetum near the river, containing almost every species of British willow'. Today, big gunneras, rodgersias and rheums abound, alongside feathery persicarias, typha and specimens of *Onoclea sensibilis* (sensitive fern) and *Chelone obliqua* (turtlehead). The native bog bean, *Menyanthes trifoliata*, grows in the water. The nearby presence of the river enhances the liquid feel, while a fine 18th-century ram's head urn lends appropriate dignity to this farthest reach of Oxford's botanical cabinet of curiosities.

TOP LEFT The border visible in the foreground contains plants – mainly medicinal – which were grown in 1621, when the garden was established.

TOP CENTRE Late summer: pink annual cosmos with asters behind.

LEFT The autumn border, designed by Nori and Sandra Pope, makes use of *Verbena bonariensis* and *Dahlia* 'David Howard', with banana leaves beyond.

ABOVE Double *Dahlia* 'David Howard' is offset by its bronzy foliage.

Pembroke College

'THAT COLLEGE SO POLITE and shy...' so John Betjeman described Pembroke in his long poem *Summoned by Bells*, adding that even though the college discreetly hides itself away in the city centre, it nevertheless seems to have more character than older and showier foundations 'splendid in the High' such as Univ or Queen's. Pembroke indeed proves a surprisingly attractive place for those who can find it, tucked away behind St Aldate's Church, as if shrinking back from the overbearing presence of Christ Church and Tom Tower, puffing out its chest across the road. Pembroke's entrance sends out the opposite message, for its lodge is squeezed into a corner where two buildings meet. In fact the college's frontage was even more obscure and insalubrious until the 1830s, when several old houses south of St Aldate's Church were finally pulled down, allowing carriages to reach the entrance lodge for the first time. For a period in the 18th and early 19th centuries something was made of Pembroke's entrance, given that visitors would drive up towards the elegant baroque facade of the old Master's Lodgings (1695), facing St Aldate's. This was described in *The Gentleman and Lady's Pocket Companion for Oxford* (1747) as 'a handsome modern Edifice [with] the Appearance of a Gentleman's House as much as any thing in Town.' But that aspect was lost with the Gothic remodelling of the college frontage, including the Lodgings, in 1829, which did away with any sense that the east-facing facade was a 'front'. Today, one has to say that the best thing

Native foxgloves in the cottagey Master's Garden, where the sword-like leaves of irises are mirrored by a spiky variegated yucca in the background. The Lodgings occupy 16th-century almshouses originally associated with Cardinal College (later Christ Church) across the road.

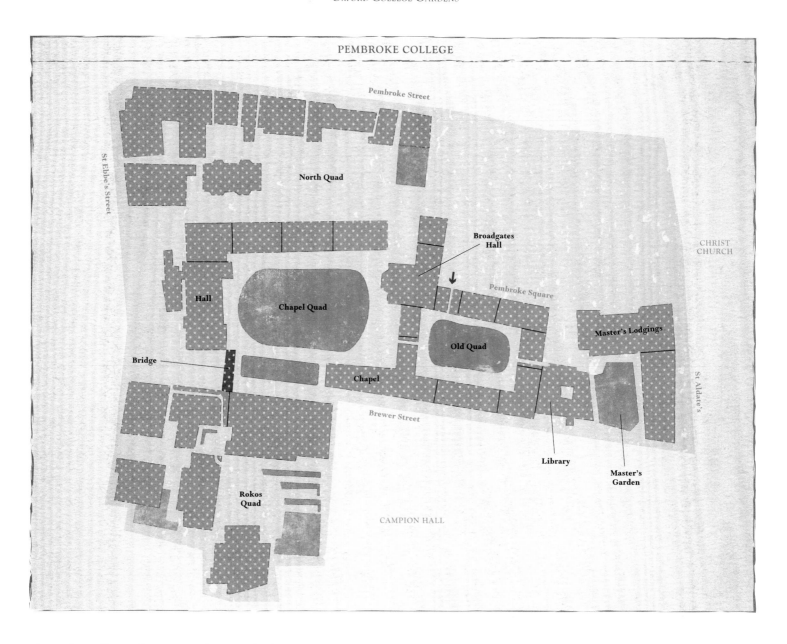

about the college's frontage is the view back across Pembroke Square towards St Aldate's and Tom Tower.

Outwardly undistinguished, then, Pembroke in fact boasts a quietly impressive roster of alumni headed by Samuel Johnson, the 18th-century poet, dictionary-maker and perhaps the greatest of all Oxford's sons, whose rooms were on the second storey directly above the lodge. Soon after his arrival he gave the master the memorable excuse that he had not finished his work because he had been sliding on the ice in Christ Church Meadow. According to his friend and biographer James Boswell, the great man recalled that he had given this excuse 'with as much nonchalance as I am now talking to you. I had no notion that I was wrong or irreverent to my tutor.' Said Boswell: 'That, sir, was great fortitude of mind.' Replied Johnson: 'No, sir, stark insensibility.'

The fact that the lodge is not in the centre of a range but at one end, makes the entry into Old Quad feel like a peep around a corner. But this has its advantages. In many colleges the symmetry of this first quad can seem overwhelming as one

emerges at the centre, making any plantings look like window dressing, literally. At Pembroke the oblique view into Old Quad means that the double tier of window boxes (47 in all) plays a powerful perspectival role, exaggerated by bright floral colour. Looking into the quad at a diagonal makes all the difference – relatively low in height (19th-century alterations did not entail a third storey, as nearly everywhere else in Oxford) and faced with stone that is exceptionally warm in tone, it appears quite homely and welcoming. The almost domestic effect is augmented by the fact that the slate roofs are visible above the customary battlements. Old Quad was completely refaced with new stone in 1829, when it was still a gravelled court. (It was grassed over only in the 1920s – late, for Oxford.) The planting, which changes every season, is identical in each window box. In 2012, for example, it consisted of the blowsy *Fuchsia* 'Blue Mirage', the soft pinks and vivid magentas of verbena, diascias, pelargoniums, lobelias and Surfinia petunias, plus the overflowing green and gold leaves of plectranthus. These are the best window boxes in Oxford. Fuchsia standards flank the doorways while the beds by the walls contain climbing roses, ceanothus, *Hydrangea anomala* subsp. *petiolaris*, heliconia (lobster claw) and clematis, as well as ferns and large, purple-leaved cannas, the latter being something of a horticultural signature for Richard Markham, head gardener for the past 20 years. Like David Leake at Corpus Christi, Mr Markham works entirely alone and has developed his own style, which lends the college a distinct horticultural personality.

Situated in the south of the city hard by its ancient wall, Pembroke had a little bit more room to play with than many other colleges at its foundation in 1624. There was a cluster of academical halls on this site for several hundred years before Pembroke appeared. The refectory of the biggest and most important of these, Broadgates Hall, was physically retained as part of the college and its entrance doorway can now be found, in altered form, at the north-west corner of Old Quad, while the great bay window of Broadgates Hall protrudes into the eastern side of Chapel Quad. It is one of the best examples in Oxford of a pre-existing medieval academical hall which was not taken down by the new college, as nearly all others were, but integrated into its fabric. (Brasenose had as close a relationship with the hall of the same name out of which it sprang – but not close enough to stop it demolishing it.) In this case it can be said that Broadgates Hall became Pembroke, which is possibly why the entrance lodge was sited so unconventionally – to provide immediate access into it. (There was originally a passageway that performed precisely this function.) Broadgates Hall was formerly known as Segrim Hall, with records going back to the 1100s, which makes it one of the very oldest of the academical halls. Several other academical halls were spaced along what was Beef Lane running westwards, and these were amalgamated into the new college. Beef Hall was one of them, and there was a Mutton Hall (which became St Michael's Hall) and a Veal Hall (later Cambyes Lodgings, today the site of Staircase 8).

BELOW Old Quad, celebrated for its window boxes (here, pink petunias and ivy), with the foliage of *Ricinus communis* in the foreground.

Several of these halls possessed gardens which stretched the 100 metres/300 feet or so southwards to the city wall, while the college also set about buying up land in the immediate vicinity (a process that continued up until the early 21st century, as we shall see). This tract was used by the college to create three separate garden strips divided by walls – the easternmost for the 'commoners' (undergraduates), with the Master's and Fellows' Gardens farther west. In the mid 19th century those historic divisions were erased and the whole became Chapel Quad, with only a small portion of the Fellows' Garden retained and closed off at the south-west corner. It was only at this point that the last of the old academical halls here was finally demolished – they survived at Pembroke far longer than in most places. There is a good engraved view of these ancient buildings – which include Durham Hall and Mine Hall – still standing in 1837, in James Ingram's *Memorials of Oxford*. The halls were fronted by a rectangular courtyard, with the college gardens over the wall on the south side. Several of the halls

clearly retained their identities for at least half a century after that, because a number are labelled on the 1878 Ordnance Survey map of Oxford.

David Loggan, in his 1675 engraving of the college, attempted to 'correct' or conventionalise the college's appearance, by placing the lodge in the centre of Old Quad's north range, but that was never the case. What he does show, however, is that Pembroke was apparently a fun place to be in the 17th and 18th centuries, a notion buttressed by testimonies from students (including Dr Johnson, who described the college in his time as 'a nest of singing birds'). Loggan depicts a bowling green in the south-west corner, with a game in progress. A long tunnel arbour bounds it to the north, providing an entrance into the Fellows' Garden, an unpretentious space with another shorter tunnel arbour and a sundial parterre (though as so often, Loggan does not show all of the space). More than half of the strip that is the Master's Garden appears to have been devoted to vegetables,

the rest a small lawn with trees. The Commoners' Garden was divided into four hedged sections, either laid to grass or vegetables, with that at the southern end containing a curious low rectangular mount topped by a large arbour in the shape of a rectangular prism. It's an unusual shape for a decorative feature and may have doubled as a fruit support.

The most interesting structure in Pembroke's garden was a pavilion against the wall in the south-west corner of the college's land, just south of where the dining hall is today – where the small Fellows' Garden now is. This building was nicknamed 'the pagoda' on account of its domed roof and became the most delightfully eccentric little 'summer common room' in Oxford. (There were several of these in Oxford's colleges – Merton's, for example, also survived into the 19th century.) It is depicted in more or less the same form in engravings of 1701 and 1744, and stood until 1869. Rowley Lascelles, in his 1821 book about Oxford, mentions it: 'Westward of the Chapel is the garden, in which is a pleasant common-room, and an agreeable terrace-walk formed on the city wall.'

Touring his old college, Dr Johnson recalled card games in the pagoda and also playing cricket in the college gardens (when he was not sliding on the ice, presumably). It seems the students would also help themselves to the produce; there is a story that Johnson, noticing that there was just one fruit left on the college's fig tree, posted a notice above it stating 'Johnson's fig' – which some other wag promptly amended to 'A fig for Johnson'. (There is a similar story told about Dr Kennicott's fig at Exeter College, which casts doubt on the veracity of both

stories.) The poet and great garden-maker William Shenstone, another 18th-century alumnus, planted a mulberry in the gardens during his time at the college, and Gilbert White, the natural historian, visited Pembroke to make a special study of some Guernsey lizards which had been released there. (The college has an old connection with the Channel Islands.) The Commoners' Garden was renamed Chapel Court in 1732 with the construction of the new chapel on the south side, a compact exercise in Anglo-baroque by Oxford master-mason William Townesend, whose father had earlier been employed on Old Quad. An engraving in the *Oxford Almanack* of 1744 shows the Commoners' Garden to be a large, L-shaped expanse of gravel or compacted earth, with the Master's and Fellows' Garden enclosures still walled off, but with the emphasis now mainly on leisure as opposed to production, with paths around grass plats. By the time of William Faden's 1789 map of Oxford, the garden closest to the chapel has become a court, while the two remaining gardens retain their basic formal layout even at this late date, with an allée of trees running down the middle of the westernmost, the Master's Garden. The last extant illustration of this mid-17th-century garden layout is in W. M. Wade's *Walks in Oxford* (1817) – the landscape craze that had affected other colleges (such as St John's and Wadham) had completely passed Pembroke by.

The tripartite garden scheme was finally swept away in 1846–50 when the fine new college hall was constructed at the western end of Chapel Quad together with an imposing accommodation range, the New Building, along the northern perimeter. The old academical halls were demolished to make way, the garden walls taken down and the whole quadrangle laid to grass.

The highlight of any tour of Pembroke is arguably the transition into Chapel Quad, since the vista is so dramatic, unexpected and open after the intimacy of Old Quad. Again, it is the corner siting of the gatehouse which is crucial here, since it entails a sudden 90-degree turn into a dark covered passageway. The variation in levels (there are three steps up from Old Quad) enhances the feeling of excitement as one walks up and into the green spaciousness of the quad, with the magnificent hall straight ahead hoving into view, the architecturally intriguing chapel on one's left and a sense of openness up and over the battlemented wall that runs along the southern perimeter. The sheer size of the lawned area – this was once known simply as the Grass Quad and is still almost field-like – offsets the dining hall to fine effect. The feeling is of width and refreshment, with none of the cramming-in which is so often found at colleges. These qualities of space and scale make Chapel Quad one of the unsung garden glories of the university.

A large, open space such as this can easily cope with big plantings. Against the hall, choice specimens of choisya, elaeagnus, buddleia, escallonia, philadelphus and hydrangea have bulked up to considerable size, with hebes and fuchsias offsetting them lower down. There is blue and white wisteria around the Senior Common Room doors to the north and several thriving abutilons, with their luscious downturned pink flowers, against the New Building adjacent. Climbing roses abound. A fine actinidia to the right of the hall steps is also worthy of note. Amid all this, self-seeded foxgloves add a sense of spontaneity, together with oriental poppies and scented nicotiana (tobacco plant).

The most intense plantings in Chapel Quad can be found around Broadgates Hall, on the eastern side, where more delicate plants combine including sculptural silver echinops, aquilegia, the larger alliums, salvias, lysimachia, phlomis and more unusual subjects such as the herb *Calamintha nepeta*. Mr Markham is fond of the striking, strap-leaved phormiums

in bronze and green shades, and a particularly fine example defines the corner by Broadgates Hall. (Massed phormiums are also used to good effect in the tiny Library Quad, east of Old Quad.) Against the wall deep red roses mingle with the purple floral stars of *Solanum crispum*.

The college expanded northwards in the early 1960s when it was able to close off Beef Lane altogether, demolish the houses along it and move its northern boundary up to Pembroke Street, where a run of old houses was converted into undergraduate accommodation. Much of the character of these buildings has been retained, and today North Quad stands as one of the most successful such exercises in 20th-century amalgamation and consolidation in Oxford. The various landscaped spaces do not hang well together, but curiously that is an advantage in the end because it emphasises the disparateness and individuality of all the buildings – evidence of obvious 'planning' can engender a more institutionalised feel.

In a way this quad is also a throwback to the very earliest days of the university, when whole streets (notably School Street in the centre, where the Radcliffe Camera is now) would have been given over to small academical halls in buildings that were formerly houses or tenements. In Pembroke's North Quad, students are once again packed together like sardines in houses, only now they are defined as staircases as opposed to halls. (This is also the case, to a lesser degree, in Wadham's Back Quad.) It may sound absurd to outsiders, but even individual staircases within colleges can seek to preserve and guard their own character, leading to friendly rivalries with neighbours. And it was the same case with the old academical halls. *Plus ça change* etc., etc.

The disparate spaces of North Quad nevertheless represent a challenging environment for any planting designer, and more muscular plantings have been essayed. For example, there is now a mature shrubbery in the large bed by the path leading to Staircase 12; here a purple hazel, weeping pear and a pair of Judas trees lend structure to a vibrant mix of smaller perennials including alliums, sedums and astrantia. Plans are afoot to develop the potential of the paved enclosed garden in front of

what is now Staircase 18, which abuts another small shrubbery containing a fine arbutus (strawberry tree). Meanwhile the dark, north-facing aspect of the New Building is enlivened by a large clematis (in which a family of ducks nests every year) and a fine *Garrya elliptica*, with dangling catkins in winter.

One of the richest moments of all comes just around the corner, where outside Staircase 8 is a large semicircular raised bed containing a choice mix of small-leaved pittosporums, *Festuca* and other grasses, elegant *Euphorbia characias* 'Silver Swan', lavenders and numerous penstemons. And then there is the private sanctum of the Master's Garden, secreted behind the 'new' Master's Lodgings which today occupy Cardinal Wolsey's almshouses (originally part of Christ Church) opposite St Aldate's Church. This is one of the most romantic and authentically cottagey gardens within Oxford University, with numerous salvias ('Hot Lips' stands out), achilleas, roses, verbascums and a marvellous yellow phygelius (long, trumpet-shaped flowers) which has turned itself into a climber.

Finally, mention must be made of the new Rokos Quad, a full-sized quadrangle south of Chapel Quad which is reached via a glass-sided footbridge across Brewer Street. It is almost unheard of, today, for a college to be able to build at this scale on acquired land next to the main college site. One unexpected garden bonus to have arisen is the resurrection of a short avenue of limes planted in the 1860s in the narrow sliver of the Fellows' Garden west of the chapel. Previously these were rather 'lost' but now this pleasant passage from Chapel Quad

up to the footbridge, underplanted with vinca and other shade-loving plants and atmospherically lit at night, constitutes an effective little garden feature in its own right.

The new quadrangle itself, opened in 2013, does not have particularly distinguished garden spaces within, for reasons of space – just a small lawn and some terraced beds overlooking it. Its main horticultural recommendation is the view it has opened up over Campion Hall, the Jesuits' college next door. This is of interest because it was designed in 1936 by Edwin Lutyens, who otherwise did very little work in Oxford. The garden is a simple rectangle of lawn with a circular pool sited directly opposite steps leading up to the hall's entrance, flanked by box hedges and a pair of wide herbaceous borders. The garden – particularly its deep borders – is perfectly in scale with the facade of the college, as one would expect from Lutyens. Pembroke's new quadrangle 'borrows' the view to Campion Hall most expediently, to the benefit of both.

LEFT Purple foxgloves and a red-flowered salvia in the Master's Garden.

ABOVE This rarely reproduced engraving, from the *Oxford Almanack* for 1744, shows the space that is now Chapel Quad formally divided into three separate gardens – for the master (far right), fellows (centre) and undergraduates (left, though it is hardly a garden by this point). The corner pavilion at top right, known as the pagoda, served as an outdoor common room and was fondly remembered by Samuel Johnson. At bottom right is a range of old academical halls which were not demolished until the mid 19th century.

The Queen's College

O FFICIALLY IT'S THE QUEEN'S College, and that is how the college always announces itself (website included). But everyone calls it Queen's. The queen in question is not in fact Caroline of Ansbach, wife of George II, who imperiously surveys the High Street from her eyrie in the rotunda that crowns the gateway at the centre of a mightily impressive 18th-century baroque frontage. The college is far older than its architectural style might imply, named in honour of Queen Philippa of Hainault (1314–69), who acted as regent for periods during her husband Edward III's long reign and bore at least 12 children, including the Black Prince. The chronicler Jean Froissart (admittedly in her employ) described her as the 'most gentle Queen, most liberal, and most courteous that ever was Queen in her days'. The college's founder, in 1341, was Robert of Eglesfield, a mere chaplain in the queen's court, who hailed from Cumberland. He specified that students from there and from Westmorland should be given priority. As a result the college developed a strong bias for students from the north-west, and latterly from the north of England more generally.

Eglesfield was admirably ambitious about educational standards: to begin with he proposed an 18-year-long course on theology for students, the plan being that they would return to Cumberland as among the most learned priests in Christendom. In fact Eglesfield produced the most interesting personalised set of statutes of any Oxford college, specifying that students and fellows would be summoned to dinner by trumpet (they

Front Quad, with clipped box balls marching alongside the central path leading to hall and chapel.

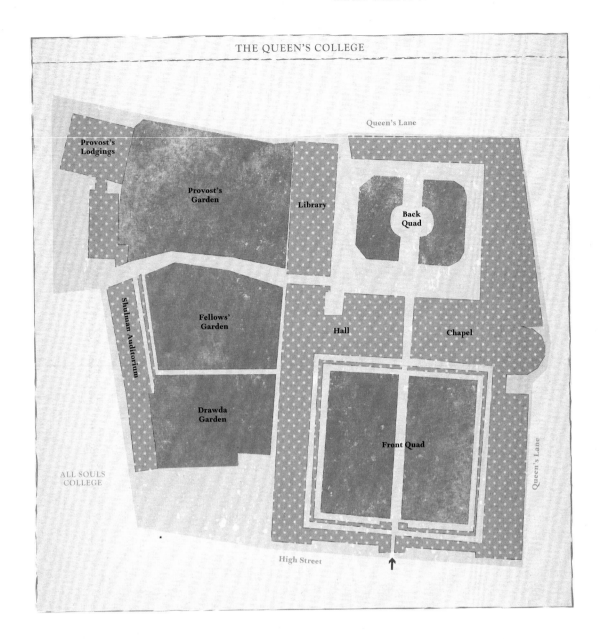

THE QUEEN'S COLLEGE

Queen's Lane

Provost's Lodgings

Provost's Garden

Library

Back Quad

Shulman Auditorium

Fellows' Garden

Hall

Chapel

Drawda Garden

Front Quad

Queen's Lane

ALL SOULS COLLEGE

High Street

RIGHT By the library is a gateway to the Provost's Garden. This was for many years the bowling green, and the garden is still open for use by all members of college.

still are on special occasions), that fellows and scholars would wear blood-red robes in honour of Christ, that 72 poor boys should be housed as choristers, and that the sick and disabled of the streets of Oxford ought to be admitted to hall on a daily basis. He lay great emphasis on courtly behaviour, specifying that French as well as Latin should be spoken in hall, and that scholars' hair should be washed regularly.

Of course there was not the money to facilitate all of these ambitious notions. As a younger son, Eglesfield was not even able to use his family's coat of arms without the addition of a distinguishing detail, which is why one of the three red eagles used on the college crest bears a gold star on its breast. For some in Oxford, there is a whiff of pretentiousness surrounding (The) Queen's College, which is deemed to be striving too hard to make an impression – not least architecturally – in this city of false modesties.

The extraordinary architectural set piece dominating the High Street today dates from the early 18th century. Before that, the college was far more modest in aspect, consisting

of a series of old buildings – including shops and cottages – that extended across the current college site and were used as accommodation. The gateway to the college was not on the High Street but around the corner, on Queen's Lane, which gave on to a cobbled-together quadrangle uniting chapel, hall, kitchen and Provost's Lodgings. It all looks positively ramshackle by the time of David Loggan's 1675 engraving in *Oxonia Illustrata*, when Queen's was evidently the most decrepit and unprepossessing college in all of Oxford. The buildings are mean and cramped (with the exception of one new range to the north, of 1671), while the engraving also shows a small garden of two lawns surrounded by young box trees in the north-west corner of the college, near the kitchens, and farther west of that a tiny grove with mature trees. We know that in 1358 the college appointed one John Godspede as its gardener, or *ortolanus* – the first named gardener in the annals of Oxford University. These gardens would have been made out of sections of the long garden plots that stretched behind the houses on the High Street, which the college had

purchased in the 14th century. Much of the first quadrangle at Queen's was built on top of these medieval gardens.

All of this was to change in a matter of decades after Loggan's map, when the college would undergo a dramatic metamorphosis from ugly duckling to regal swan. First came the library (1693–96), one of the finest buildings in all of Oxford, which went up to the north of the existing quad, and then the decision was taken in 1700 to demolish the rest of the college and rebuild it in its entirety, thanks to a bequest from a rich old member. Nicholas Hawksmoor was consulted as architect, though his plans, while of influence, were not realised. The result is a college of notable architectural homogeneity achieved in an elegant and restrained if rather austere fashion.

Front Quad is a startlingly formal environment, the great hall and chapel straight ahead snapping to attention thanks to a centrepiece of four massive Tuscan columns. Its south side, the back side of the college's front, is revealed to be a screen

only – like a Hollywood set – with a covered passage within but no rooms bar the tiny porter's lodge. The identical east and west ranges are tall and imposing, with two storeys of lofty sash windows and a cloistered ground floor which is not so much monastic as palatial. What is there for the two panels of lawn in this quadrangle to do, except to lie back and think of England? (The north of England.) The central path is lined with box balls pacing out the steps to hall and chapel, a better idea than the lines of pelargoniums and other gaudy annual flowers that have been used in the past. The garden team have concluded that there is no point in trying to make a space like this seem more homely or friendly by means of colourful flowers – better to just go with the flow.

LEFT A view back towards the entrance lodge, with Queen Caroline of Ansbach in her rotunda (though she is not in fact the queen celebrated in the college's name).

ABOVE Back Quad continues the austere theme to good effect. Not a flower in sight.

It's the same story in the college's second main quad. Back Quad is dominated by the library on its west side while some nondescript early-Georgian blocks enclose it north and east. One has the sense that an awful lot of architecture has been squeezed into a small space. A single lead urn on a pedestal, itself set on a stepped plinth, is all that adorns the quad with its segmented lawn. The urn always contains some species of architectural plant, such as cordyline. Again, there are no jolly annuals in window boxes or trees in pots to unburden the space of some of its Augustan restraint. It's a kind of horticultural nihilism which ought to be applauded in this context.

There are a few homelier horticultural touches to be found within this college, though they are not usually accessible to visitors. Turning left (west) in the airy passageway in front of the library takes one out towards the large Provost's Garden, which is bookended by the library at its east end and, to the west, by the rear of the Georgian Provost's Lodgings, shaded by a large copper beech tree. There are deep and well-stocked herbaceous borders down both sides of the lawn, and a narrower bed at the foot of the wide terrace in front of the library. Somehow the institutional feel that can blight principal's or master's gardens has been avoided here. The Provost's Garden can be viewed through the iron gate to the left of the entrance to the library.

Two other gardens are tucked in behind the west range of Front Quad. They can be reached from the northern side via a walled lane which delightfully still runs through this part of the college (a remnant of the medieval layout). There used to be three gardens here, but the so-called Nun's Garden was in 2011 used as the site for the 120-seat Shulman Auditorium, a barn-like structure that has been inserted into the space extremely sensitively. East of this is the Fellows' Garden, a simple lawn enhanced by some of the most subtle and delicate planting in Oxford's college gardens, with pulmonaria, epimediums, acers and a good variety of flowering shrubs. A wall running east to west, terminated by a holm oak that dominates this part of the garden, divides it from the Drawda Garden, which takes its name from the old building called Little Drawda on the western side. It's a fairly utilitarian space, with lawns and paving and little by way of planting, used in summer as a de facto beer garden by students spilling out from the adjacent college bar.

Like Robert of Eglesfield back in the 14th century, The Queen's College today evidently takes seriously the discipline and general deportment of its undergraduates. In recent years the dean has posted strict rules regarding behaviour in the college's gardens and quadrangles, reproduced opposite as a historical record.

ABOVE One of the arcades running down the sides of Front Quad, creating a cloister-like effect.

RIGHT A notice from the dean regarding behaviour in Queen's quadrangles, posted on noticeboards in Trinity (summer) term, 2011.

From The DEAN
The Queen's College, Oxford OX1 4AW

Behaviour in the College Quadrangles and Gardens
Summary of Regulations for Trinity Term 2011

I. Students are not permitted to walk, sit or lie on the grass in the Front or Back Quadrangle at any time (with the exception specified in VII).

II. Students are welcome to sit on the steps in the Front Quadrangle in an orderly fashion, conversations and noise should be kept at a reasonable level not to disturb others. No sunbathing is allowed.

III. Eating and drinking (non-alcoholic drinks only) in the Front Quadrangle is permitted during daytime as long as waste is immediately and completely disposed of in the rubbish bins provided. Please exercise extra care not to spill food or drinks while eating in the Front Quadrangle.

IV. Generally, drinks should not be brought out of the Beer Cellar area. However, drinks bought from the Beer Cellar may be consumed in the cloisters in front of staircase I, II and III after 18:00. Noise is to be kept at a reasonable level. No drinks to be consumed outside the JCR, OTR or the Dining Hall.

V. Finalists who have finished their exams are allowed to use the cloisters and steps in the Front Quadrangle for brief, civilised celebrations directly subsequent to their final exam.

VI. The Back Quad (steps in front of the library and around the flower column) and the alcoves of the Dining Hall and Chapel may not be used for lounging, eating or drinking.

VII. Croquet and bowls may be played at the following times in the Front Quadrangle only, if the condition of the lawns allows for it:
Weekdays: 13:00 – 17:00 and 19:00 – 21:00
Sundays: 13:00 – 17:00 and 19:30 – 21:00
No more than 4 players at the same time on the lawn on either side of the Front Quadrangle. Appropriate shoes to be worn on the grass.

VIII. The Provost's Garden may be used subject to the rules established by The Provost:
Mondays – Saturdays: 11:00 – 17:30
No food, no drinks, no games, no loud noise

IX. Smoking is not permitted anywhere in College except for the Beer Cellar yard. Smoking in the quadrangles will be reprimanded with an instant fine.

From
The Dean
The Queen's College, Oxford OX1 4AW

Rhodes House

NOT A COLLEGE: THIS intriguing building and its garden, situated just north of Wadham on the Parks Road, is the headquarters of the Rhodes Trust. That is the organisation which administers the Rhodes Scholarships, established in 1902 according to the will of the industrialist Cecil Rhodes, the son of a Hertfordshire vicar who went on to make his fortune in South Africa. It now supports around 80 postgraduate students annually from the USA, Australia, South Africa, Canada, India and six other countries, who are billeted at one of the university's colleges, though they can use Rhodes House's library and other facilities. With no students around to scuff it up, Rhodes House slightly has the air of an immaculately empty showpiece with more the ambience of a country-house hotel than a typical college.

Rhodes House sits within a coherent late Arts and Crafts design that convincingly ties it with the house. It was all designed by Herbert Baker, a British architect who had carved out a hugely successful career in South Africa, and who had already designed Rhodes's Cape Town house and garden at Groote Schuur. Baker's style was eclectic: he blended elements of the fashionable, vernacular-inspired Arts and Crafts style (old Cotswolds manor houses) with Queen Anne-inspired neoclassicism and – in South Africa at least – elements of Dutch colonial architecture, such as decorative gables. The freedom with which he plundered these different architectural traditions was not always to the taste of his peers in England (notably Edwin Lutyens, a friend and collaborator with whom

The main herbaceous border, combining yellow achilleas, orange tagetes and the tall wands of *Stipa gigantea* grass.

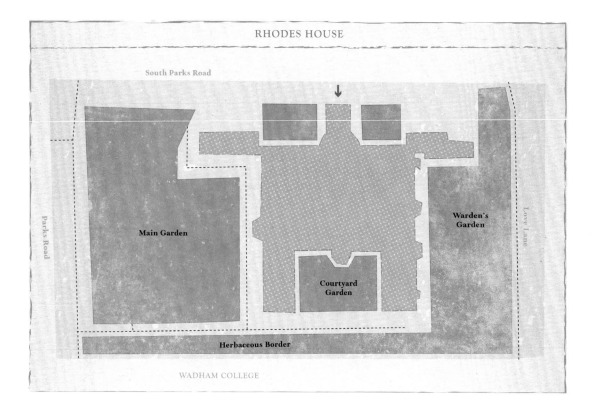

RHODES HOUSE

South Parks Road

Parks Road

Main Garden

Warden's
Garden

Love Lane

Courtyard
Garden

Herbaceous Border

WADHAM COLLEGE

RIGHT The new Mediterranean plantings in the courtyard garden feature *Euphorbia characias* and the feathery grass *Stipa tenuissima* (in the foreground), as well as *Melianthus major* and strappy-leaved phormium at the back.

he fell out spectacularly). In some ways Baker's style was more in tune with the Beaux Arts approach that was in the ascendancy in the United States when Arts and Crafts was in Britain; so perhaps it is fitting after all that he was the architect chosen to create the headquarters for Rhodes's imperialistic dream of an institution, which would turn out tyros with the intellect and moral character to lead the world.

The land on which Rhodes House and its garden were built was acquired from Wadham College in 1927; it was originally part of what is now known as Wadham's private fellows' garden. Baker's design was for an H-plan building in the monumental Arts and Crafts manner, with great lattice windows, tall buttresses and a steeply pitched and tiled roof. The row of dormer windows protruding from the roof is a reference to traditional collegiate architecture, as is the sheer scale of the exercise. There are several neoclassical interpolations that provide variety, such as the balustrade around the roof. Most striking of all is the rotunda with its tall, imposing portico and double row of Ionic columns, which now marks the entrance to the building and initially gives it something of the air of a mausoleum. Some have found this grafting-on of neoclassical features to a more traditional form of British architecture to be vaguely offensive, but it seems perfectly appropriate in the context of the urban environment of Oxford University, where a fake 17th-century manor house would surely have been anachronistic and clichéd. As it is, Rhodes House seems to offer its postcolonial clientele a one-stop-shop of great British architecture, from the 17th-century Jacobean manor house to the 18th-century Palladian mansion, neatly packaged up in an Arts and Crafts wrapper.

The garden is straightforwardly Arts and Crafts in its appeal, however. The space accorded to it is generous, occupying some 0.8 hectares/2 acres to the east and west of the main building, though the stiff rectangularity of the main garden spaces perhaps imparts a rather institutional feel that Baker might have avoided by means of a more subtle landscape design. His best garden idea was the courtyard terrace, open on one side, which is set within the southern part of the building. This courtyard device had proved popular among Baker's generation of architects, from Edwin Lutyens to Charles Voysey. He did not include a pool, however, and avoided any feeling of the Italianate in the decoration, a common theme in other gardens of this style and period. In fact the original idea was for this to be a simple plaque of lawn, to echo the form of a traditional college quadrangle. The northern entrance is offset by plain panels of mown grass, while the substantial symmetrical gardens to the west and east of the building were made as lawns dotted with trees, with herbaceous beds at the base of the building and beneath the low walls bordering pathways. Old yews and a large horse chestnut on the west lawn are remnants from the Wadham period. The garden on the eastern side of the building is the private Warden's Garden, with a sunken lawn, rose arch, cut-flower garden and ornamental potager.

A long border against the southern perimeter of the estate, flanking what was conceived as the entrance drive, was made as the showpiece of the garden. It is intriguing that the noted planting designer Norah Lindsay was at first engaged to create a scheme, though nearly all her work had disappeared within a decade as it was mostly herbaceous (while an avenue of yews

she planted in the Warden's Garden was dubbed too dark and finally removed in the 1940s). Lindsay liked to operate in that uncertain area between house guest and paid advisor, travelling the country to oversee the upkeep of the designs she formulated during discussions with the owners over luncheon or dinner. So it is interesting to find that she was paid £5 a day for 15 days for her work at Rhodes House, and that the total cost of the garden was £1281, with £450 of that spent on turf.

The herbaceous border was substantially enlarged in 1959, its depth doubled to 4 metres/14 feet and extended by some 9 metres/30 feet to the present length of 53.5 metres/176 feet. Today it is perhaps the most appealing facet of the garden at Rhodes House, and one of the finest borders in Oxford in high summer. It is planted according to Gertrude Jekyll's theories of border design, in that it starts 'cool', with white and pink flowers, such as phlox, cosmos, asters and lavatera, and becomes progressively 'hotter' as it moves towards the centre, with pink and magenta salvias, *Persicaria* 'Red Dragon', purple agastache

and colonies of daylilies in orange, yellow and copper shades. The centre is most intensely coloured, with tall orange and ruby dahlias, sweet peas in scarlet and vivid pink, and in August and September, towering yellow sunflowers and *Rudbeckia* 'Herbstsonne' above ribbons of helenium and veronicastrum. These are supplemented by annual rudbeckias in burnt oranges, toffee browns and golden yellows, as well as tinges of burnt red from burning bush, purple shiso and California poppies. The claret leaves of the vine *Vitis coignetiae*, and crimson Boston ivy act as backdrop. In recent years sub-tropical tender perennials such as bananas, *Sparrmannia africana*, papyrus and several varieties of the castor oil plant, *Ricinus communis*, have been added. Its origin as a border by an entrance drive is recalled today by the large ornamental gateway (1951) which gives on to the Parks Road to the west. How many visitors hurrying along this long straight road towards Keble, the Pitt Rivers Museum or the university's Science Area, must suddenly stop in their tracks as they find a glorious horticultural vision

bursting into view through black railings. In spring there are substantial tulip displays here and throughout the garden, which have in recent years tended towards the moodier end of the spectrum, with deep reds, magentas, purples and the near black of the variety 'Queen of Night'. The shrub border at this season is awash with snowdrops, yellow aconites, white and mauve wood anemones, egg-yolk narcissi, bluebells and the occasional self-sown snake's head fritillary.

Head gardener Neil Wigfield has instigated an unusual method of support for his shrub border in the summer months: a 'corset' of twigs from coppiced silver birch saplings, made in spring and designed to be a third of the eventual height of the plant at its time of flowering. The construction process can take up to six weeks to complete, and initially resembles an abstract sculpture as it snakes through the undergrowth. This border features a great diversity of shrubs, including weigela, abelia, deutzia, corylopsis and crab apples, underplanted with swathes of aquilegia, *Zizia aurea* (golden alexanders) and ferns. Hydrangeas, hypericum and fuchsias extend interest into late summer and autumn. Elsewhere in the garden, walls and borders are planted romantically and in profusion, the predominant colour notes being the creams and whites of

roses, white foxgloves, irises and *Clematis montana*, together with the blues of herbaceous geraniums, delphinium, aconites and cascading wisteria.

One big change occurred in 2005, when the lawn of the central courtyard became infested with chafer grubs, killing the turf and ruling out any possibility of resowing. The lawn was replaced with a most effective gravel garden, with massed plantings of euphorbias contrasting well with vivid orange tulips in spring, and enlivened in winter with ceramic pots containing winter-flowering wallflowers, grasses and evergreen bergenia, ivies and *Lonicera nitida*. Other parts of the garden are lit up by the coloured stems of willow and cornus in winter, all of which helps make Rhodes House well worth a visit at almost any time of year. The horticulturally minded visitor should not miss William Morris's tapestry *The Romance of the Rose* which hangs in a corridor inside the house, a glorious vision not just of climbing roses but of tulips, too.

LEFT A hot moment in the border, with several orange dahlias, including 'David Howard', fuchsia, orange tagetes and the purple foliage of *Ricinus communis*.

ABOVE A gentler episode: white cosmos, pink Japanese anemones, yellow-leaved cornus and solidago.

Somerville College

OR YEARS THIS COLLEGE had something of a 'speakeasy' feel: there were two ways in, but neither entrance was impressive in style and you would never have known there was a college lurking behind. The first, to the west, was little more than a hole in the wall next to a public house on Walton Street; the second, to the east, was a carriage-drive entrance with a small gatehouse facing the Woodstock Road. This was the set-up inherited at Walton House, the Regency villa which was chosen, in 1879, as the 'temporary' home for the new women's hall. It quickly became accepted as a permanent base, however, and was decisively purchased from St John's in 1881. The carriage drive proceeded east to west along a narrow strip of land just north of St Aloysius Church. The eventual acquisition of additional land in this north-eastern part of the site, and its translation into the homely Darbishire Quad, is one of the great triumphs of planning at any Oxford college, creating as it did both an effective entrance and the sense of a college which opens up and widens out dramatically before the visitor's very eyes.

But for now, in 1879, the nascent college was faced with the declining years of a large suburban house of rural aspect, with dilapidated stables along the driveway – the empty boxes still bearing the names of departed horses – and a house in need of urgent repair. Madeleine Shaw Lefevre was the first college principal and she remembered Walton House in the college logbook of 1879:

The main herbaceous border – a happy mix of crimson *Crocosmia* 'Lucifer', orange daylilies, the blue globes of echinops and the great round seed heads of *Allium cristophii* – with the Margery Fry Building behind.

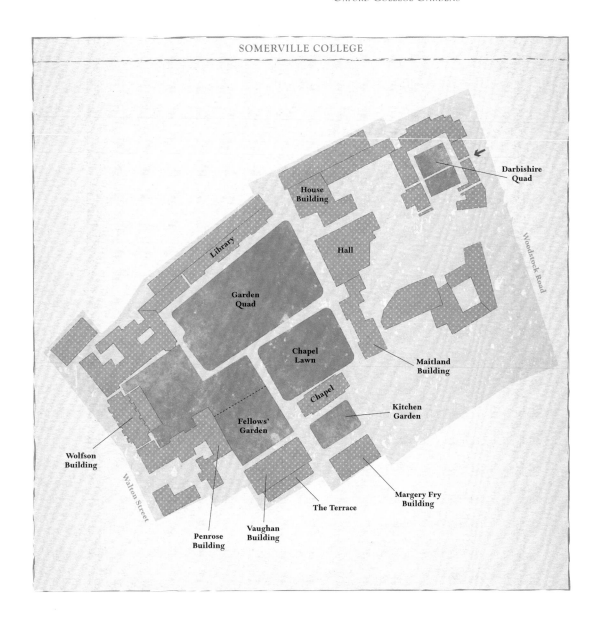

SOMERVILLE COLLEGE

RIGHT Agaves in pots nestled inside one of several well-sited modern sculptures dotted about the garden. In the background is the Maitland Building.

It was approached from St Giles' the Woodstock Road by a private road densely overshadowed with trees. The grey square stone house covered with wisteria and other creepers had a very countrified aspect. Near the house, the ground widened out into a large garden well planted with fine old trees, and the field beyond bright with buttercups and the apple trees in blossom added to the rural effect of the place.

It is probably fair to say that the founders of Somerville College – a breakaway institution with no formal links to the Church of England – were at the no-nonsense end of the spectrum, and unlike at St Hugh's, for example, the feeling of an existing domestic garden was not successfully integrated into the college fabric. There was a lawn extending across the area where the library and Library Lawn are today, while the orchard was to the south, in the area now overlooked by the Maitland Building. The land to the west was designated as kitchen gardens, and was also the site of the old gardener's house. It appears that the garden was essentially laid to lawn

with mature trees and shrubs, with little by way of herbaceous planting. The 'field beyond' and the kitchen garden would have given it something of the air of a smallholding. So to be judicious, this was never an ornamental garden like the one inherited by St Hugh's. What we have today is essentially a series of spacious lawns with trees (most of them on the main asphalt path leading east-west) and one enclosed garden area (the Fellows' Garden) overlooked by a variety of red-brick buildings – pleasant enough and airy, if strongly institutional in atmosphere.

There were 12 students at first, ranging in age from 17 to 36. One servant was employed in the house (always known as 'House' by Somervillians) and there was one gardener. A lawn tennis court was laid out immediately – the college got serious about this sport very quickly – and among the first gifts the college received was a lawn-roller from a female supporter who was married to a fellow of Corpus Christi. A composite engraving of college scenes made in its first year shows the tennis court and also, somewhat surprisingly, cattle grazing right next to wisteria-clad Walton House. As Miss Lefevre

recalled, 'for the first few years two cows and a pig formed part of the establishment, but these were later replaced by a pony and a donkey which might be seen disporting themselves in the field, adding to the picturesque and homely character of the place.' The pony, named Nobby, became something of a college personality, since he was available for usage by undergraduates, attached to a small basket carriage. Students of the 1880s would use him for jaunts in the local countryside or for longer journeys during the vacation (on one occasion to Land's End and back) and mastery of his ways was seen as something of a rite of passage.

There does seem to have been some gardening, of a genteel kind, going on at Somerville in the early days. A former undergraduate of the 1880s recalled 'a vision of [Miss Lefevre] in the garden, her dachs at her heels, prodding with a small garden fork round the tubers of the irises which grew in profusion where now the library buildings stand. She catches sight of me and beckons me to her to say: "You know, my dear, to do well irises should be moved every three years." ' Miss Lefevre also instigated the Somerville tradition of garden parties, when important guests were invited and students were expected to play at being hostesses. They were required, too, to take turns in the arrangement of flowers in the House, which Miss Lefevre felt ought to be part of an education, together with necessary elegance in dress and comportment, in which area she led by example. Miss Lefevre was on friendly terms with art critic John Ruskin in the 1880s – perhaps because of her elegance in dress and comportment – who despite being opposed to women's colleges on principle, was a frequent early visitor to the hall. (It became a college in 1894.) Ruskin wrote an inscription in a copy of one of his books during one of these visits: 'So glad to be old enough to be let come and have tea at Somerville and to watch the girlies play at ball.' What a strange man he was.

Named after Mary Somerville, the 19th-century scientist and early supporter of women's suffrage, this college was the academic powerhouse among the early women's institutions; its long list of eminent alumni would include Indira Gandhi, Margaret Thatcher and Dorothy Hodgkin. Notwithstanding its intellectual standards, the importance of domestic niceties

in the early years of the women's colleges is perhaps reflected in the way 'flower balconies' were seen as a necessary addition to the south-facing student rooms in the extension to the House that was built in 1881. (It has to be said that the genteel, 'ladies' college' feel of Somerville dissipated on the retirement of Miss Lefevre in 1889.) Of the women's colleges, Lady Margaret Hall and St Hilda's had the riverside and boating (later rowing), while land-bound Somerville concentrated on tennis, hockey and even basic keep-fit, as recalled by a former student of the 1890s: 'I have also a vivid recollection of a gym instructor man, coming on Wednesday afternoons to drill a handful of volunteers, headed by our Classical don, Miss Lorimer, who all dressed in peculiar tunics [and]…wound up their afternoon's exercise with a run in single file through the garden.' Another form of exercise, albeit unorthodox, was the Somerville fire drill, which attained legendary status in the college's early days. It appears to have involved throwing oneself out of a window of the House while clutching a rope.

Darbishire Quad, which today's visitor sees first on coming in to Somerville, was designed by Morley Horder (who mainly worked in domestic settings) and opened in 1933. It occupied the site of several houses on the Woodstock Road that the college was able to buy up in the 1920s and then demolish to make way. This is essentially a low-slung quad of Arts and Crafts appeal, though the square-rubbled Cotswold stone used has perhaps come out a trifle murky. The transition between the busy Woodstock Road and this vision of village content is extremely effective and not dissimilar in terms of shock value to the sensation at Magdalen, which fronts a similarly busy road at point-blank range. The gables in the roofs and the friendly fenestration create a homely feel that is only increased by the sight of the gentle curve of the archway into the next quad. The arch was something remembered from the original Walton House drive and incorporated into the new scheme. There are two parcels of lawn surrounded by plain and jolly cottage plantings with plenty of annuals such as osteospermums, begonias and salvias next door to fuchsias and hydrangeas for formal presence. But it is the low walls around the quadrangle, against flagstoned paths, which really make the scale attractive. Lavender peeps over the wall and

floods the paths, geraniums and hellebores mass in cottagey corners, and one could almost be at Kelmscott Manor, William Morris's Cotswolds home. Its small size makes one feel this could be a mini college or permanent private hall, with just a few scholarly monks or nuns wandering about – but the visitor is soon to be disabused of this idea; this is a small portal into a big place.

Sometimes the Oxford colleges seem to specialise in balloon-popping moments in their gardens, and the second quad, through the promising arch, is nothing more than a dispiriting car park with nasty signage. But then the visitor emerges into Garden Quad, which is the name given to the large expanses of lawn surrounded by mainly red-brick buildings, put up at intervals during the 20th century. There is the library to the north (right), the dining hall to the east and various residential halls ranged about, with the 1960s concrete Wolfson Building (by Arup Associates) at the far western end, against Walton Street, striking an effective modernist note. It

was on these lawns that both Siegfried Sassoon and Robert Graves convalesced when the college was requisitioned as a hospital in the First World War. (Somervillians went to Oriel for the duration.) There was a huge Atlas cedar on the lawn for years, and when it blew down to everyone's consternation in 1976 Harold Macmillan came and planted a new one, which is doing very well. Several abstract sculptures are extremely well placed, too.

But it is the planting beds in front of the Maitland Building, and those close by associated with the chapel, which are Somerville's garden glory. Big groupings of perennials – inulas, echinops, orange heleniums, alliums, anemones, hollyhocks, sedum, salvias – have been allowed to surge up and establish their positions in the border, remaining *in situ* even after death, their seed heads and drooping forms playing an active part in the display into late autumn. It's a very contemporary look, in tune with the 'New Perennials' theme in British gardening of the past 20 years or so. The chapel (1935) provides a superb

backdrop, though the chapel lawn to the north of it does have a slightly leftover feel. The college website claims that Garden Quad has been landscaped, but the very use of this term (which is never used by those 'in the know') generally indicates that there has in fact been no overall planning at all. As at most Oxford colleges, there is evidence of horticulture at Somerville but not of landscape design.

There is a pleasant surprise (or not, depending on one's view of modern architecture) around the corner, with the concrete Margery Fry and Vaughan buildings rearing up at the southern border of the college, against Little Clarendon Street. Steps lead up to a large and barren terrace where one then finds a remarkable garden space tucked between the chapel and the Fry Building. This is a well-ordered kitchen garden complete with herb patch, cold frames, greenhouse and sheds. A row of espaliered apples ('Golden Reinette') creates a decorative barrier on the western side. And wonder of wonders, there is also a cut-flower garden. Do Somervillians still have to learn flower-arranging? (Probably not, it is true.)

From here there are views down into the Fellows' Garden, which is overlooked by the Vaughan Building and the red-brick Penrose Building. The latter looks as if it presides over the space but was actually built a few years after the garden was laid out in the 1920s. Descending to ground level again the visitor can turn the corner by a hedge to be faced by a classic English country-house scene, with herbaceous borders popping up – hollyhocks and cardoons in dramatic conversation, with verbascums, bergenia and hemerocallis too – a lawn, low terraces, a brick wall bordering the north, wisteria against the house and a sundial encircled by *Alchemilla mollis* and cranesbill geraniums. It all looks a little dishevelled at times, and the garden must fight against its surroundings, like a dowager duchess who finds herself in a council flat, but the Fellows' Garden, open to all, provides a valuable sense of an enclosed garden in a college otherwise of wide open spaces.

The standard of horticulture is kept up throughout this large college site. The library is fronted with magnolias and a blue-themed border (agapanthus and lavender), while the Park Building has its own abundant borders, with *Verbena bonariensis* springing out by the front door to welcome students home. Near here is a large bank against the main lawn topped by big stipa grasses underplanted with ivies and alchemilla – another modern note. There is also an intriguing bed directly in front of the new Brittain-Williams Room, which opened in 2013 as an extension along the front of the Wolfson Building. The planting here forms a kind of alpine meadow with plants such as dianthus in gravelly soil, with some Mediterranean species including lavender thrown in as well.

There is an awful lot of good gardening being done at Somerville – jolly hollyhocks! – but at the moment the landscape design within which it has to perform is not quite up to scratch. Perhaps one day a benefactor will come along who wishes to improve this aspect of the college's fabric and make sense of the disparate spaces, as opposed to simply endowing yet another shiny new building. But I don't want to end on a dud note: Somerville is an uplifting place, and the planting – especially the borders near the Maitland Building – is among the best that can be found in the Oxford colleges.

St Anne's College

S T ANNE'S, THE FIRST of the all-female colleges to accept men, prides itself on thinking big, thinking differently and thinking ahead. The problem has been that the funds have not always been in place to realise those thoughts. Several key building projects have had to remain partially completed or shelved, and different initiatives have popped up as various bequests, endowments and donations have come over the horizon. The result is a spectacularly diverse arrangement of buildings and spaces in a triangle of north Oxford land sandwiched between Woodstock Road and Banbury Road, bounded on the north by Bevington Road.

The overall theme, architecturally, is modernism, but it appears in so many stylistic guises and in such sharp juxtapositions that it makes even that capacious term seem redundant. Yet fascinatingly, somehow everything at St Anne's hangs together – possibly more the result of luck than judgment, given there has never been the opportunity to create a credible masterplan.

There is no evidence of any landscape planning at St Anne's, and its garden areas can be characterised as infills, squeezed in between the various new buildings. But there are some effective moments. The best of these is the main college lawn, at the centre of what is in effect the principal quadrangle. The lawn is overlooked from the east by the handsome concrete blocks of the twin Wolfson and Rayne buildings, designed in 1960 by the architectural firm of Howell, Killick, Partridge and Amis

Modern additions such as the Claire Palley Building, 1992 (on the left) slot in with the existing Victorian villas, such as the Principal's Lodgings on the Woodstock and Banbury Roads (in the background). The tiled summer house is one of several incongruous remnants of the original gardens to these houses.

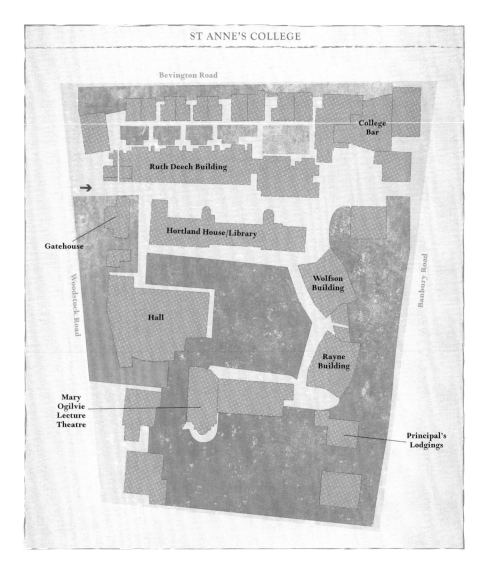

(HKPA). The frontage of these buildings, with three storeys of balconied rooms, bulge out attractively across the lawn, which is shaded by the mature trees the college insisted should be left unmolested by the building plans. These trees – notably an old cedar, oak and copper beech – are a little large now, creating rather too much shade, while the shrub plantings around the base of the buildings also appear somewhat overgrown and over-bulky. But essentially this remains as successful a space as it appears in the earliest photographs.

The space the lawn occupies today was at one point going to be the site of a huge artificial lake, 200 metres/700 feet long. This was to be the centrepiece of a masterplan commissioned by the college from HKPA, which originally included two more identical residential blocks plus an 11-storey accommodation tower to the north. The lake itself was to boast a music room on an island. Of this ambitious scheme only the Wolfson and Rayne buildings, and the college Gatehouse, were ever realised.

St Anne's began life in 1879 as the Society of Home-Students, which was 'a manifesto and not a location', with no physical identity, though there was a common room on Ship Street in Oxford. The initial aim of this worthy initiative was to enable women to study at the university without having

to live on college premises. In reality nearly all lived in rented lodgings or in the boarding houses gradually acquired by the college after the Second World War. Initially women were simply allowed to attend lectures, chaperoned, but from 1920 the university started awarding degrees.

The college's great early benefactor, Amy Hartland, a Canadian non-graduate, noticed in 1932 that two houses were up for sale simultaneously, at 35 Banbury Road and 56 Woodstock Road. The generous gardens behind these north Oxford villas created the potential for new building, and St Anne's instigated a policy of purchasing as many houses as it could in the vicinity, much as St Hugh's had been doing already for several decades, a little way north. The only potential problem was that the freehold to all these buildings belonged to St John's College, opposition from whom could potentially hinder developments. In the event, the college down the road turned out to be a good friend to St Anne's, offering the opportunity to acquire all the relevant freeholds as they became available.

The first college building to be created was, fittingly enough, the college library, which is located in Hartland House (1937), a late work by Giles Gilbert Scott, who was also responsible for the New Bodleian Library in Oxford, Liverpool's Anglican Cathedral and the power station in London that became Tate Modern. It is an interesting and attractive building which fuses Scott's tendency towards monumentalism with a certain homeliness and even whimsy – the beavers adorning the building are the college's symbol, chosen because of that animal's industry and communality coupled with its desire to return to its own private lodge. (No students lived on site until 1964.) It is recorded that the then principal, Grace Hadow, took personal charge of planting around the new building – dwarf roses and 'rock plants' are mentioned.

The college took the name of St Anne's in 1942 and gained full college status a decade later. The dining hall of 1959, conceived in a perhaps over-polite English-modernist style,

formed the second side of the rectangle which would become the 'quad'. A large willow next to it has grown up to create a curtain of foliage that acts as a sort of visual aperitif. In a story typical of the college's self-deprecating humour, former students recall how one of the old garden walls running down the middle of what is now the main college lawn was removed on the eve of the Queen's visit to open the new dining hall, in order to make St Anne's appear more venerable. It's an amusing story, but it was also to prove quite a profound move in the landscape history of the college. With the addition of the Wolfson and Rayne buildings five years later, which allowed students to live in college for the first time, St Anne's heart was complete.

Since then the story at St Anne's has been one of frenzied bedroom building, as the college has expanded and changed, admitting men, too, from 1979. Various new buildings have been put up in the past few decades – though slightly controversially, there was never to be a chapel at St Anne's. The Ruth Deech Building (by New York shiny-skyscraper specialists Kohn Pedersen Fox, completed in 2005) features dramatic stairways that descend to lawns on the site of the back gardens of the red-brick houses to the north along Bevington

Road, which all belong to the college now. There are plantings here of euphorbia, lavender and grasses; they emphasise a certain corporate feel.

Several of the larger Victorian villas acquired by the college have become seminar rooms, most of them in the southern part of the estate. In this nether region, the college dissolves into a deranged daydream of dislocated back gardens. The outsider has a faint sense of trespass here, like some thief in the night or Burt Lancaster in the film *The Swimmer* (1968), who passes from one garden to the next to try out the swimming pools. The residue of gardens that once occupied these sites only adds to the feeling of incongruity – a summer house here, an ornamental pool there, cottage flowers, denuded herbaceous borders, small ornamental trees. At St Anne's you can now move from deconstructed late-Victorian suburbia to generic Hong Kong modernism in the blink of an eye.

At the turn of the 21st century, the college felt the urge to demolish. St Anne's has long considered its frontage on Woodstock Road to be problematic, since it is somewhat unfocused and underwhelming, with a low brick wall, parked cars and two mismatched modern buildings. The first is the Gatehouse, which is idealistic modernism of the 1960s; the second is the western end of the long Ruth Deech Building, which is shiny corporate modernism of the 2000s. The Gatehouse, with its protruding rectangular windows, is very much of a piece with HKPA's Wolfson and Rayne buildings, and was most welcome at the time because it provided a number of additional student bedrooms above the porter's lodge. But the college has decided it must go because it is no longer fit for purpose, arguing that getting rid of it will reveal the western end of Scott's Hartland House, effectively creating a new front for the college. These plans were initially turned down, as efforts were made to secure listed-building status for the Gatehouse, which is arguably a more important building, architecturally, than the new one next to it. Listed status was not granted, however, and at the time of writing permission to demolish has been given. So St Anne's may yet have its new/ old face to present to the world. Or at least to the Woodstock Road. Perhaps there might be an opportunity, too, for a new landscape design to complement this new face?

St Catherine's College

'**D**OES ST CATZ ACTUALLY have a garden?' an architectural-historian friend asked. That got me thinking. Of course it has a garden. But a simple rebuff is not good enough. My instinctive rejoinder – perhaps a little defensive – was that Oxford's great modernist college is in its entirety essentially a designed landscape or garden with buildings set within it. To anyone focused primarily on architecture, the very reason why St Catz (as it is universally known) might appear not to have a garden is precisely because the landscape setting fits with the built elements so snugly, creating the impression of a seamless whole. That was the intention of the college's Danish architect, Arne Jacobsen, and that is its effect today.

St Catz, which was constructed between 1960 and 1964, is a little rough around the edges nowadays but it remains substantially authentic as the idealised vision – almost a *Gesamtkunstwerk* – of its architect. It is well known that Jacobsen designed not just the buildings but every aspect of the college right down to its last detail: the salt and pepper pots, cutlery, door handles, ashtrays, furniture, and also the garden, specifying on a plan where individual plants should go. (Jacobsen apparently forgot about the need for wastepaper baskets, however – they were someone else's choice in the end.) The college has recently added a slew of new buildings and a car park in the northern part of the site, but has had the good judgment not to try and upstage the original design with these expensive additions, leaving Jacobsen's plan largely unmolested

Arne Jacobsen's rational fenestration on the long, western accommodation range, with Barbara Hepworth's 1959 *Figure (Archaean)* on the lawn in front of the canal.

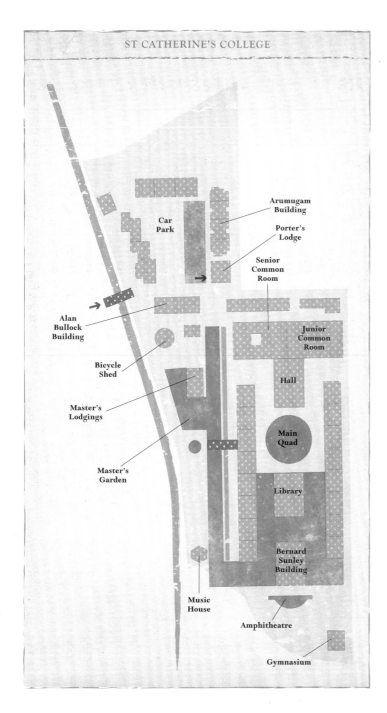

ST CATHERINE'S COLLEGE

Arumugam
Building

Car
Park

Porter's
Lodge

Senior
Common
Room

Alan
Bullock
Building

Junior
Common
Room

Bicycle
Shed

Hall

Master's
Lodgings

Main
Quad

Master's
Garden

Library

Bernard
Sunley
Building

Music
House

Amphitheatre

Gymnasium

and extrapolating his architectural vocabulary across the new areas. This means that the visitor today can still perceive the architect's intention with some clarity, appreciating it (or not) as Oxford University's greatest modernist statement.

That statement was seen as necessary by the governing body of St Catz because – as with the women's colleges half a century earlier – there was a pressing need for it to assert its own personality within the university. St Catz achieved collegiate status in 1962, when the first undergraduates moved into a college which was at that point still a building site. (These pioneers were nicknamed the 'dirty thirty'.) But St Catz had been in existence in some form since 1868, when it began as the Delegacy for Unattached Students – that is, undergraduates who were not affiliated with a specific college. The idea was to relieve students of the burden of paying rents

and battels (bills) to colleges by boarding in lodgings in the city itself, thereby radically reducing the overall cost of an Oxford degree. That was the impetus, though in the event the Delegacy proved almost as attractive to nervous foreign students and the incurably shy as it was to the impecunious. Almost immediately the irresistible Oxford urge to form social groupings took hold and the Delegacy started to gather regularly in St Catharine's Hall on Broad Street (now part of Hertford College). Identifying itself as St Catharine's, or St Cath's, and starting up a boat club, the institution's road to collegiate status now looks inevitable in hindsight. (With a slight name change: it substituted the 'a' for an 'e' to become St Catherine's Society in 1931, while the shortening St Cath's became St Catz.) Hindsight, of course, is wonderful – the modern college really came about because of the vision and persistence of one man, historian Alan Bullock, who was censor (principal) of the old St Catherine's from 1952 and went on to become the fully fledged college's first master.

From the start a college with a contemporary ambience was envisaged. There were to be no restrictions as to the nationality of the potential designers (and there was predictable criticism in the press when Jacobsen 'the foreigner' was finally selected). A small group of university high-ups – including Maurice Bowra, Warden of Wadham – travelled to Denmark to look at seven of Jacobsen's projects, returning full of enthusiasm, unanimous that he was the man for the job despite the fact they had not actually met the exacting designer at this point (as he was away in Paris when they visited). Jacobsen accepted the commission and came to England to gain some idea of what an Oxford college was. He visited a few and looked at some plans, but appears not to have done any in-depth research. This was no bad thing, because in the event he exercised a light touch with his references to traditional collegiate architecture, with no hint of pastiche or mock humility.

This would have been unthinkable, anyway, for Jacobsen, schooled in the doctrines of architectural modernism and deeply influenced by the Dutch modernist pioneer Mies van der Rohe. But while Mies was not an adept when it came to designing gardens and landscapes, Jacobsen proved to have a feel for the medium. He evidently appreciated that the Oxford

colleges are not merely sequences of disassociated buildings realised in a wild variety of period styles (the sense one gets, reading most architectural guides). He saw that they are held together by their landscape setting, focused on the paradigm of the quadrangle. Jacobsen took the idea of the quadrangle, and of the traditional trinity of buildings clustered around it (chapel, hall and library), and played with it. He deconstructed the college formula and then built it up again in a rational modernist manner.

Jacobsen retained the concept of a college quadrangle by placing one massive circle of lawn at the heart of his plan. The Main Quadrangle is overlooked from north and south by the block-like (but not 'heavy') dining hall and library, while two long, glass-walled ranges flank the space and in fact continue along almost the entire length of the original college complex. These identical ranges are organised in the traditional collegiate way as staircases, as opposed to floors and corridors, eight staircases to each range, while the covered walkways

that run beneath the cantilevered bays are a subtle reference to the cloister tradition. Most Oxford colleges present an orderly facade to the world, and one that is not demonstrative in architectural terms; Jacobsen was clearly responding to this with his buildings, which convey the impression that the real riches are hidden within, out of sight. The external facades of the two long ranges allude to collegiate design in their regularity and generally fortress-like aspect. There would be no chapel at St Catz (for this was to be a modern college) but there is a bell tower, realised in the concrete which was used throughout for the college's distinctive construction of pillars and beams. Jacobsen may have utilised certain elements that typify an Oxford college, but the arrangement, form and the materials employed were intended to appear unfamiliar, exciting and new.

The whole college is organised on the principle of a rectangular 'module' of space, 3 metres/10 feet by 2.4 metres/8 feet, which was used as the basic building block across the

entire 3.2-hectare/8-acre site. There are no instances of paving slabs, bricks or glass panes cut to fit in corners, as with most building projects, and even the planting beds conform to this template. It is this, just as much as the unity of the materials, that creates the impression of a seamless overall design. The minimalist spaces around the buildings were not conceived as blank or empty areas but were carefully engineered in exactly the same way as the architecture. At St Catz there is no leftover space – it is all dynamic. The grid is most obviously disrupted in two places: the roundel of grass in Main Quad, and the striking circular bicycle shed, which was always the first thing visitors saw.

'Was' because the college's recent alterations included the move of the porter's lodge away from the middle of the western accommodation range, which gives straight on to Main Quad. The new lodge is in the Arumugam Building, a little way north of Jacobsen's original college. Visitors arrive from Manor Road to the west, an offshoot of St Cross Road, itself an extension of

Longwall Street running north alongside Magdalen. Victorian red-brick suburban houses suddenly give way to this dream of modernism, as the visitor crosses a mill-stream tributary of the River Cherwell via the unassuming Napper's Bridge. (Jacobsen's original intention was to put the entrance lodge here, which would have been better.) The visitor now proceeds straight on, past the large new car park to the left – planted with *Ligustrum lucidum*, paper birch, and blocks of lavender and sarcococca – to report in to the porter's lodge. In front of the Arumugam Building is a long panel of lawn, the setting for *Unbroken Taichi Flow 1*, a massive abstract sculpture by the Taiwanese artist Ju Ming. It is then necessary to double back and enter the college at the side of the Alan Bullock Building, which was constructed in the 1980s and hides the landmark bicycle shed from view. This orientation is not particularly clear and in any case one is naturally drawn south across an open area of granite setts, with some recently planted *Sophora japonica* trees.

What catches the onlooker's attention here is the dynamism

of the rear side of Main Quad's western range as it shoots away due south, and the sparkling canal or moat which prefaces it. The vista down the whole 190-metre/623-foot length of the water garden was only opened up in 1968 – it was not Jacobsen's intention that one should catch sight of it here. But it is such a dramatic vista that there is a convincing argument for it to be the opening salvo of Jacobsen's design. There are waterlilies on the moat and *Tamarix, Ficus* (fig), *Cotinus* and *Indigofera heterantha* tumbling over the walls which flank it for about 40 metres/130 feet until the accommodation block itself begins. The vertical concrete pilasters and dark glass of the west range march away into the distance, while the third element is a perfect strip of lawn that leads the eye past holm oaks and ginkgos to a verdant fringe of mature trees. In the distance, on the grass, a tall abstract sculpture can be seen, unmistakably a work by Barbara Hepworth: it is *Figure (Archaean)* (1959), the title referring to a geological aeon. Formerly students were able to use several overlooks or balconies built into the wall above the water, but these are currently closed off. Some mature trees are placed about this lawn – but not too many – including a large *Salix babylonica* 'Tortuosa' (corkscrew willow) and, visible from within the Master's Garden, *Davidia involucrata*. Farther south are specimens of *Cornus controversa, Gleditsia triacanthos* 'Sunburst' and a group of columnar *Fagus sylvatica* 'Dawyck'.

This trio of long narrow strips formed by the water, west range and grass establishes the horizontal orientation of Jacobsen's design, which is key to his successful integration of landscape and building at St Catz. Architecture is usually a vertical component in a site's design, creating a tension with the horizontality of the landscape plane, historically often viewed by architects as little more than a platform. Jacobsen understood that architectural and landscape elements could work in harmony, balance and alignment with each other. He essentially allowed his architectural interventions to be dictated by the feel of the landscape he was working in, rather than design his buildings and then try to insert them into a landscape.

To enter the college the visitor must leave the vista and proceed right (west) around the rear of the Alan Bullock Building, which itself features some interesting planting across three small courtyards centred in turn on a *Eucryphia* x *nymansensis*, an *Acer palmatum* 'Osakazuki' and a mature dawn redwood (*Metasequoia glyptostroboides*). The visitor passes the bicycle shed, realised in the distinctive tan-coloured brick used throughout the college. It proved impossible to source the Danish natural-clay brick specified by Jacobsen, and this artificial substitute has not weathered well in some areas. To one's right (west) is the mill stream, while the Master's Garden is situated to the left, with a short run of trees against its wall: *Sorbus aucuparia* 'Fructu Luteo', *Gleditsia triacanthos* 'Rubylace', and *Malus baccata* (Siberian crab apple). Then one reaches the original entrance to the college, marked by a turning circle with a silver maple (*Acer saccharinum*) on its island, for cars can proceed no farther.

That this modernist college is reached via a bridge across a moat is a wonderful *coup de théâtre* on the part of the architect. There is no precedent in Oxford's collegiate history for this feature – even Christ Church cannot boast a moat – but it has proved a huge success in that it announces the college with fanfare and a hint of glamour. I shall never forget first visiting St Catz one night as an undergraduate – brought along by friends, not as part of some architectural tour. The lights of the college, reflected in the water, twinkled and sparkled and there was a genuine feeling of excitement as one crossed this most improbable moat into a palace of glass and concrete that truly was like nowhere else in Oxford.

The use of a substantial body of water by Jacobsen was perhaps his master stoke, above and beyond his overall architectural design. Oxford is a watery city, surrounded by flood meadows and criss-crossed by a great river and its various tributaries, as well as the canal. But only a handful of the colleges have been able to make good use of water in their gardens. The location chosen for the new college was Holywell Great Meadow, a 10-hectare/25-acre site owned by Merton and used for a while in the early 20th century as a rubbish dump (causing its own problems when a garden was being made; tons of topsoil had to be brought in). Jacobsen's low-slung design somehow retains the openness and flatness of the flood meadow. It is almost as if the college has emerged from the marsh – rather than landed like a spaceship, this being the

usual jibe about modernist buildings. The moat defines at the outset the college's landscape context – both natural and man-made – and contributes to the feeling that the buildings are somehow floating above it on a great concrete plinth.

The bridge brings the visitor straight out into Main Quad, having crossed the surprisingly short distance through the narrow accommodation range. A cedar of Lebanon has been planted off-centre in the quadrangle lawn, asymmetry being a key principle of modernist design. There was a bit of a saga surrounding this cedar. Jacobsen originally specified this species because he felt the form of its almost horizontally spreading branches would complement his overall design. For some reason the college thought it was a good idea to advertise publicly for a suitable tree to be donated, which they did in the pages of the *Sunday Telegraph* newspaper. In the end a mature tree from an Oxford garden was chosen and transplanted to St Catz in 1964, its great size necessitating an articulated lorry, the temporary closure of the Woodstock Road and the removal

of several walls in college in order to get it in. The tree survived for less than a year. It was replaced by not one but two trees – another large specimen, this time from a more reliable source (Exbury Gardens in Hampshire), and a 60-centimetre/2-foot back-up tree, which duly did much better than the bigger one. St Catz now has one cedar, as per Jacobsen's instructions, though there is a suspicion it is not a true cedar of Lebanon at all but a sport.

Jacobsen came up with his planting plan (sadly lost) in 1963, as building work was reaching an end. He always said that his design for St Catherine's could only be judged after a decade or so, when the plantings had matured – an indication of how seriously he took this aspect of the project. It is no surprise, then, that he was as exacting about planting as he was about everything else to do with the college. He specified exactly the number and breed of fish to be put in the moat, for example; and the fellows nearly revolted when he proposed putting markers in the carpet design of the Senior Common

Room (SCR) so that the chairs would not be moved one inch from their original positions. It appears there was to be no wiggle room, literally, for the fellows of St Catherine's College. Jacobsen nevertheless earned the respect of those he worked with in Oxford. A taciturn and slightly obsessive man, he did not socialise and totally dedicated himself to work. St Catz was his last major project, and he was in no mood for compromise. Several Oxford figures noted how impressive and commanding he was even when silent, though his taciturnity may have had something to do with the fact he spoke no English – probably a considerable asset when having to deal with the fellows of an Oxford college. Jacobsen did listen and rethink when faced with good evidence, however. The plant scientist Barrie Juniper was advising the college informally about its garden; he went on to become a fellow and first Keeper of the Gardens. He pointed out that while Jacobsen's planting ideas may have been suitable for dry Danish conditions, they were not appropriate for a sodden Oxford water meadow. The planting plan was

completely revised, which was the beginning of the college's quiet appropriation of the horticultural aspects of the college.

Like many Scandinavian and northern-European modernists, Jacobsen was suspicious of colour as too decorative, preferring muted shades in solid chunks such as the dark green of yew hedges. Jacobsen's view was that horticultural elements should be treated as architectural building blocks, and if they did not function in that way they should be omitted. His English colleagues found this difficult to accept from the outset, and there were several arguments early on after flowering plants such as roses were added without the architect's permission. Jacobsen reportedly likened one such colourful planting to 'a dog's cemetery'. But the Great Dane should have lightened up

OPPOSITE The yew-backed amphitheatre, situated behind the lecture theatre, and the gymnasium visible through the trees.

ABOVE A cercidiphyllum (katsura tree), next to the eastern range, is one of the now mature trees that enhance the college's modernist architecture. Jacobsen's signature walls and yew buttresses can be seen behind.

a little. The architectural austerity of St Catz is today leavened somewhat by the addition of serious horticulture in the form of trees, shrubs and some herbaceous material. The plantings can be discovered in the little garden areas north and south of Main Quad, formed by repetitive use of the principal garden motif: short runs of brick wall 2 metres/6 feet high, interspersed with clipped yew hedges of exactly the same dimensions. This forms an oscillation between architectural (hard, mineral) forms and landscape (soft, vegetal) forms, so that the division between them becomes blurred. Main Quad itself is enlivened by specimen trees – a mulberry, tulip tree and katsura – while the SCR garden, to the north-west of the quad, is prefaced by *Magnolia kobus* and a *Paulownia tomentosa* (foxglove tree) underplanted with hellebores. The dining hall is now almost completely covered with Virginia creeper, which lights up the quad in autumn, offset by white nicotiana below.

The principal garden areas to the north of Main Quad are around the Senior and Junior Common Rooms (JCR). The SCR garden is the only part of the central college site kept segregated and private, and within it is another katsura, *Acer palmatum* 'Sango-kaku' and *Melia azederach* (bead tree), with creamy white *Rosa* 'Madame Alfred Carrière' on the wall. The JCR has a row of Jacobsen's signature brick walls, this time with benches attached to them, and several large planting areas on the terrace outside the glass-walled bar. Subjects here include *Exochorda × macrantha* 'The Bride' (pearl bush), *Melianthus major*, *Abutilon vitifolium* and *Clematis texensis*. The area is shaded by specimen trees such as *Koelreuteria paniculata* (golden rain tree), *Acer griseum* (paperbark maple), *Acer capillipes* (snake-bark maple) and *Prunus maackii* (Manchurian cherry). There are long views from the JCR's garden south down the entire length of the covered walkway that runs beneath the eastern accommodation range.

On the south side of Main Quad the gardening is slightly more intensive, with a number of partially enclosed gardens to be discovered. Several of these have matured and now have an almost glade-like quality. To the east of the library and the lecture theatre that sits behind it, a number of interesting trees can be seen, such as *Cladrastis lutea*, *Ptelea trifoliata* and *Halesia monticola* as well as magnolias including M. *obovata*. Tree

peonies and eucryphias add more floral interest among a variety of herbaceous plants, all arrayed in rectangular beds of uniform size. At the far south end of the raised plinth on which the college sits, the land falls away and takes on a more informal, meadow-like character. The college's Gymnasium is housed in a cuboid brick building designed by Jacobsen; it takes on something of an idealised classical air in this setting, as if one of Plato's hidden forms has been made visible. Directly behind the lecture theatre is the amphitheatre, its arc of green created by layers of yew around concrete pavers. This is perhaps the only aspect of the original design that looks ungainly and out of scale, as it appears to be squashed up against the end of the building. A grapevine, *Vitis* 'Brant', grows here, on the south wall of the lecture theatre.

There is a quieter, slightly more private feel to the garden spaces over on the western side of the library and lecture theatre, with *Clerodendrum trichotomum* var. *fargesii*, *Parrotia persica*, hamamelis, *Malus tschonoskii* and, in the Middle Common Room garden, *Rosa* 'Old Blush China' and *Hydrangea villosa*. Finally, one can come out on to the lawn by the moat and enjoy the modernist Elysium created by the green grass, the sound of water, the scents of the shrubs and trees, and the pleasing rational monotony of the glass-walled building. Perhaps the visitor will hear 'sounds and sweet airs that give delight and hurt not…a thousand twanging instruments' from the Music House, which like the Gymnasium stands alone in the meadow, this time realised in a more complex form created by two hexagons laid across each other, and festooned with rambling *Rosa* 'Bobbie James'.

Arne Jacobsen's design for St Catherine's College is usually hailed by enthusiasts of modernist architecture as a masterpiece. It is also accorded high praise by commentators on landscape design. It can be placed in a tradition of idealistic architecture made for educational institutions that reaches far beyond Oxford, encompassing designs such as Thomas Jefferson's for the University of Virginia and Walter Gropius's for the Bauhaus. But does St Catz work on all levels?

In the modernist credo, functionalism is all. Part of the function of an Oxford college is to provide spaces in which college members can feel cocooned in pleasingly privileged

safety. At St Catz the balance between architecture and landscape is too strongly tipped in favour of the former, and the result is that the college can seem harsh and uncompromising. In its formal austerity and in the almost oppressive use of a narrow range of materials, the college that St Catz most resembles is Queen's. The sheer volume of brickwork, paving and glass on display overwhelms the landscape elements, and that can sometimes result in a feeling of alienation on the part of those who live in the college. In addition, the particular social quality of the Oxford quadrangle is entirely missing from St Catherine's – a certain inward-looking sensibility that is imparted to the enclosed cellular design of a typical Oxford college. Instead, St Catz's Main Quadrangle has more the atmosphere of the central square of a small Danish town – a civic rather than a semi-private quality. The college can also feel overbearing in that it never allows its users to 'customise' the space – for example, there are very few places where it might be possible to perch informally, or just hang around without

feeling exposed. At St Catz there is nowhere to hide, or lurk, while thinking quiet thoughts. The importance of a sense of the domestic and of the need for informal social spaces in an Oxford college was not fully appreciated by Jacobsen, whose underlying modular system apparently allowed no room for happenstance and spontaneity. This cannot detract from the originality of the design and the verve with which Jacobsen reinterpreted the traditions of collegiate design in terms of both landscape and architecture. St Catherine's stands today as *the* modernist college of both Oxford and Cambridge, and will surely be judged ever more kindly by posterity.

ABOVE The tonal contrast between yew and brick reflects the fruitful balance of hard and soft materials in the college as it has aged and developed – in full accordance with Jacobsen's wishes. Scillas are among the bulbs to complement the concrete and brick in spring.

St Edmund Hall

TEDDY HALL, AS EVERYONE in Oxford calls it, is indeed as cute as a teddy bear – at least outwardly. Conceived on a dinky scale, it modestly hides itself away in a side street in the shadow of grand Queen's College on the High. Indeed it was for centuries in the academic shadow of its neighbour, too, the Queen's fellowship nominating the principal of what was seen as a subsidiary site. But this college is venerable, certainly, not least as the only collegiate survival among the academical halls of Oxford – lodging houses, essentially, which predate the colleges proper. The first recorded reference to St Edmund Hall is in 1317, though it is believed to have existed several decades before that. Because most colleges did not begin to accept students (as opposed to fellows) until the mid 16th century, the Hall can, slightly mischievously, lay a claim to being the oldest educational institution for undergraduates within the university. The very suggestion makes some members of other colleges condescend to the Hall even more energetically. 'But it's not even a college,' they splutter. A better argument would be that many if not most Oxford colleges can trace their origins back through the academical halls extant on the same site, so this game of recalling earlier foundations could go on and on.

St Edmund Hall is immune to such jibes, in any case. It wears its hall status as a badge of pride, and was awarded full equivalence with colleges in 1957. In reality, some of the denizens of 'Hall' (as college members like to call it)

More village green than Oxford college? Charming Front Quad, with wisteria and a *Magnolia grandiflora* against the north range, location of the original 14th-century 'Hall'.

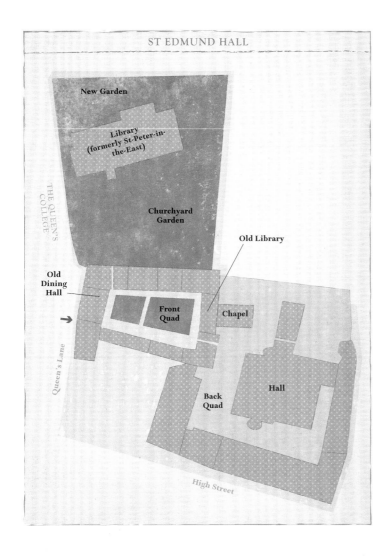

ST EDMUND HALL

New Garden

Library
(formerly St-Peter-in-
the-East)

THE QUEEN'S COLLEGE

Churchyard
Garden

Old Library

Old
Dining
Hall

Front
Quad

Chapel

Queen's Lane

Hall

Back
Quad

High Street

are not cuddly at all, but more akin to real bears – koalas perhaps – for the Hall is probably best known within the university for the ferocity and skill of its rugby players, or 'rugger buggers', while its undergraduates watching boat races on the river have developed a terrifying way of cheering on their college, by incanting the word Hall at great and monotonous length, drowning out everyone else. So much for cuddly Teddy Hall. On the intellectual side it could hardly be called senescent either: St Edmund Hall has long harboured dissenters and freethinkers, its non-collegiate status allowing Nonconformists such as Methodists access to an Oxford education. As a result its members have occasionally exhibited a slightly fanatical bent, creating furious ructions and religious disputes. The approach to the college is one of the most delightful in Oxford. Queen's Lane is possessed of a slightly surreal, country-lane air, notwithstanding the fact it is nanoseconds from the busy High Street. This effect is mainly the result of the homely presence of the Church of St Peter-in-the-East, its small tower drawing you forward, and the way the lane curves attractively to the left and out of sight, as if a village green with cricket match might be happened upon just beyond (rather than the back end of Queen's). This church, in fact, now has a special role to play in the life of the college.

ABOVE The door to the library, with clamouring *Rudbeckia* 'Herbstsonne'.

RIGHT Looking north in the churchyard, a rogue orange *Euphorbia griffithii* 'Fireglow' pleasingly disrupts the mauve moment created by purple aquilegias and *Allium hollandicum*.

As befits this modest and down-to-earth place, the lodge is unassuming in the extreme, resembling a corridor with porter's offices attached. Coming through a doorway, rather than the usual collegiate gate, it almost feels as if you are entering a private residence.

Front Quad seems to be preternaturally blessed with a sunny disposition, breathing contentment and ease even when the sun is not shining. It is a small quadrangle with a higgledy-piggledy feel, the college equivalent of a Cotswolds village, an effect produced by the haphazard assortment of building styles, most of it dating from the late 17th century. The north range, to the left, is the site of the original hall (of which only a fireplace survives), while the range to the right is low, gabled and domestic in style. Rustic stonework abounds. Behind the visitor who has just arrived, the old college dining hall is integrated into the west range, alongside the entrance lodge. Fittingly enough, the tiny hall is probably today the one which is most redolent of those at the old academical halls, which had a more domestic feel.

What really catches the eye in Front Quad, though, is the two-storey library almost straight ahead in the east range, a miniature exercise in late-17th-century neoclassicism – tall columns flanking a doorway and high windows, the whole topped with a neat little pediment. This was put up in short order between 1680 and 1686 by a reforming principal bent on attracting a better class of undergraduate to the Hall. The library may not have turned out to be the key to the college's financial success, as its progenitor had hoped, but it is nevertheless its greatest adornment. The mason-architect – Bartholomew Peisley – is not well known, and one cannot imagine a fancy London designer putting his name to such a tiny accoutrement, but St Edmund Hall's library is one of the most attractive small buildings in Oxford. The fact that it is not in the centre of the range, but squeezed into a corner, only adds to its charm.

The charms of the Hall were not lost on 19th-century visitors, to judge by *The Oxford Visitor* guidebook of 1822, which includes a delightful engraving of Front Quad embowered in delicate shrubs and small trees, with a simple plank bench on the grass. Front Quad today is filled with two panels of lawn and a wellhead which covers the original medieval well-chute: another village-green moment. Against the walls are wisteria, honeysuckle and magnolias while cheerful cottage flowers in beds by the walls (cranesbill geraniums, pink daylilies) and window boxes (red pelargoniums of course) add to the country feel. Even the college bar in the northern range looks like a snug in a village pub. Above the east range straight ahead, the 20th century looms in the form of the buildings of the college's 1968–70 extension along the High Street (which involved the demolition of several masonic lodges).

Turning to the left, the visitor can leave Front Quad through what feels like a service passage in the north-west corner. This takes one into the churchyard of St Peter-in-the-East, a typical medieval tower church which mainly dates from the 12th to the 14th centuries. When this building came in to the college's hands in the late 1960s, the first idea of the fellows was to use it as the college chapel, obviously

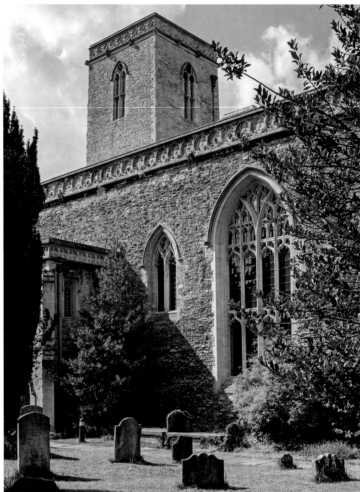

enough, but this proposal was pooh-poohed as impractical – by none other than the college chaplain – and an alternative idea was put forward. Why not convert it into a new library? The plan was approved, and in 1970 the project was realised. The churchyard then contained several hundred tombs and headstones amid its yews, a proportion of which were removed by a team of volunteer undergraduates at the time. The result is a churchyard that doubles as a place of repose and refreshment for college members. A garden, no less. It is highly successful, and does not have a spooky, defunct or redundant air, despite the controversial addition of a bronze sculpture of a skeletal St Edmund reading a book on a bench.

The area immediately behind the church-turned-library has recently been converted into a new garden space, the wide paved pathway swirling around the corner of its east end, with hollyhocks and persicaria straining in the slips. The path goes on to encircle an island bed defined by low box hedging underplanted with cranesbill geraniums, while

Miscanthus sinensis 'Zebrinus' sprouts from the centre. More border plantings – hydrangeas (including *H. quercifolia*), ferns, euphorbias and a large fig – help create a secluded and meditative corner, the main colours being white, green and purple. If one of the functions of a college garden is to create a space that transcends the everyday and thereby soothes the addled brains of scholars, then the unusual garden of St Edmund Hall can be deemed a considerable success.

OPPOSITE TOP LEFT Two flowers interlocked: a purple and a white iris.

OPPOSITE TOP RIGHT The Church of St Peter-in-the-East became the college library in 1970.

LEFT Recent planting behind the church includes a circular bed frothing with the foliage of *Euphorbia characias* and variegated *Miscanthus sinensis* 'Zebrinus', plus the purple flowers of geraniums and *Verbena hastata*.

ABOVE The dinky (old) library in Front Quad was completed in 1686. The wellhead covers the original medieval well-chute. Modern 'Teddy Hall' looms beyond.

St Hilda's College

AS MIGHT BE IMAGINED, the new women's colleges were viewed with great suspicion by some in the Oxford University establishment. In the case of St Hilda's, that outsider status was redoubled because the college, founded at the end of 19th century, was seen as something of an interloper even among the educational sorority of the women's colleges. There were doubts expressed or inferred as to the motives and objectives of Dorothea Beale, a visionary and ambitious headmistress of Cheltenham Ladies' College, a school she had turned from provincial mediocrity into an academic powerhouse that was of national importance in the late Victorian period and beyond. There were insinuations that Miss Beale was not serious enough about education, that she was content for her girls to study at Oxford in a relatively casual way. Elizabeth Wordsworth, Principal of Lady Margaret Hall, was also concerned that the proposed low fees would undersell the women's halls and thereby attract the 'wrong' sort of girl. On the other hand there were fears that St Hilda's might become some kind of finishing school for the girls of Cheltenham Ladies' College, though this was never explicitly stated.

Dorothea Beale had few allies, then, in the early female academic establishment in Oxford, but she did have a powerful friend in the Provost of Queen's College, and it was his support which was to prove decisive. The college opened in 1893.

Fears about the new college were soon shown to be unfounded, as St Hilda's knuckled down with the rest of the

Its river frontage makes St Hilda's prime punting territory – it even boasts its own 'dock'. A riverside walk is the best garden moment in the college, with roses such as 'Compassion' adding to the romance.

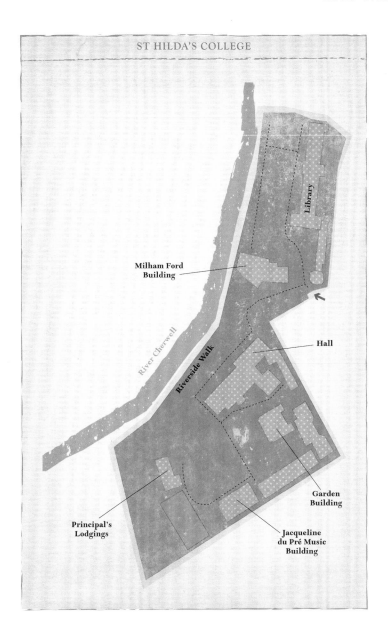

ST HILDA'S COLLEGE

Library

Milham Ford
Building

River Cherwell

Riverside Walk

Hall

Principal's
Lodgings

Garden
Building

Jacqueline
du Pré Music
Building

women's colleges and punted above its weight in academic terms. But even the college's location has ensured that it retains a sense of apartness: it hovers at the eastern boundary of the city, off a side road on the 'wrong' side of Magdalen Bridge, as opposed to being ensconced in comfortable north Oxford, where all the other women's colleges are. The site was also quite unlike that of all the other women's colleges: it is a small and awkward sliver of land overlooking the River Cherwell, with no opportunity for the creation of a large garden cobbled together from existing back gardens. Although the college did expand substantially, southwards, through the 20th century, the spaces inherited proved tricky and St Hilda's was never able to create the kind of bucolic setting enjoyed by St Hugh's or Lady Margaret Hall.

In any case all was not lost, in garden terms: the situation at St Hilda's was and is saved by the college's delightful riverside location. Of all the colleges, only St Hilda's and Wolfson feel as if their principal college buildings are actually 'on' the

river, with lawns tumbling directly down to the banks of the Cherwell as it makes its way towards Magdalen Bridge.

Cowley House, the building which formed the nucleus of St Hilda's (and now known as Old Hall), was built in the late 18th century for a great Oxford botanist, Dr Humphrey Sibthorp. In the 1860s it was enlarged, with a new Gothic wing, by Professor Benjamin Brodie, whose house guests at this time included novelists Elizabeth Gaskell and George Eliot, the latter describing Cowley House in her journal as a 'pretty place near the river and bridge'.

A photograph taken in the 1890s shows the imposing Gothicised St Hilda's Hall (as it then was) and its familiar sloping lawn down to the river, with mature trees including cedars set in the grass, and shrubs in beds by the house. A gardener was among the staff employed by Miss Beale at the outset, and we know that an existing croquet pitch was immediately turned into a grass tennis court. The garden in front of Old Hall today is essentially the same as it was

then, only the cedars are of course much larger, and there is a cottagey herbaceous border down at the foot of the lawn facing the river, with rudbeckias, delphiniums, white roses, sedum and cranesbill geraniums.

Gardens and gardening do not seem to have loomed large in the history of St Hilda's, the emphasis outdoors being more on tennis, boating and walking. As Esther Burrows, principal from 1893 until 1910, recalled, 'Women students were customarily out of doors between lunch and tea, to the advantage of their health.' The boathouse was a destination for picnics, and the St Hilda's boat, provided by Miss Beale, was regularly in use. Before anyone could get into a boat, they had to prove they could swim 15 metres/50 feet. The first college punt was acquired in 1905, and canoeing was another popular pursuit; punting skills were to become a matter of pride for all St Hilda's students. There was also a rifle range in the grounds, for St Hilda's had its own rifle club in the first decades of the 20th century. A member of the college council

donated a silver goblet as a prize for revolver shooting, with the suggestion that 'if any of our students go to the colonies they might find that art useful.'

More gardening opportunities arose after 1921, when the college was able to acquire neighbouring Cherwell Hall (formerly Cowley Grange), which it renamed South Building. The recorded flower and vegetable gardens at the property did not survive, but the college did make the most of its riverside potential, creating over time a delightful garden of terraces down to the river and a pleasant riverside walk. This is today the finest garden adornment at St Hilda's, with cistus, cotoneaster and especially shrub roses setting the tone, providing welcome relief from the heavy emphasis on car parking and asphalt roads in other parts of the college. There is a fleet of punts moored at a little dock down on the river, and in summer this passage of the Cherwell is action-packed.

ABOVE Poppies (LEFT) are among the plants to inhabit the wildflower meadow in front of the Principal's Lodgings (RIGHT).

St Hugh's College

S t Hugh's is exactly 1 kilometre/ 0.6 miles north of St John's, but Oxford undergraduates cocooned in city-centre colleges generally consider it to be situated somewhere in the vicinity of Dundee. That's their loss, because St Hugh's possesses one of the most attractive estates in the university. It has always been the pleasantest of the former women's colleges. Much of its ambience is created by the extensive college gardens, which cover about half of the substantial 6.5-hectare/16-acre site, bounded by the Banbury and Woodstock Roads to east and west, and St Margaret's and Canterbury Roads to north and south.

The key to the peculiarly tranquil, quasi-domestic atmosphere at St Hugh's is the spaciousness and evident maturity of its grounds. This arises from the fact that the new college building (1916) was constructed on the site of The Mount, a large and well-established property on the Banbury Road, itself surrounded by 1.8 hectares/4.5 acres of existing gardens. The sense that St Hugh's is a house set in its own large garden has never been supplanted, even as the college has erected more buildings and expanded across all the neighbouring properties in the block. In fact the site is nicknamed 'the island' on account of its atmosphere of cut-off tranquillity.

St Hugh's started small, like all the women's colleges; in 1886 just four students occupied 25 Norham Road, a semi-detached house. The nascent college rapidly expanded into neighbouring properties until by 1912 it was decided that proper college premises elsewhere were required. The Mount

Lawn, avenue and double border in front of the library (left) and the Mary Gray Allen Building (on the right).

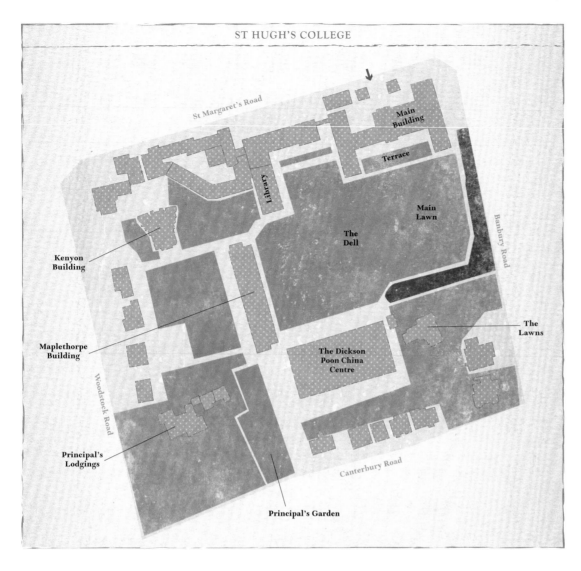

ST HUGH'S COLLEGE

St Margaret's Road

Main
Building

Terrace

Library

Main
Lawn

The
Dell

Banbury Road

Kenyon
Building

Maplethorpe
Building

The Dickson
Poon China
Centre

The
Lawns

Woodstock Road

Principal's
Lodgings

Canterbury Road

Principal's Garden

RIGHT Narcissi and tulips blooming in the vicinity of the rose arch and dell by the south lawn, features left over from the 19th-century garden inherited by the college.

BELOW Men have been admitted to St Hugh's since 1986. They include *Man Lifting Bricks* near the Maplethorpe Building, sculpted by Marcus Cornish and 'sponsored by a leading brick manufacturer'.

FOLLOWING PAGE Tulips and narcissi announce spring from the beds in front of the Main Building terrace. In the background is the sundial dedicated to Annie Rogers, the fellow who did most for the garden in its early years, as *Custos Hortulorum*.

was found to be up for sale and the college acquired it with a view to demolition, using borrowed money and despite the fact that University College owned the freehold. The gamble paid off and St Hugh's today has one of the largest undergraduate populations in Oxford.

The red-brick Main Building – as it is still called – is an unremarkable exercise in the homely Queen Anne style which was then in vogue, especially for institutions such as schools and colleges. The original entrance to The Mount was on Banbury Road, but the new building was given a frontage on St Margaret's Road to the north. This reorientation may have been partly for horticultural reasons: the college council had always envisaged 'a house with grounds', as the official record has it, and even in 1916 there is a statement concerning the beginnings of 'what we hope will be a very beautiful collegiate garden'. Could it be that the new college was built facing north because of the opportunities a south-facing garden site afforded, especially for the substantial terrace garden which remains its glory today? One of the college's most influential figures at the time was Annie Rogers, a tutor who went on to become the fellow in charge of the garden, and she would certainly have

had a say in such matters. (The ladies involved with the so-called Trianon Adventure, revolving around claims of supernatural activity in the gardens at Versailles, were both academics at St Hugh's at this early period. See page 314.)

The other key to the success of the garden at St Hugh's is the pragmatic way the college has either integrated or obliterated existing Victorian garden features left over not only from The Mount but also from the gardens of neighbouring properties acquired slightly later (houses such as The Shrubbery and The Lawns – the clues being in the names). There are in fact the ghosts of at least nine gardens lurking in the shrubberies and lawns at St Hugh's, and most of them have been reconstituted to make a pleasingly flowing and amorphous ground plan, with no obtrusive evidence of former boundary lines. It's a matter of gliding from lawn to shrubbery to avenue...and very romantic it is, too – though in the early days the sturdy and strait-laced academics of St Hugh's would never have conceded that. Presumably romance has occurred here, though – when the university laid down its rules governing the behaviour of female students in 1920, the grounds of a student's own college was one of the few areas where she was allowed to be

with a male unchaperoned. This was probably an oversight on the part of the authorities.

The quickest way out to the terrace, the garden's chief adornment, is straight through the front door of Main Building and out on to the south side (though this route is not open to visitors; when leaving by the building's west door, one must turn left and left again). It is here that the feel of the college as a domesticated institution comes into its own, thanks to the terrace itself and the sweeping main lawn it looks across, with mature trees including *Aesculus parviflora* and a *Magnolia x soulangeana* given by the Junior Common Room to celebrate the Armistice of 1918. One has to admire the way St Hugh's makes no attempt whatsoever to look like an Oxford college in the traditional sense – something which cannot be said of any of the other newer colleges in the university.

The paved terrace consists of four rectangular planting beds edged in box, fronted by a low retaining wall and twin herbaceous borders. It is generously proportioned and a much-appreciated suntrap in spring and summer. There is also a long border against the six bulging bay windows of Main Building, a sheltered spot where a remarkable orange-flowered pomegranate tree flourishes. The terrace beds contain standard roses in various colours (including 'Tickled Pink' and 'Just Joey'), with bearded irises in spring, the central pair of beds also featuring planted ornamental urns. Oriental poppies, alliums, geraniums and cistus contribute to the desired jewel-like effect. A few outcrops of lavender are all that remain of the garden's original incarnation as a sort of alpine garden, when hundreds of small plants grew in crevices in the paving – veronica, saxifrages, campanulas, phloxes and especially helianthemums. By the 1920s the terrace was apparently being overcome by weeds and it was completely re-paved in order to suppress them. Today the borders at the front of the terrace feature shrub roses, stachys, agapanthus, anchusa, rudbeckia and many other perennials maintained in the traditional English manner as a cottage-style 'tapestry' planting. It is resplendent with tulips in spring.

Moving out on to the lawn, the visitor is drawn right (west) and into 'the dell', the remains of a feature that belonged to The Mount. This still retains its Victorian atmosphere, with ferns, erythroniums in spring, and winding paths. The undulating

terrain is evidence of the site's use as gravel pits in earlier days, and it is possible that the mount which gave the earlier house its name (and which was demolished with the house in 1916) was the result of spoil from these excavations. An old rose arch from the 1920s has been quite successfully integrated here, yet another disembodied feature finding a home in the garden. (There are no plans, however, for the reinstatement of the college pigsty, which was in existence until 1933 – perhaps the last example of a college keeping livestock on site. One of these pigs was designated as a perk for the gardener.) There is a fine old avenue of beeches running north-south, as well as good specimens of weeping silver pear (*Pyrus salicifolia* 'Pendula'), strawberry tree (*Arbutus unedo*) and a flowering cherry (*Prunus avium*). More good herbaceous plantings can be found in the vicinity of the library, where there is a double border and a herb garden for the college kitchen. The three-strong gardens team, who ride around college in a little buggy, obviously take great pride and care about their work.

Despite the presence of the red-brick villas which the college bought up in the first half of the 20th century, the western part of the college is now rather campus-like, dominated by new buildings and extensions including the Maplethorpe Building and the Kenyon Building. These corporate-modern edifices look across landscaped or non-landscaped areas that are almost devoid of character. The worst decision has been to place a bicycle park in the middle of the lawns. To the south, the Dickson Poon China Centre opened in autumn 2014 on the site of the old tennis courts. It features a central courtyard in the form of a generic oriental-style garden of bamboos, boulders and *Fatsia japonica*. This clichéd scheme must count as another opportunity missed. There are, however, some good trees in the western gardens at St Hugh's, including an Atlas cedar, a pair of fastigiate hornbeams and an avenue of *Prunus serrula* – but they struggle to make much of an impact in the confused surroundings.

The south-west corner of St Hugh's contains the Principal's Lodgings (formerly The Lawns) and garden, as well as the Fellows' Garden, which reopened after restoration in 2011. Its central lawn is flanked by shrub and perennial plantings and mature trees including a *Paulownia fargesii*, magnolias and a tulip tree.

At the lawn entrance to the terrace are two massively overgrown conifers – which should probably be taken down – shading a sundial dedicated to the memory of Annie Rogers. Rejoicing in a typically formal Oxford title, *Custos Hortulorum*, the doughty Miss Rogers presided over the horticultural development of St Hugh's from the moment it arrived at its new home until her death in 1937. After 1921, when she retired from tutoring, she was able to devote much of her time to the garden, with generations of St Hugh's students recollecting her as a fixture on the terrace, in the shrubberies and flower beds, wont to pop out suddenly from behind a bush and engage students in conversation about new plants or other garden curiosities. As one ex-student recalled: 'Miss Rogers on a blustery autumn day, wearing four coats, each shorter than the one beneath it, and a man's trilby hat, surveying the progress of some alterations with majestic dignity and judgment.' She was well known for visiting Oxford gardens, such as Dr Bidder's rock garden at St John's, and taking cuttings whether invited to or not, dropping them into a partially opened umbrella or instructing the long-suffering St Hugh's gardener, trailing in her wake, to procure them. Eccentricities aside, the horticultural tone at St Hugh's was set by Miss Rogers, who was a proponent of Arts and Crafts gardening as practised by Gertrude Jekyll and William Robinson, especially their informal style of woodland gardening. Miss Rogers was probably the most notable gardening academic at Oxford until, in our own times, Robin Lane Fox (of New College). One of her foibles was a certain overconfidence on a bicycle and she was unfortunately knocked off and killed one dark night on St Giles' as she made her way to a meeting of the Archaeological Society. But the garden at St Hugh's lives on as her legacy.

ABOVE LEFT The Maplethorpe Building is one of a number of recent architectural additions to the college, which is today one of the largest in the university, numerically.

ABOVE RIGHT The summer house in the Principal's Garden, with a magnolia flowering above and tulips and hellebores in the foreground.

St John's College

WITH SPIKY GABLES TO the third storey, St John's presents a dark, forbidding and archaic appearance along its exceptionally broad west-facing frontage on St Giles', itself the widest thoroughfare in central Oxford. The church of St Giles lies nearby, marooned in the centre of the road and encircled by dizzying bus traffic, much as St Clement Danes sits on its island on the Strand in London. The college's somehow ancient and venerable aspect arises partly at least as a result of its striking juxtaposition with the facade of the Taylor Institution (known as the Taylorian), which looms large across the road, attached to the Ashmolean Museum, each of its four giant Ionic columns fantastically topped by a large female statue. The facade's towering scale and over-the-top classicism seems overweening here and somehow at odds with the sober, withdrawing tone of most college architecture. It is as if the Taylorian were a worldly starlet, thrusting her ample bosom in the general direction of St John's, the high-minded young cleric, who is nevertheless mesmerised.

This was, indeed, very much a clergyman's college for much of the 19th and early 20th centuries. Today, it is best known as the richest Oxford college, the owner of tranches of land in north Oxford and – one of its greatest trophies in undergraduate eyes – the Lamb and Flag public house next door. Christ Church runs it a close second for assets and income, with the rest far behind.

From the spacious lodge, Front Quad presents an

Canterbury Quad, perhaps the most refined quadrangle in all of Oxford. There is no floral interest – just a simple lawn – but elegant arcades connect architecture to landscape and so create a coherent whole.

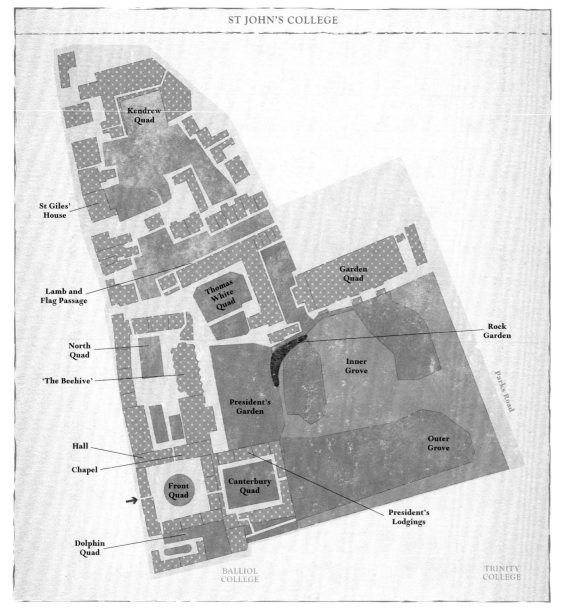

ST JOHN'S COLLEGE

Kendrew
Quad

St Giles'
House

Lamb and
Flag Passage

Thomas
White
Quad

Garden
Quad

North
Quad

Rock
Garden

'The Beehive'

Inner
Grove

President's
Garden

Parks Road

Hall

Outer
Grove

Chapel

Front
Quad

Canterbury
Quad

Dolphin
Quad

President's
Lodgings

BALLIOL
COLLEGE

TRINITY
COLLEGE

RIGHT Shrubs and a stopping place in the Outer Grove: handsome oak-leaved *Hydrangea quercifolia* at the front, evergreen elaeagnus and *Corylus avellana* 'Contorta' against the building.

FOLLOWING PAGE The secret Gooseberry Garden is kept locked and is strictly reserved for college fellows and their guests. *Magnolia grandiflora* and wisteria overlook the circular pool and box-edged beds.

As if to increase the sense that the college always has its eye on you, the President's Lodgings, located at the north end of the east range, actually look over this quadrangle. In fact the first thing to greet visitors to St John's is a stern black sign on the lawn immediately in front of the lodge enjoining us to 'Keep Off Lawn', a message which becomes all too familiar to the chastened visitor, as such signs multiply in the college's precincts.

The planting is kept simple here, as in St John's other quads: window boxes with red geraniums (pelargoniums, botanically) and petunias along

uncompromising, slightly severe aspect: a roundel of lawn surrounded by paving stones and – unusually – panels of pebble-work up to the walls. This austere space creates an impression of industry and seriousness, the sense that this is not a college in which to dawdle (or indeed, one in which even to contemplate a third-class degree – for St John's has for several decades now vied with Merton for the reputation of the most academic, or 'cleverest' college). This is one of Oxford's older quadrangles, begun in 1437 when it was the College of St Bernard, though there were alterations and additions in the following century, after the foundation of St John's in 1555. In 1616 William Laud, then president of the college, oversaw the installation of a crenellated pediment all around this quad and also along the St Giles' frontage of the college. It is these crenellations, together with the regularity of the fenestration, which lend remarkable homogeneity and continuity – as well as considerable elegance – to Front Quad, emphasising too the circular motion of the central lawn. It is as if the quad is whispering 'Get on, get on – haven't you got work to do?'

the eastern range, and a magnolia and flowering shrubs on the northern, hall and chapel side. As ever in Oxford quadrangles, the ratio of vegetation to stonework decisively influences the overall tone. Here it is all about rational thought as opposed to irrational organic profusion.

St John's is principally aligned along a west-east axis, with its second quadrangle, the jewel-like Canterbury Quad immediately behind Front Quad, and the college gardens beyond that – for this is a college which does possess 'gardens' in the more conventional sense. But before proceeding straight on towards them, the visitor can turn right and enter Dolphin Quad from the south-west corner of Front Quad. This addition to the college was built in 1947–48 and from a landscape-design point of view is notable chiefly for the grandiloquence of its bicycle sheds – a pair of them facing each other across this sliver of a quadrangle. Resplendent with Ionic columns, these portals outdo anything at any other college by way of velocipedal stabling.

Canterbury Quad, a splendid if effortful confection of

the English Renaissance constructed under Laud's auspices between 1631 and 1635, has a claim to be the greatest architectural jewel of all Oxford quadrangles. One curiosity is that it is not quite in alignment with Front Quad – so as to avoid blocking the light into the chapel's east window. Its east and west ranges – those which one sees on entering – are highly decorated, while the remaining two are relatively plain. The decorated ranges boast a dramatic two-storey elevation, each with an architectural centrepiece holding sculptures in niches. The lower sections are classically arcaded with elegant Tuscan columns, eschewing any medievalist cloistral savour and aiming instead at a flavour of continental intellectualism – more Petrarch than Bede. The slender columns support semicircular arches, with ornamental busts in the spandrels between the columns. There is quite an iconography to these busts, ambitiously encompassing as they do the entire span of academic study and moral probity. Perhaps it is symbolic that these lofty denizens looking down on the quadrangle are

quite out of the reach, and usually above the sight line, of the students. More easily identifiable are the bronze statues in elaborate alcoves above the east and west porticoes: Charles I and his queen, Henrietta Maria. Archbishop Laud was a strong supporter of the Stuart cause during the English Civil War and was ultimately executed by Puritans at the Tower of London in 1645.

This quad was constructed over part of the original college garden but there is nothing horticultural about it – and neither should there be, given the singular quality of the architecture. (The mason was a colleague of Inigo Jones.) Canterbury Quad does, however, have a landscape component in spatial terms, because the arcades on the ground floor have the character of garden loggias giving on to the simple lawned quadrangle. The dialogue between east and west facades is of course played out in the space between, which is the quadrangle itself. It means that the attentive visitor is caught in the middle, in the invisible web of their architectural conversation. This is,

LEFT The celebrated rock garden, constructed in the 1900s by the college bursar and renovated several times since. Today it comprises various Japanese maples, dwarf columnar evergreens and of course bulbs and diminutive alpine plants such as blue *Omphalodes verna*, *Lewisia cotyledon* hybrids, iberis, alyssum and sempervivum.

RIGHT The foliage of *Vitis coignetiae* colours the south wall of the Outer Grove, and a strawberry tree (arbutus) opens its flowers above the bench.

however, another part of St John's where lingering does not appear to be encouraged. Canterbury Quad always seems to be empty. It suffers from a desiccated, scholastic air. This arises from the fact it was evidently conceived as an exercise in architecture as opposed to a place for people to use.

The transition from here into the college gardens is one of the most dramatic in all of Oxford, a real Alice-in-Wonderland moment, as one is inexorably drawn to a small dark portal at the eastern end of the quad. The visitor bursts forth to face a large lawn or meadow fringed with trees, almost forming a grove at its farthest end. (Indeed, the component parts of the college's garden have always been known as 'groves' and the garden master – the fellow with responsibility for the garden and its budget – is known here as Keeper of the Groves.) It is an immensely refreshing sensation to come out to this lawn, and generations of St John's students will have appreciated the literal breath of fresh air their groves offer, hard by the college library which occupies the upper storey of the east range overlooking the space.

The garden as a whole is roughly divided into two parts, with the addition of the private President's Garden occupying the space north of Canterbury Quad. The character of these two main areas has remained essentially constant since the land for them was acquired in 1600. The lawned area or Outer Grove was always simpler, even during its baroque incarnation in the early 18th century, its more informal character defined by trees and lawn, while the rectangular garden to its left (north), known as the Inner Grove, was more elaborately and densely planted. There is a marvellous depiction of the college's groves in William Williams's *Oxonia Depicta* of 1733, which this engraver privileges above all other Oxford gardens bar Trinity's and Wadham's. He shows the Outer Grove with four plats enclosed by high, clipped palisades of trees, while the emphasis within the Inner Grove was on the sensation of walking under trees. A foreign visitor, Zacharias Conrad von Uffenbach, in 1710 described the gardens as 'a very large square with grass and garden-walks, and on the left-hand side a fairly spacious but wild garden with trees and paths'.

Thomas Salmon, in his 1744 guidebook to the universities, reserves high praise for the grove at St John's:

The inward Garden has evry thing almost that can render such a Place agreeable as a Terrass, a Mount, Wilderness, and well-contriv'd Arbours; but, notwithstanding this is much more admired by Strangers than the other, the outer Garden is become the general Rendezvouse of Gentlemen and Ladies every Sunday Evening in Summer: Here we have an Opportunity of seeing the whole University together almost, as well as the better Sort of Townsmen and Ladies, who seldom fail of making their Appearance here at the same time, unless the Weather prevents them.

The 'Terrass' mentioned here – running the width of the eastern end of both groves – remained an important feature of the garden well into the late 20th century.

The formal division between the Inner and Outer Groves was obliterated in 1770–78, when Robert Penson, a local nurseryman, assisted the fellows in the creation of the naturalistic scheme that is today's inheritance. There was a persistent story that the great landscape designer Lancelot 'Capability' Brown was engaged at St John's. One 1794 guidebook claimed that the 'celebrated Mr Browne, by removing a few embarrassing, overgrown Chestnut trees, has so changed the Aspect of this Garden, that few can at present vie with it.' The appearance of this garden was never exactly 'Brownian', however. An unpublished watercolour of the 1790s (in a bound volume of 'Views' in the British Library) shows the area around the exit from Canterbury Quad with an island bed centred on a conifer and a deciduous tree, with more than a dozen different shrub varieties clearly differentiated, being admired by two gowned and mortar-boarded fellows.

There is a circular walk around the Outer Grove which allows one to appreciate the forms of choice trees such as the Lucombe oak that leans out over the lawn, a paperbark maple, Indian horse chestnut and *Quercus canariensis* (Algerian or Mirbeck's oak) and cork oak, while a pair of mature copper beeches flanking the far end lend the whole considerable dignity (something of a watchword at this college). There is also a plantation of rhododendrons and camellias, in acid soil transported to the garden for the purpose, and groupings of mahonia. A frisson of Yunnan.

Moving from the Outer to the Inner Grove the visitor notices a distinct tonal change, for here smaller areas of mown lawn are enclosed by plantings of specimen trees, such as weeping beeches and groups of Japanese maples among more conventional birch, yew and chestnut. There is a private, enclosed and domestic feel to the space, as one follows winding paths that create a pleasing sensation of becoming lost (or almost). The climax, at the eastern end of the grove, is a massive cut-leaved beech which drapes its considerable skirts over the path, forming a sequestered green cathedral of filigree leaves that no visitor will want to leave.

At the Inner Grove's western boundary, the college's justly celebrated rock garden hugs the curving wall to the President's Garden. It was constructed in about 1900 by Henry Jardine

LEFT *Crocus tommasinianus* and varieties of Dutch crocus in the lawn of the Inner Grove, with the buildings of the early 1990s Garden Quadrangle visible beyond.

RIGHT David Loggan's engraving shows the layout of the college garden in 1675. The ground plan has not fundamentally changed: the Outer Grove is top right, beyond Canterbury Quad, the Inner Grove is to its left, and the President's Garden occupies the space to the left of Canterbury Quad.

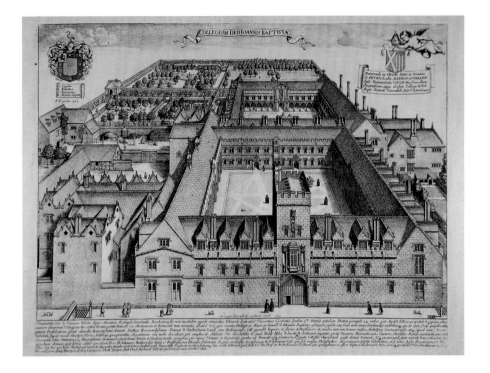

Bidder, the college bursar, whose name on a plaque on the wall here is now in danger of being obscured by a rampant cotoneaster. The St John's rock garden was much appreciated by the celebrated alpinist and wit Reginald Farrer. He was a Balliol man at the turn of the 20th century, and there is no evidence he contributed to the garden's design at any point – though one can understand why such an idea has been put forward, since the careful deployment of rocks here does seem to follow his naturalistic precepts, based on the observation of alpine meadows. This alpine scene was kept nicely in scale by Dr Bidder, nothing like the 'mini-Matterhorns' constructed elsewhere at the time. Perhaps it influenced Farrer, rather than the other way round? It became the thing for dons of Bidder's acquaintance to send him alpine specimens discovered on their holidays – the President of Trinity gave him a gentian, for example. The rock garden developed into an outdoor cabinet of alpine curiosities: a catalogue of 1913 listed some 700 species. Many of the saxifrages and other plants were lost in the 1976 drought, and in 1985 a consignment of large quarry stones slightly altered the character of the garden, giving it more of a landscape and less of an ornamental feel. It is kept in good order today, with many of the plants labelled. They include sempervivums, gentians, dianthus, erica, veronica and erodiums, and on a larger scale dwarf varieties of evergreen species such as *Picea*, *Thuja* and *Abies*. The presence of a number of colourful mature maples nowadays makes this almost more of a Japanese garden than an alpine rock garden.

Visible from the Inner Grove, and an adornment to it,

is the Sir Thomas White Building – distinctive modernism of 1972–75 from Arup Associates. This open quad is filled now with mature trees; however, the decision to allow undergraduates to chalk up rowing victories on the walls of this important modernist building is to be regretted. Near here is the President's Garden, still occupying the same site as depicted by Williams in the 18th century, but now wholly domestic in feel, with a lawn and trios of silver birch. (It is destined to be partially built over to make way for an extension to the college library.)

The Garden Quadrangle of 1994, designed by Richard MacCormac, features some serious gardening, including a mirrored roof garden with substantial Mediterranean-themed plantings which might be predictable (euphorbias, acanthus, lavender, rosemary, sages) but are holding up well. A central light well features a number of ivies which have been allowed to hang down almost to ground level below, an arresting sight.

There is a secret garden connected to the groves at St John's, which, in the best traditions of secrecy perhaps, is not open to the public. The rectangular Gooseberry Garden runs behind the south range of Canterbury Quad and is reached via a (locked) door in the south-west corner of the Outer Grove. Created in 1985 for the private use of the college fellows, it is an atmospheric and effective formal space with an appealing 1950s feel, focused on a circular pool shaded by a magnolia, with box-edged semicircular beds containing blue agapanthus and yew domes at each end. There is no evidence of any gooseberries. Yet another secret locked door in the wall opens directly on to another world: Trinity College.

Trinity College

I T IS ALWAYS INTERESTING to compare the modern form of Oxford's college gardens with how they appear in old engravings. In the case of Trinity College, one illustration is so astonishing that any appraisal of its garden must always be referred back to it. That image by William Williams, published in his *Oxonia Depicta* of 1733, shows in fine detail what would have been by far the most ambitious baroque garden layout to be realised at any college – including those of New College and Wadham. The engraving depicts a formal parterre of magnificent proportions marching away from the college buildings, its strong east-west axis accentuated by the lines of slender conical topiary trees which punctuate it like pinnacles on a cathedral. The garden is arranged in three long rectangular sections. The largest is the parterre proper, with seven compartments – two of them more ornate, centred on mounds – and heraldic beasts on the tops of posts flanking the central path. (The beasts look like griffins, as per the college arms.) The second consists of files of perfectly identical lime trees arrayed like soldiers on parade, four abreast. (Parts of the college's celebrated lime avenue lingered on into the 1990s.) The last is a Wilderness – not 'wild', since wilderness is a specific though rather fluid term in the garden-history lexicon – of clipped and shaped evergreens organised into arabesque patterns to form what we would today describe as a maze or labyrinth.

The top corner of the Williams engraving is rightly reserved for an illustration of the elegant wrought-iron gates installed

A peek into tree-studded Front Quad, bounded to the west by Balliol's stripey chapel.

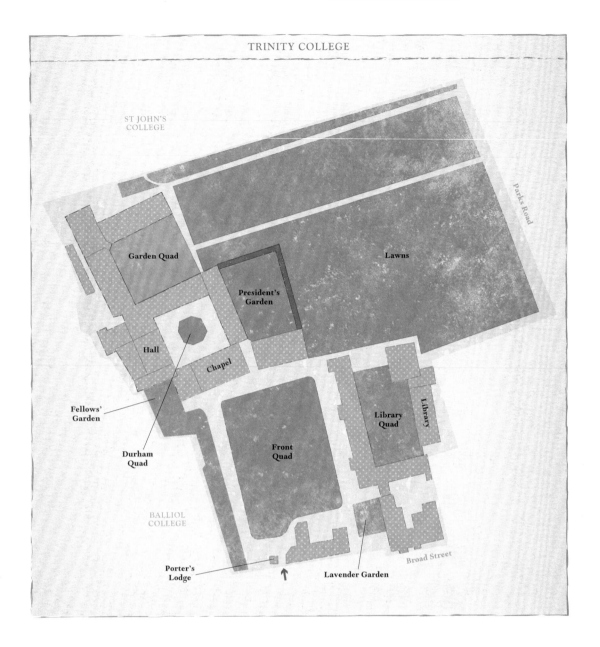

TRINITY COLLEGE

ST JOHN'S
COLLEGE

Garden Quad

President's
Garden

Lawns

Hall

Chapel

Fellows'
Garden

Durham
Quad

Front
Quad

Library
Quad

Library

Parks Road

BALLIOL
COLLEGE

Porter's
Lodge

Lavender Garden

Broad Street

to create a *clair voyée* from what is now the Parks Road on to this splendid scene. (One 18th-century guidebook to Oxford relates the unlikely story that when the massive stone blocks to make the gate piers were first sawn in half, a live toad hopped out of one of them – a variation on the idea that toads came out of stones, which was still just about current.) Any formal garden is long gone, but the view into Trinity through these gates is still one of the most magnificent surprises the city has to offer. The great lawn sweeps up to the Garden Quadrangle as if to the wing of a noble house, hidden in plain sight within the heart of Oxford. This vista somehow never fails to delight, no matter how many times one has seen it.

The college accounts imply that Trinity's formal garden was installed after 1706, when it would have been by no means old-fashioned. King William III's Privy Garden at Hampton Court had been laid out in this baroque formal style in 1701 – and today in its restored state provides a useful guide to the feel of Trinity's garden as it could have been at this time. By the late

1730s and 1740s, however, fashions were changing: 1733, the year the engraving was published in *Oxonia Depicta*, was also the year in which the Whiggish Lord Cobham of Stowe began to re-landscape his formal garden in a more naturalistic manner, with the help of William Kent. But he was in the vanguard and therefore in the minority. Many owners of estates – especially those who equated the new landscape garden with the Whigs gathered around statesman Robert Walpole – deliberately persisted with formal parterre gardens at this period. The formal topiary garden at Levens Hall in Cumbria, which survives in decorously overgrown form, was kept up in this style. It is perfectly possible that an Oxford college of Tory outlook might still in the 1730s have aspired to a garden in the high baroque manner harking back to the time of William and Mary and Queen Anne, the last of the Stuart monarchs, in the period immediately before the arrival of the House of Hanover and the wholesale dismissal of Tories from government and the bureaucracy. It is this context which makes the Williams engraving of Trinity's

grand formal garden in situ in 1733 seem plausible, despite its old-fashionedness – it was in part a political statement.

But what of the evidence 'on the ground'? There is a useful description of the college garden in *The Gentleman and Lady's Pocket Companion for Oxford* (1747):

The Gardens of this College are large and well laid out, containing about three Acres of ground. They are divided into three Parts: the first, which we enter from the grand Quadrangle, consists of fine Gravel Walks and Grass-plats, adorned with Ever-Greens, and the Walls entirely covered with them, as those in other College Gardens generally are; the Walks adjoining on the South were lately laid open to the Garden, and thereby much improved.

While it is not quite clear how the 'three Parts' of the garden are divided up, it sounds as if the the main garden featured grassy plats and was enclosed by evergreen walls, and possibly – if it was

'adorned with Ever-Greens' – ornamented with topiary figures. John Pointer, in his guidebook to Oxford of 1749, records:

The College garden is very pleasant, kept in extreme good order, planted with every variety of evergreens, and the walls all round cover'd with Green Yew in Pannel-work. Here was a wilderness extremely delightful with a variety of mazes, in which 'tis easy for a man to lose himself. Here and there in this Labyrinth are plac'd Benches, inviting students to sit down and study. In the middle of all is a neat Fountain with Artificial Flowers on the Surface of the Water. But this Wilderness is now alter'd to an open Grove.

This clearly refers only to the Wilderness area, and how it was made less formal – 'alter'd to an open Grove' – over the decades. There is no mention of a grand parterre garden to vie with Hampton Court's in its magnitude, though again 'every variety of evergreens' is mentioned, perhaps indicating

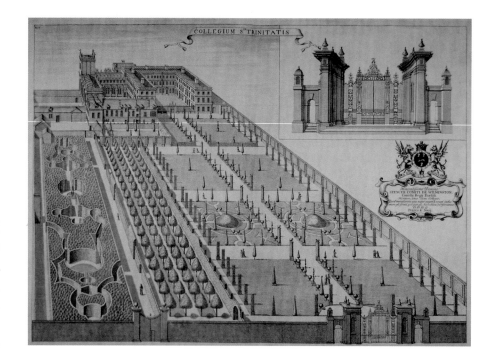

topiary. A speculative engraving in the *Oxford Almanack* for 1756 shows the (unexecuted) plan for a newly designed Garden Quadrangle. There is no formal garden visible at all in the foreground – no topiary, just lawns and a central pathway.

William Faden's 1789 map of Oxford was based on surveys made in 1750. This tells a similar story about the main garden, showing simple grass plats, though it does show a line of posts defining its north and south edges. (These posts turn up in several subsequent engravings.) It also clearly depicts the lime walk and the form of the Wilderness – an east-west serpentine walk through (yew) hedges with three clearings or *ronds-points* along the way. It seems as if in time the Wilderness became less and less formal – more like a structure of interconnecting glades – with floral interest too. Witness the description in *Oxford: A New Pocket Companion* (1794): 'The Southern Division is a Pleasing Solitude, consisting of shady Walks, with a Wilderness of flowering Shrubs, and disposed into serpentine Paths.'

The approving comments of Humphry Repton, who visited Trinity in 1794, and of the poet Robert Southey in 1807, also appear to focus on the Wilderness area. Repton commended 'the ancient style of gardening very properly preserved', noting the 'hedges and straight walks'; while Southey remarked on 'a wall of Yew, which encloses it on three sides, cut into regular pilasters and compartments. What Southey seems to be describing is a great undulating yew hedge, the overgrown remains of the yew 'walls' around the garden, which would have appeared pleasingly old-fashioned, as such hedges still do today.

Early 19th century sources echo the story, with Chalmers' *History of the University of Oxford* (1810) recording how 'the larger division…is laid into grass-plats', while *Walks in Oxford* (1818) by W. M. Wade states that 'the northern division is laid out in the airy style of modern landscape gardening, while the southern exhibits in its wilderness, its narrow winding walks, its trim hedges and its superabundance of formal yew, the fantastical taste of Queen Anne's time.' We are given a glimpse of some superabundant yew in *The Oxford Visitor* (1822) by J.

and H. S. Storer, which includes two engravings of Trinity's garden showing the old yews, some 4.5–6 metres/15–20 feet tall, on the south side of main garden, distorted into wonderful shapes. These would appear to be the overgrown remnant of the yew 'walls' planted at least 100 years earlier.

Yet still, across the course of some 70 years, not a single commentator mentions the existence – or the even pre-existence – of the great parterre garden we can see in the Williams engraving. Why? Multiple visitors over the decades mention the baroque garden elements at New College and Wadham, and there are several visual sources. Trinity's great garden is illustrated only once and is never described in detail by anyone. The college benefactors' book for 1709 records how part of a legacy had been used 'to embellish the public garden (lately the grove) and lay it out in a new design'. But the extent of that design is not specified. In fact the only real indication we have that this formal parterre existed at all is the Williams engraving, an image which has, perhaps understandably, proved irresistible to posterity.

But since such engravings sometimes contained speculative elements, and that this was a widely accepted form of licence, is it possible that the formal parterre was never even made? The college accounts mention the acquisition of trees, but not decorative heraldic beasts on posts or the construction of mounts. Perhaps it was the case that the Williams engraving was aspirational; that the impulse for its publication in *Oxonia Depicta* was essentially political; and that the Wilderness and lime avenue were the only elements ever actually implemented.

This does not take away from the magnificence of Trinity's gardens today. The great east garden is best approached as the climax of a walk through three complementary quadrangles. Trinity is unique among the city-centre colleges in that it is apparently set in the midst of its own substantial gardens. The impression is strongly conveyed at the main entrance, on Broad Street, where the college buildings do not abruptly rise up where the pavement ends, as with other colleges (such as neighbouring Balliol), but is set some way back, viewed across a large lawn with mature trees. The blue-painted railings, quaint entrance lodge, associated 'estate cottages' and gravel sweep of entrance drive are more in line with what one might expect of a large private house of Georgian character. The building which catches the eye as one looks north across the lawns is the perfectly proportioned chapel of 1694, one of the happiest small neoclassical buildings in Oxford, with a fine tower topped by female statues representing theology, medicine, geometry and astronomy. The roof of the chapel itself is decorated with urns containing imitation topiaries in green copper.

The chapel forms the south range of Durham Quad, the oldest part of Trinity and the site of Durham College, an institution founded by that city's cathedral for the education

of its monks. It was almost derelict by the time Sir Thomas Pope acquired the site in 1554 as a perk of his role in Henry VIII's team overseeing the dissolution of the monasteries. Perspicaciously he founded the college the following year and died four years later without ever having actually visited it. Trinity was initially known as a college for north-countrymen, though the regional link faded over time. Pope was a Catholic sympathizer (evidently a pragmatist, too, given his role in the destruction of England's monastic tradition) and, as has been indicated, the college became a haven for high Tory supporters of the Stuart succession and crypto-Jacobites – many of whom had estates in the North. Trinity's political leanings have since added spice to the college's historic rivalry with Balliol next door, which views itself as progressive. There is indeed

LEFT William Williams's 1733 engraving of the college garden and its east gate (TOP RIGHT). Of the three principal elements, we know that the maze-like Wilderness (LEFT) was planted, as was the double lime avenue (CENTRE) – but where is the evidence for the great parterre (RIGHT)?

BELOW The long border on the north side of the college lawn – yellow ligularia partnered with scarlet *Crocosmia* 'Lucifer'.

something a little landed and lofty about Trinity, a character perhaps exaggerated by its landscape setting, set slightly aloof from the urban goings-on of Oxford. Perhaps it was this that inspired some Balliol students to break in to the Trinity junior common room one night in 1963 and lay a lawn across it, using real turf and even a sprinkling of daffodils. The pranks played between these colleges are among the most elaborate and ambitious in the university and there appears to be an element of donnish approval about it all. The Gordouli is the name given to the cheeky song performed by Balliol students 'over the wall' at Trinity from their Garden Quad after celebratory dinners in hall.

The garden in front of the college is known as Front Quad, though it bears no resemblance to a quadrangle in the classical sense. For many centuries Trinity could only be reached by a narrow, high-walled lane leading from Broad Street straight up to the west end of the chapel – a rather insalubrious entrance. There were gardens on either side of this lane, which were both productive and ornamental; they are shown on Loggan's 1675 engraving of the college. His overall map of the city of Oxford in *Oxonia Illustrata* has rather different detail regarding these garden spaces, including a remarkable strip of small parterre gardens – presumably of evergreens and gravel – running alongside the lane. Perhaps in response to the successful use of wrought-iron gates at the eastern end of the college, in 1737 a new set of gates was added to the Broad Street frontage and the way in widened so that carriages could come right up to the chapel. A turning circle was created – a large oval of lawn surrounded by gravel, visible on Faden's map of 1789. This developed into the large open area of lawn visible in photographs of Front Quad in the 1880s. Specimen trees were planted at this time and today the area almost has the feel of a miniature arboretum, with a huge *Magnolia grandiflora* in front of the chapel, a pair of Atlantic cedars, an old catalpa, liquidambar, *Pinus virginiana*, *Cryptomeria japonica* 'Elegans', *Gleditsia triacanthos* 'Sunburst' and various other trees which I have not had leisure to identify. (While I was examining said trees, a lady who was crossing the grass of Front Quad at a diagonal – a fellow I assume – politely but firmly told me to get off the lawn.)

Trinity's Fellows' Garden is small but dignified: a private, high-walled space set just to the west of Trinity's chapel, with views across and up to Balliol's candy-striped chapel, too. There is a lawn, good herbaceous beds, and palms (*Trachycarpus wagnerianus*) underplanted with salvias. A pool set at its south end contains heraldic beasts in limestone that spout water. On the other side of Front Quad is a new Lavender Garden designed by head gardener Paul Lawrence, focused on an armillary sphere. A simple layout featuring only lavender and box hedging, it is an attractive and uplifting sight for pedestrians on Broad Street, who can spy it through the railings.

Trinity's first quad, proper, is Durham Quad, which contains the college's oldest architecture, though the early Georgian north range sets the tone. An admirable innovation is the raised octagon of Portland stone sitting in the centre of the quad, the setting for a lawn of perfectly mown stripes, each exactly a foot (30 centimetres) wide. Window boxes with annuals in the college colours of blue and yellow, and rows of tubs with lavender or salvias, constitute perfectly weighted neoclassical gardening which is appropriate to the architectural setting. The grass was recently painted blue (temporarily) as part of the preparations for the college's Commemoration Ball.

Moving north, the visitor enters the paved Garden Quad, its north range originally a free-standing building designed by Sir Christopher Wren in the late 1660s. The south and west sides were made in sympathetic style and all three ranges joined together to create a quad of sunny and open disposition, with views east to the great garden beyond. Screened by railings, the garden is not clearly visible until you pass through an archway festooned with the luxuriant, scarlet-flowered *Campsis* x *tagliabuana* 'Madame Galen'. The railings are clothed in a variety of climbing shrubs and fronted by a row of silver-grey cardoon thistles, which adds a striking contemporary note. Four beautiful 18th-century lead vases on plinths lend considerable elegance to this space, which is perhaps the most genteel and refined of all Oxford's quads. This is a gentry college, after all.

Trinity's lawns jet away into the distance as one enters the eastern garden. Today the main horticultural interest lies in

the two great borders flanking it to north and south. These are now being gardened in a way more in tune with the 'New Perennials' school of gardening, with an emphasis on drifts of plants to create layers and less of the 'tapestry' effect of the traditional colour-themed English herbaceous border. The north bed, backed by dark holm oaks and yews, features a wide range of herbaceous subjects including solidago, sedum, achilleas, heuchera, echinops, *Verbena bonariensis*, helenium

and salvias, as well as white roses and various ornamental grasses, which get larger as one progresses towards the gates at the east end of the garden, where persicarias, buddleia and daylilies up the ante. The area to the south that was once the Wilderness, and is still so termed, is in summer an informal expanse of limes and yews and winding paths, set amid some of the college's 1960s accommodation blocks. It comes into its own in spring, when thousands of bulbous plants – tulips,

anemones, winter aconites, fritillaries, narcissi, crocuses – create a fine display.

The President's Garden is secreted behind a wall in the south-western corner of the main garden, behind Durham Quad, a pleasant blend of mown lawns and shrub borders. It has always occupied this spot. The college records of the mid 16th century reveal that several enclosed gardens were inherited from Durham College, in addition to the grove (the site of the main east gardens) which originally extended to twice its present size. The President's Garden was enlarged

PREVIOUS PAGE The college lawns, leading to the east gate, with the Warden's Lodgings at Wadham visible beyond. The old yews to the right are probably the remnant of formal 18th-century plantings. On this afternoon the garden was open to the public for charity under the National Gardens Scheme.

ABOVE The recently installed Lavender Garden in the south-east of the college, visible to passers-by. In the distance can be spied (top left) Exeter College's Antony Gormley sculpture, sited on top of a building in Broad Street.

and enclosed in 1614, while a tiny garden to the north of Durham Quad, just 10 by 19 metres/11 by 21 yards, was used as the Fellows' Garden for the first century of Trinity's existence (until the advent of Garden Quad).

Trinity's grove and gardens were notable long before the realisation (or not) of grandiose baroque garden plans. The grove was reached via a passageway in the pre-Wren north range of Garden Quad. In 1560 a new gate to a new garden in the grove was installed and eight keys cut; it was specified that there was to be one given to the president and one each for seven senior college fellows. A covered walkway made of privet is mentioned. In 1580 another garden was made and another eight keys cut, and at this point a gardener was employed. Expenditure at this time is recorded for roses in 1581, plum trees in 1587 and rosemary and paved alleys in 1594. It is likely that much of this activity was focused on ornamenting the college's smaller enclosed gardens, as opposed to the grove itself.

Loggan's 1675 map indicates that the grove at that time was quite densely treed, with straight and criss-cross paths and a small mount at its north-eastern corner. During the Civil War garrison years, when Royalist soldiers came to live in Oxford with their wives and families, one Trinity man described the grove as 'the Oxford Hyde Park, the rendezvous of the nobility

and gentry'. The influx of women could be disconcerting. The antiquarian John Aubrey was at Trinity in the 1640s and in his 'brief life' of Dr Kettell, the college's most celebrated president, he describes the time of the Siege of Oxford: 'Our Grove was the Daphne for the Ladies and their gallants to walke in, and many times my Lady Isabella Thynne (who lay at Balliol College) would make her entry with a Theorbo or Lute played before her. I have heard her play on it in the Grove myself, which she did rarely.' Aubrey goes on to relate how Lady Thynne and her friend Mistress Fenshawe liked to tease the old college president, who gave them short shrift, and how they would 'come to our Chapell, mornings, halfe dressed, like Angells'. What curious angels. From Aubrey's account it sounds as if the chaplain of the College of the Holy and Undivided Trinity may not have had the whole and undivided attention of his congregation.

LEFT The view south into Library Quadrangle, with a specimen beech tree: *Fagus sylvatica* 'Dawyck Purple'.

ABOVE Pink hydrangeas create a frou-frou moment in Front Quad.

University College

BANG IN THE MIDDLE of the High Street, 'Univ' as it is generally known, is the most urban in feel of Oxford's colleges, squeezed between the High to the north and Merton Street to the south. It is a no-nonsense and utilitarian sort of place, notwithstanding the statue of Shelley which the college had the brass neck to accept in the 1890s – even building a special domed room for it – having sent down the great Romantic poet for his atheistic and generally bad behaviour just 80 years earlier. Indeed, the very name University College seems curiously devoid of character. But its full title is perhaps more evocative: the Master and Fellows of the College of the Great Hall of the University of Oxford. This reflects Univ's foundation as a hall, *Aula Universitatis* (university hall) – while the fact it was able to adopt this straightforward name is an indication of the college's antiquity. Univ is generally held to have been founded in 1249, making it credibly the oldest of the college foundations in Oxford. So its 'boring' name came about simply because it had no need to use any other. The lack-of-personality tag is not helped by the supremely generic nature of its frontage on the High Street: a long run of Oxford-Gothic gables and chimneys, with a low tower in the centre and a statue of Queen Anne in a niche above the gate. It is one of the most forgettable of college facades because there is so little to distinguish it from any of the others – except for its sheer scale, perhaps. The Queen's College, on the opposite side of the High Street, comprehensively upstages Univ with its own marvellous

Shadows on the lawn and wisteria on the walls in Radcliffe Quad, a quintessential Oxford college scene.

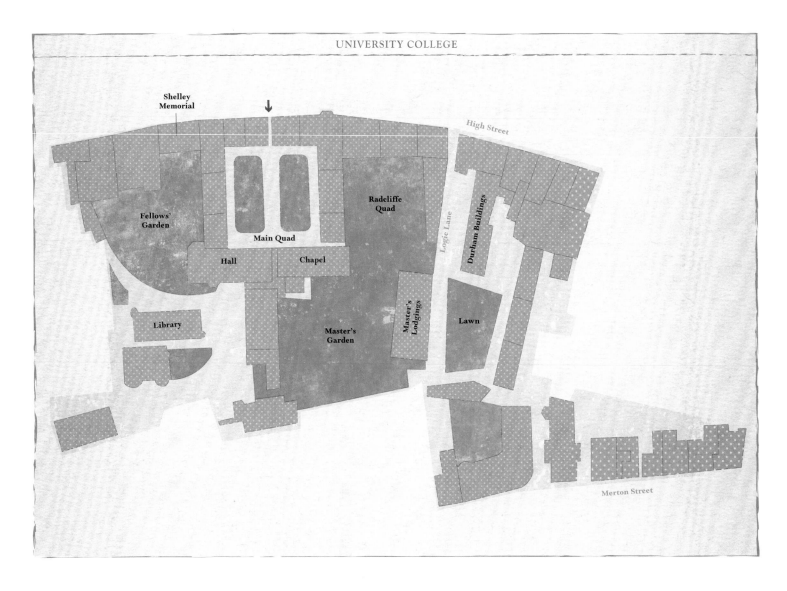

UNIVERSITY COLLEGE

Shelley Memorial

High Street

Fellows' Garden

Main Quad

Radcliffe Quad

Logic Lane

Durham Buildings

Hall

Chapel

Library

Master's Garden

Master's Lodgings

Lawn

Merton Street

cupola containing a statue of another 18th-century queen: Caroline of Ansbach, wife of George II.

The college site is split into two halves by the rationally named but irrationally wending Logic Lane, which makes its way north-south through the middle of the college. Most visitors will see only the older, western side, since the eastern portion is mainly comprised of student rooms above High Street shops or in the 20th-century Goodhart Building. (You have to be made of strong stuff to study at Univ: Examination Schools, the nemesis of all students, is right next door.)

Univ's entirely symmetrical and conventional Main Quadrangle reinforces the idea that this college somehow acts as a template for others. The reality is that it was a follower rather than a leader in terms of quadrangle design. The college moved to its present location in 1332, having probably started life on land now occupied by Brasenose College. The original medieval quadrangle on the High Street site was about a third smaller than the present one, which was built across a period of some 45 years after 1631, when the college unexpectedly inherited the estate of a childless landowner. The reason for the delay in completion was a combination of the upheaval of

the English Civil War and a lack of funds. (The master wrote numerous begging letters to ex-students, much as colleges still do today.)

There were actually two plans proposed for the new quadrangle. The first, which was rejected, was radical in its neoclassical detailing and could have been the first baroque building in Oxford. This plan survives in the college archive, with the words 'refused as inconvenient' written on the back. The second, executed plan was conventional Gothic and very much in thrall to the newly built quadrangles at Wadham and Oriel. The chapel is on the left and the hall on the right as one looks south across the quad, each with its own doorway. There was a 'frontispiece' in the middle of this south range, with a modicum of classical decoration, but it was timid stuff compared with Wadham's (and was anyway superseded by full-on Victorian Gothic in the 19th century). The college owns a cardboard model of its Main Quadrangle, made at the start of the rebuilding process, which can be positioned to show different possible permutations, including a cloister that was never constructed. It is thought to be the earliest such architectural model in existence.

The direct, confident and unpretentious flavour of this college is reflected by the way a straight path cuts right across the middle of the quadrangle and up to the twin doorways. The path is lined by contrasting annual bedding plants, which are changed frequently through the season. There is wisteria against the west wall. One curiosity of the quad is the statue of James II, in Roman emperor garb and pose, set in a niche in the tower. It is one of only two known statues of this unfortunate monarch; the other stands outside the National Gallery in London. Dating from 1687, Univ's is the residue of a master who was a Catholic convert and ardent supporter of the king. James II was of course removed from power the following year at the so-called Glorious Revolution (when the master was also obliged to remove himself from Univ). It is touching that the college has left this statue in position – showing loyalty to its former master if not necessarily to the deposed king.

Moving west, the visitor passes through the oddly antiseptic atmosphere of the Shelley Memorial, set in a room off a passageway. It is as if the poet has been decontaminated

for college consumption, as he lies there in the position he was found in on the Ligurian beach. The poet John Betjeman called Basil Champneys' domed chapel-of-rest 'municipal baroque'. One emerges with a sense of relief into the Fellows' Garden, an uneven rectangle with Gilbert Scott's Gothic library at its southern end. This building significantly reduced the size of the garden when it was constructed in 1861. Shaded by a mature horse chestnut and tulip tree, this is now a pleasant grassy space with a substantial border along the back of Main Quadrangle's west range, incorporating yellow inula, orange crocosmia, daylilies and hydrangeas. The garden was first laid out in 1809 after the demolition of Deep Hall, one of the medieval academical halls on the site, and a mid-19th-century engraving in the annual *Oxford Almanack* shows it to be in basically the same form now as then. Going farther back, we know that two other halls on Univ's site, Spicer's

BELOW The Master's Garden by the east end of the chapel. The shrub border visible across the lawn includes roses, yucca, peonies, variegated cornus and weigela.

271

Hall and Ludlow Hall, had between them a pleasure garden ('*disportum*') and a herb garden ('*herbarium*') in the late 14th and early 15th centuries. According to the bursar's rolls these were amalgamated following the removal of a wall in 1391, so it appears there was a precedent for a garden in this part of the college. The sheltered courtyard in front of the library is attractively arrayed with climbers and tender plants in pots, including *Edgeworthia chrysantha*, *Jasminum mesnyi* and *Plumbago auriculata*.

The original Fellows' Garden occupied the area now reserved for the private Master's Garden, south of the chapel. This surprisingly large space features a long herbaceous border with iris in spring, and asters and penstemons a key note later. Cornus, viburnum and pineapple-scented *Cytisus battandieri* are among the shrubs here, while a trio of *Betula utilis* var. *jacquemontii* (Himalayan birch) were planted to replace a mulberry which fell in 2002. The garden is overlooked by the Master's Lodgings (1879), a pleasing Victorian-Gothic building by G. F. Bodley. Few records survive but it appears that there was some adornment to this garden in the late 17th and early 18th centuries (a summer house is recorded in 1710), as well as an avenue of walnut trees running south which was known as a 'grove' – very much what colleges wanted at the time – and is remembered in the name of Grove House on Kybald Street.

To the east, Radcliffe Quad has a déjà-vu effect on the visitor, in that it was built in exactly the same Gothic style as Main Quad. That was one of the inviolable terms of the bequest which paid for its construction, in 1716–19, when Queen's College just across the High would have been taking shape in a much more of-the-moment baroque neoclassical style. Perhaps the main architectural impact of this new quadrangle is that it increases the college's markedly uniform frontage on the High Street to some 90 metres/300 feet in width. Wisteria is the prime horticultural note, though there are other climbers including *Akebia quinata* (chocolate vine), while a large *Robinia pseudoaccacia* marks the end of the quad's southern portion, which is closed off by a wall. There is a wrought-iron gate just here (locked) that leads into the Master's Garden and a view of the eastern end of the chapel.

Logic Lane, closed off at the High Street end where a short bridge provides a connecting passage, is an interesting curiosity, with the faux-Tudor, half-timbered Durham Buildings and, halfway along, the Goodhart Building of 1962, with its 'concrete cloister' and a simple lawn to the front. The landscape architect Sylvia Crowe laid out several areas in this part of college, including Cecily's Court, though none of this can be seen by visitors today. Another of Univ's hidden spaces is the Bob Thomas Garden, named after a former garden master of the college and situated behind houses that look on to Merton Street. It features climbing roses and shrubs such as azara and calycanthus.

Univ may have an urban feel by dint of its city-centre location, but a glance at a ground plan of the college today reveals that almost half of its acreage is taken up by gardens or quadrangles. The college has been able to keep its garden areas largely intact by means of imaginative expansion into adjacent blocks and buildings, a good policy which has also helped preserve the unique ambience of a number of other Oxford colleges.

University Parks

I N THE CONTEXT OF the riches of Oxford's college gardens, it is all too easy to overlook the Parks, situated between Keble College (to the west), the university's Science Area (south), the River Cherwell (east) and the Victorian garden suburb of Norham Manor (north). This is a place of great refreshment and relaxation, much used by town and gown alike. Free and open to all every day of the year (except Christmas Eve), the Parks has none of the strictures and opening-time eccentricities of the colleges, which operate as their own little worlds and can feel a little overbearing at times. One is only ever a visitor in an Oxford college (unless you count among its privileged members) so it is impossible to relax completely, however interesting or delightful the surroundings. The Parks allows for anonymity and asks no questions of its users. Picnics are allowed, ball games are positively encouraged and there are no 'keep off the grass' signs. The Parks also has sheer size on its side – at about 30 hectares/75 acres, this is a place where it is easy to lose oneself in the pleasantest way, transcending for a while the quotidian worries of life. No college garden can offer quite that.

The University Parks was to be a high-minded high-Victorian innovation. Most of the land was originally owned by Merton College; the western portion had been used as a recreational space within Oxford since the early 17th century, while much of the eastern part was under the plough. The area would therefore have had a far more open character than it does now. The term 'Parks' was habitually used in Oxford to

The River Cherwell and the footbridge to Marston – one of numerous tranquil passages to be discovered.

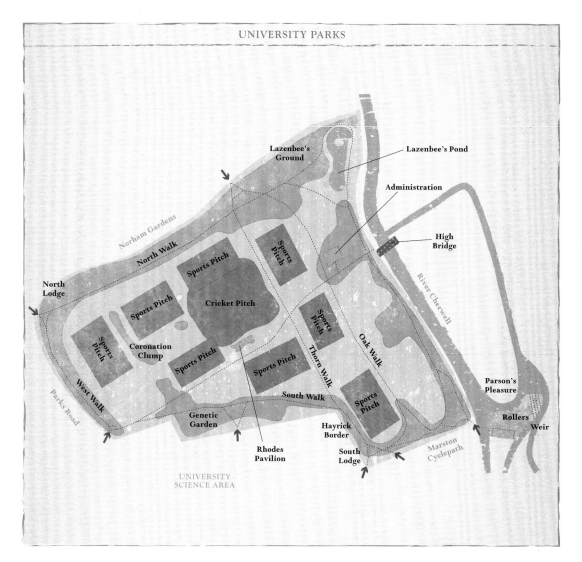

UNIVERSITY PARKS

Lazenbee's
Ground

Lazenbee's Pond

Administration

High
Bridge

Norham Gardens

North Walk

North
Lodge

Sports
Pitch

Sports Pitch

Sports
Pitch

Cricket Pitch

Sports Pitch

Sports
Pitch

River Cherwell

Coronation
Clump

Sports
Pitch

Sports Pitch

Thorn Walk

Oak Walk

West Walk

Sports Pitch

Parks Road

South Walk

Parson's
Pleasure

Genetic
Garden

Sports
Pitch

Rollers

Weir

Hayrick
Border

Rhodes
Pavilion

South
Lodge

Marston
Cyclepath

UNIVERSITY
SCIENCE AREA

RIGHT Another mood by the Cherwell – at the south-eastern corner of the Parks, towards Parson's Pleasure (historic nude bathing spot) and the rollers (used for transporting punts safely around the weir).

describe a swathe of fields and countryside that spread in an arc across the northern edge of Oxford city. It is so-labelled on old maps and crops up in various texts. This perhaps explains the curious pluralisation of the term today, which is after all used to describe one piece of land. The modern park, which duly became known as 'The Parks', was initially conceived as an adjunct to the new University Museum of Natural History and in 1860, when all of the land had been acquired by the university, the committee in charge suggested that it be developed as an arboretum, so it might have an educational and scientific aspect as well as a recreational one. The need for a university cricket pitch was also an early priority. James Bateman, owner and designer of the extraordinary fantasy garden at Biddulph Grange, Staffordshire (who had been at Magdalen), was asked to come up with a plan for the park which integrated these elements. Bateman was not just a fantasist but a serious horticulturist; his proposals included a circular perimeter walk, a large lake, an avenue of wellingtonia trees connecting the museum with the park, and two cricket pitches, as well as specimen trees for the arboretum. The leading practical garden stylist of the day, Robert Marnock, was to implement the plan. But it was immediately rejected by the university as

too expensive, and only ever partially realised. The original parks committee promptly disbanded and in 1864 the university's Hebdomadal Council recommended that 'eight to ten acres of the Parks Estate be planted with belts, clumps and single trees at £50 per acre', and that 'a walk be carried round the whole enclosure of an average width of not less than twelve feet'. This was far less ambitious than Bateman's scheme, and left a 16-hectare/40-acre hole in the centre of the site, but a start was made the following year when the university allocated £500 for trees to plant in the Parks.

With no sense of an overall design, the University Parks was developed in a piecemeal manner, and that is how it has continued ever since. Today there are no fewer than ten Parks Curators – taken from the ranks of the university – who are charged with overseeing the space in collaboration with the Parks Superintendent. The lack of a clear plan at the outset, coupled with the need for formally segregated sports pitches, has resulted in a park with no strongly discernible character today, despite its considerable horticultural and arboreal assets. One has to conclude, when one looks at Oxford's biggest park in the context of other public parks of a similar date in Britain, that the 19th-century university missed a golden opportunity as a result of its own short-sightedness and parsimony.

The average visitor to the Parks today will neither know nor care about any of that, because so many aspects of this space are first class, thanks to the work of Superintendent Walter Sawyer and his team (who also look after a number of the college gardens on a contract basis; see page 315). Trees are of course the principal interest here. There has been a great deal of replanting through the 20th century, especially after the

depredations of Dutch elm disease in the 1970s, which killed off the large collection of elms that formed the nucleus of the original arboretum. Today, the North Walk offers perhaps the richest arboreal pickings, running from the North Lodge (1866) in the north-west corner of the park all the way down to the pond and the Cherwell at the eastern end. There is a wide variety of unusual and more familiar trees to see. They are not all labelled by name but they do have tags, and the Parks' useful website lists them all alphabetically and by location. Among these trees are Mongolian lime (*Tilia mongolica*, NW4), white ash (*Fraxinus americana*, NW7), a huge Turkish hazel planted in 1868 (*Corylus colurna*, NW20, also NW34), tree of heaven (*Ailanthus altissima*, NW30), smooth Arizona cypress (*Cupressus glabra*, NW52) and a number of different oaks. Seven wellingtonias were planted near North Lodge in 1888, perhaps as a belated nod to Bateman's original planting plan. The red-brick Victorian villas of Norham Gardens overlooking the north end of the Parks became among the most sought-

after houses in Oxford in the late 19th century, when many of the university's professors lived there, perambulating around the Parks' walks on summer evenings with their families. In the 1920s huge crowds (often 8,000 strong) were drawn to the Parks to hear military bands play, while it has also been the venue for vast tea parties celebrating events such as royal jubilees or weddings. A more recent innovation is the university's Quidditch pitch, for inter-college matches of the ball game described in the Harry Potter series of books.

The second principal avenue, informally lined with a variety of trees, is the West Walk running north-south alongside the Parks Road at the western perimeter. Here one can spy a fine old *Sophora japonica* (WW2), the hop hornbeam with its long catkins (*Ostrya carpinifolia*, WW14), incense cedar (*Calocedrus decurrens*, WW17) and a range of hawthorns and unusual hollies, including the Highclere holly (*Ilex* x *altaclerensis*, WW1). The South Walk's more unusual offerings include yellow catalpa (*Catalpa ovata*, SW11) and

RIGHT Wild ducks on Lazenbee's Pond. The noise of ducks is a near-constant presence in the Parks.

Lucombe oak (SW25), while Lazenbee's Ground in the north-east of the park has a number of evergreens – deodar cedar (LG11), Corsican pine (LG14) – mingling with the likes of *Carya tomentosa* (LG19) and *Populus trichocarpa* (LG12). Cedars are indeed one of the strengths of the tree collection, with good mature specimens of cedar of Lebanon and Atlantic cedar dotted about.

The university cricket field occupies the centre of the park, its pavilion on the south side realised in the same Picturesque spirit of cottage orné as the north and south entrance lodges. The pavilion was designed in 1880 by Thomas Jackson, architect of Hertford and of various buildings in other Oxford colleges, and it makes for an evocative backdrop on summery afternoons. There are several themed avenues east of the cricket pitch, such as the Thorn Walk, incorporating more than 40 unusual varieties of crataegus (they thrive here), and a more recent (1980s) plantation of oaks along the Middle Walk, to replace some of the lost elms. Thorns with especially attractive orange-red autumn foliage or fruits include *Crataegus persimilis* 'Prunifolia' and *Crataegus phaenopyrum*. South of the cricket pitch is the site of the Genetic Garden, which was established in 1964 as a tool for teaching genetic science by means of plants (notably variegated subjects, hybrids and graft chimeras). The planting beds devoted to this have now been subsumed into the park itself and the scientific theme is less rigorously pursued. Nearby is an avenue of alternating catalpa and liriodendron (tulip trees).

The eastern side of the park has the benefit of water, in the form of the pond, which was enlarged in 1996 and is surrounded by cornus and artemisia, and the River Cherwell, spanned by what is known as the Rainbow Bridge (1924) about a third of the way down the eastern perimeter walk. The visitor passes arboretum areas named Picked Mead, The Leys and Diamond Ring – each with their own interest – before reaching Cox's Corner at the south-eastern edge of the park. This section was extensively planted with mainly native shrubs in the 1990s, as well as willows, alders, hawthorn and birch (including downy birch, *Betula pubescens*, CX7). Following the path east, the visitor will see the rollers – which safely convey punts around the weir – and then arrive at the historic site of Parson's Pleasure, a place which some may assume is mythic. This was the celebrated nude bathing spot for male members of the university (closed – officially at least – in 1991, when it was brought into the purlieu of the park). In a spirit of equality, Dame's Delight a little farther on was reserved for women – until it was closed in 1970.

It is easy to miss Mesopotamia, the spur to the park which extends south a little way from here on an island between two branches of the Cherwell (the name Mesopotamia referring to the area between the Euphrates and the Tigris). Once the site of a mill, it is less frequented than other parts of the Parks and has a wilder feel – though nowadays sections of grassland in the main park are also left to grow longer, to encourage wild flowers such as *Cardamine pratensis* (lady's smock), *Jasione montana* (sheep's-bit scabious) and *Lotus corniculatus* (bird's-foot trefoil).

Spring bulbs are one of the highlights of the park as a whole, with bright yellow winter aconites (*Eranthis hyemalis*)

under the beeches near Lady Margaret Gate and at South Lodge. These are followed by snowdrops (*Galanthus nivalis*) and the blue flowers of *Scilla siberica* and *Anemone blanda* beside North Walk. Crocuses, including the delicate *Crocus tommasinianus*, have naturalised along Thorn Walk, while drifts of daffodils cover the banks north of the cricket pavilion; *Narcissus lobularis* is the first variety to flower, in early February. Bluebells (*Hyacinthoides non-scripta*) bordering North Walk continue the succession. There is also an autumn bulb display, with cyclamen (*Cyclamen hederifolium*), crocus and colchicums along North Walk, colchicums in Lucas Walk, cyclamen at South Lodge, and sternbergia (autumn daffodil) flowers in the island beds near North Lodge.

Although trees are the main attraction in the Parks year-round, there are several areas of intense decorative gardening using mainly herbaceous material, backed by shrubs. The largest of these can be found just to the north of the South Lodge, which was constructed as a house for the Parks

Superintendent in 1893. The Hayrick Border (made on the site of an old hayrick) is one of the finest of all Oxford's mixed borders and is gardened on an ambitious scale, with as much emphasis on form as colour. The bright lights of crocosmia, helenium, penstemon and geranium varieties are given a sturdy context by euphorbias, acanthus, a number of big grasses (miscanthus, stipa), hollies and eupatorium, while in late summer a collection of salvias comes to the fore.

The University Parks is perhaps best viewed as a series of mini-arboretums of varying character, each of which is well worth exploring in some detail across the seasons. Appreciated in that way, its charms might be said to be nigh on inexhaustible.

ABOVE The Hayrick Border near South Lodge, with (LEFT) orange-berried pyracantha and blue perovskia, and (RIGHT) orange helenium, blue salvias, spiky eryngium and a clump of miscanthus grass.

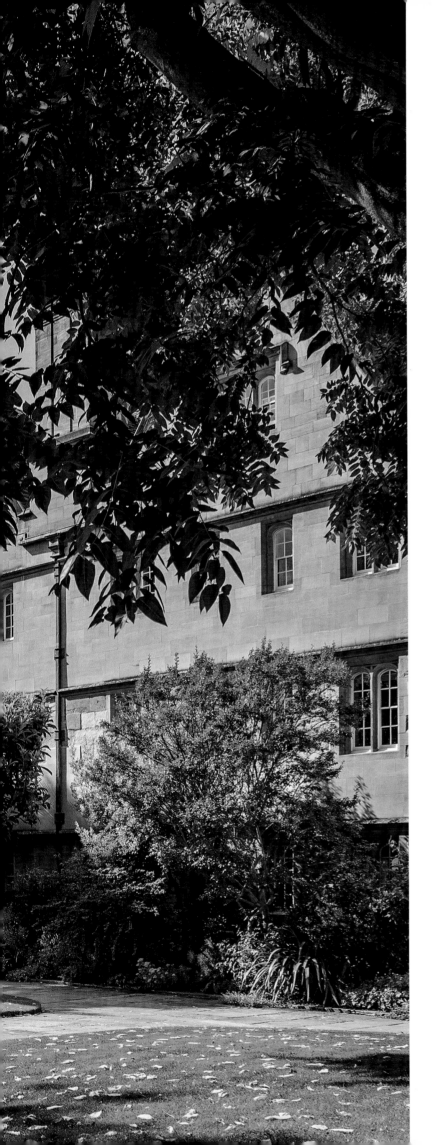

Wadham College

THE FIRST FACE WADHAM presents to the world – its facade and Front Quadrangle – is rational, orderly, smooth and entirely symmetrical. The statues of the founders, Nicholas and Dorothy Wadham, stand to attention in their niches in Front Quad, as if benignly patrolling their creation. The second face is hidden beyond: the college gardens, which delight in the unpredictable exuberance and mystery of nature. In the 17th century they were the site of the most extravagant garden of baroque tricks in Oxford; latterly they have been converted into a miniature arboretum, delicately arrayed with flowery walks.

Slightly set back from Parks Road, Wadham's imposing frontage is offset by rectangles of lawn on either side of the entrance tower and lodge – front gardens, in effect. These were originally walled areas dedicated to fruit and vegetable production, that to the left (north) being reserved for the warden. For many centuries Wadham was walled, fenced or railed along the width of its entire road frontage, with a gate in the centre and grass parterres with trees behind, but since 1925 it has been left open, the tower flanked by pairs of chimneys rising to its height, with battlements all along the facade. This uncompromising silhouette, seen to good effect as one crosses into Parks Road from the Broad, makes Wadham's frontage perhaps the most arresting among Oxford's colleges. The extreme abruptness of arrival one experiences at most colleges, where there is no preamble, is leavened here by the few seconds it takes to walk up the path to the lodge; the

Mature trees and shrubs dignify Back Quad, which was formerly used as a service area, with stables and outbuildings. Today, it is effectively the college's second quadrangle.

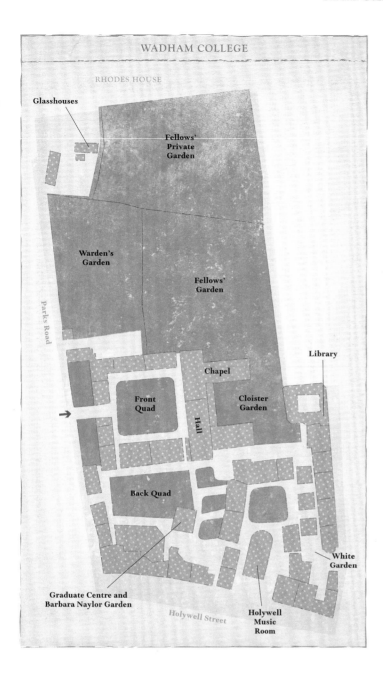

WADHAM COLLEGE

RHODES HOUSE

Glasshouses

Fellows'
Private
Garden

Warden's
Garden

Fellows'
Garden

Parks Road

Library

Chapel

Front
Quad

Cloister
Garden

Hall

Back Quad

White
Garden

Graduate Centre and
Barbara Naylor Garden

Holywell Street

Holywell
Music
Room

BELOW RIGHT The earthwork in the Fellows' Private Garden, which was reputedly built by Royalist soldiers during the Civil War siege of Oxford. The roof of the cowshed is visible through the trees.

FOLLOWING PAGE View across the roof of the Clarendon Building of the Bodleian Library, over the pink-rendered King's Arms pub, and into Wadham's Back Quad.

the door to the dining hall. This is a confection of four storeys, each level framed by twin columns in different classical orders, with the statues of Nicholas and Dorothy Wadham on the second level, James I on the next, and the whole crowned by an extraordinary starburst pediment. This segment of the eastern facade is like a sliver of fashionable classicism amid a perfected version of conventional Oxford Gothic. In the light of the neoclassical revolution in architecture which occurred in various incarnations over the next several hundred years, it now looks to be small beer, perhaps – but at the time it would have been a noteworthy statement of modernity. The quadrangle is laid to grass, which replaced the gravelled court that was in existence until 1809. There are photographs of Front Quad being used for drilling troops in the First World War, and it does indeed have something of the air of a parade ground.

A passage in the top left (north-eastern) corner of Front Quad, passing by the entrance to the chapel, leads to the Fellows' Garden, which is the place where the college lets its hair down, figuratively. Like many fellows' gardens, this treasured space is not closed off but has for years been open to all members of the college, and to visitors. Before it was made into a formal garden at the midpoint of the 17th century, the land was given over to orchards and market gardens, as it had been during the time of the Augustinian priory that formerly occupied the site. The garden today takes up a surprisingly large proportion of Wadham's acreage and is easily big enough to have been used as the site of a second quadrangle at some point, following the arc of development of most colleges. But Wadham has cherished its garden and as a result the college has just one 'proper' quadrangle, Front Quad, notwithstanding 20th-century additions. In fact, there was a horticultural element bound up with the terms of Dorothy Wadham's foundation of the college, which stipulated that it should be 'well and sufficiently furnished with apple-trees, pear-trees and other fruit trees thereupon to be of the growth of twenty-five years, fit for an orchard at the end of thirty-six years'. A Somersetshire woman speaks.

In garden history, the Wadham Fellows' Garden is important because of the various 'contrivances' recorded there, notably by the diarist, natural historian and gardener John Evelyn, who visited in July 1654. At this time, during the period leading

visitor is mentally prepared to enter Wadham, which enhances one's awareness of its dignity and presence.

Front Quad certainly encourages visitors and students to be on their best behaviour, since it is one of the starkest and most strikingly symmetrical of Oxford quadrangles. Constructed between 1610 and 1613, it displays a remarkable homogeneity in both its design and craftsmanship. This is probably because the 27 stonemasons who worked on the project all hailed from the same place, Somerset – as did the founders of the college and its first fellows. (The records indicate that most of these masons walked all the way from the quarry village of Stoke-sub-Hamdon, source of Ham stone.) The architecture mingles a medieval savour – the tall arched windows of the hall and chapel, and the crenellations all around – with bursts of what was in the early 17th century a more 'modern' and challenging classical style. This is expressed most dynamically in the central 'frontispiece' section of the east range, straight ahead, framing up to the founding of the Royal Society in 1660, Wadham was a nexus of scientific activity, with the emphasis on experimentation and demonstration. John Wilkins, the warden of the college, who was then in his thirties, invited or attracted a large number of scientifically minded men to Wadham – John Locke and Robert Boyle among them – where they enjoyed an intellectually stimulating and socially convivial atmosphere. (Wilkins was necessarily ambitious – his marriage to Oliver Cromwell's youngest sister, Robina, would not have hindered his career, especially since the future Lord Protector was also Chancellor of Oxford University from 1650.) The impression is that anything could be attempted at Wadham; the microscopist Robert Hooke, for example, in later life recalled his 'way of flying by vanes [wings] tryed at Wadham'. We may be sure that this is not some metaphorical reference to youthful confidence by way of Icarus but a record of an actual attempt to fly. Wilkins himself had at the age of 24 written a book which posited the feasibility of sending a man to the moon. This was Wadham in the 1650s.

Wilkins oversaw the creation of a garden in the latest style, having acquired most of the land it now occupies. We know that it cost £72 13s. The existing market gardens were dug over and in their stead – on the evidence of Loggan's engraving of 1675 – was made a formal design of four rectangular enclosures, each with four squares within, all planted out in box and yew, with small specimen trees around the perimeters and espaliered fruit on the surrounding walls. In the middle was a modest mount reached by some steep stairs, topped by a balustraded hexagonal platform with a figure of Atlas holding up a globe. This was a strident statement by Oxford standards at the time: most colleges were content with the creation of far simpler appurtenances such as orchards or bowling greens. (Neighbouring New College, with its own much larger mount, was the obvious exception.)

It is not clear whether this Atlas was in position in Wilkins' time, for Evelyn, during his visit to the man he dubs 'that most obliging and universally-curious Dr Wilkins', does not make specific reference to either Atlas or to the garden

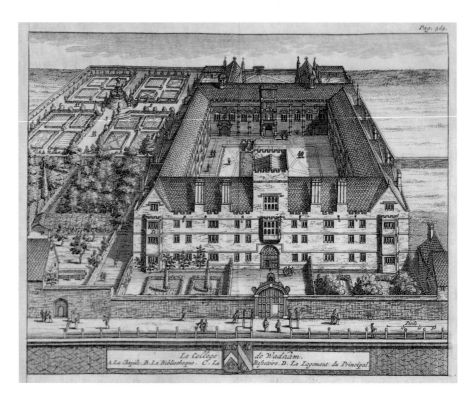

itself in his brief journal entry, only to some of the contrivances he saw there. Chief among these were 'the transparent apiaries, which he [Wilkins] had built like castles and palaces, and so order'd them one upon another as to take the honey without destroying the bees. These were adorn'd with a variety of dials, little statues, vanes, &c'. The warden presented Evelyn with a spare beehive, which was transported back to his garden at Sayes Court in Deptford; Evelyn claims that the king later came to his garden expressly to see this wonder. The evidence is that the beehive was the invention of Christopher Wren (of All Souls), a friend of Wilkins', whose drawing of a 'transparent beehive' was published the very next year. His contraption resembles three large octagonal hatboxes stacked on top of each other, with a trio of small viewing holes at each level. (Wren was not 'just' an architect but an accomplished natural historian as well.) Another source of delight to the gadget-mad Evelyn was Wilkins' 'talking statue', used to shock and delight (in that order) visitors. It worked by means of a long speaking pipe. It seems likely that this statue was in the area west of the Fellows' Garden, near to the Warden's Lodgings – in the Williams engraving of 1733 a statue is shown in one of four compartments set around a classical temple, but this area is cut off from view in Loggan's 1675 engraving. Another visitor recorded a device which created artificial rainbows by spraying a fine mist into the light on sunny days. This would have been a version – a rather primitive version – of an established element of the garden repertoire, generally found inside grottoes.

All of this does not quite add up to a baroque garden of contrivances anything like as elaborate and impressive as those made elsewhere for royal and aristocratic patrons, by masters such as Isaac de Caus. But if the college garden had been conceived as a garden of jokes in the Italian and French tradition, it would certainly have contained water tricks designed to soak the unwary. Wadham's contrivances were a novelty for Oxford, and Wilkins obviously liked to amuse and enchant his guests; but serious scientific experimentation rather than affectation was the true focus.

The garden remained in this basic form until the 1750s, when the mount was removed, Atlas having finally been knocked from his eyrie during a storm. But the biggest change came in 1795, when the last vestiges of the 16th-century garden were finally swept away and the layout was brought naturalistically up to date courtesy of Mr Shipley, the Duke of Marlborough's gardener at Blenheim Palace, in Woodstock. This period saw the removal of existing trees and the planting of new specimens, including several cedars of Lebanon and a copper beech that still stands. John Wills, who was warden at this time, oversaw the planting of various other specimens, such as monkey puzzles and a Judas tree, and these helped establish the current grove-like character of Wadham's gardens, which are not dissimilar in feel to those of St John's. A large tulip tree near the Warden's Lodgings and a holm oak are survivors from this period. The guidebook *Walks in Oxford* of 1818 described Wadham's garden as 'extensive' and 'laid out in the modern way'.

The Fellows' Garden today is a great surprise and delight, first of all because of its orientation to the north (left) of Front Quad, as opposed to directly behind it. Visitors might well feel as if they are 'sneaking in' around the side – not an unpleasant sensation. The garden is now essentially a large lawned area studded with trees, encircled by a perimeter walk lined with shrubs, herbaceous perennials and surprising floral exotica. The presence of numerous young trees adds to the impression of a garden that is under active management (not always the case in the colleges), while more venerable specimens stylishly dotted about the lawns include a large Scots pine, a giant redwood, a ginkgo and two cedars of Lebanon, in continuation of a college tradition. There is a fine *Magnolia*

acuminata – the cucumber tree – set in the border, along with a *Sophora japonica*, and nearby a trio of Chinese cedar trees, *Toona sinensis*. Another plus is the aggregate used as gravel for the paths: it is well chosen, sympathetic to the scene.

The border and walk down the western side of the garden is its greatest ornament, with numerous interesting shrubs including candy-coloured *Xanthoceras sorbifolium*, *Euphorbia characias*, mahonias, escallonias, clerodendrums and hydrangeas, as well as trees such as parrotia, a group of delicate acers, large-leaved *Paulownia tomentosa* and *Sorbus bristoliensis*, the whitebeam native to the Avon Gorge. This last is a (possibly accidental) reference to the fact that bomb-wearied working-class inhabitants of Bristol were given holidays in Wadham and other Oxford colleges during the Second World War. At the northern end of this walk, in the corner, the so-called 'nook' is a small seating area secreted within the dense cover of foliage plants such as rheums, sasa grass, rodgersias, ferns and aralias, enlivened by fuchsias in summer and the

black shiny leaves of *Aeonium* 'Zwartkop'. Planting interest continues along the northern wall, with sedums, salvias, heleniums, daylilies and numerous other flowers. All the time there are fine views back across the lawn towards the chapel and the rest of the college – architecture and landscape in harmony together.

Finally one reaches a locked gateway in the north-east corner. One is reminded that the Fellows' Garden may be a distinguished and stylish place, but it is slightly smaller than it might be, given that a portion was sold in order to institute neighbouring Rhodes House in the 1920s. It is also somewhat foreshortened by the presence of the Fellows' Private Garden to the north (entered via this gateway) and the Warden's Garden to the west, neither of which are open to the public or to students. What visitors cannot realise is that these gardens are each as large again as the Fellows' Garden itself.

The Fellows' Private Garden continues the general theme, with numerous mature trees set around a lawn – a mulberry, a metasequoia, tulip tree, walnut, younger fruit trees. At the eastern end is a raised walkway, by repute the remains of earthworks dug by Royalist soldiers in 1642. There is a delightful old cowshed built into the side of this bastion. The tradition of tortoises in this garden is, alas, in hibernation. The Warden's Garden covers a whole acre (0.4 hectares) and is one of the most impressive principal's gardens in all of Oxford, with a fine tulip tree dating to 1701, some interesting birches (including the Chinese birch and peel-bark variety) and an elegant serpentine path around the perimeter allowing one to enjoy the herbaceous borders kept up in fine fashion by head gardener Andrew Little and his colleague Michael O'Day. These two have been at Wadham for 30 and 50 years respectively, and are living proof that working at the same place for a long period does not necessarily mean being stuck in a rut. They have recently been joined by a new female colleague. Given the heavy horticultural workload in a typical college, it is not often the case that areas such as master's gardens are kept up as rigorously as the more public parts of a college, but at Wadham there is clearly one standard with no distinctions across the piece. The Warden's Garden is farther distinguished by the remnant of what were once considerable glasshouses – one of them shelters a cherished 'Black Hamburgh' vine, which the college records state was 'planted during the wars with Napoleon'. In 2014 it produced 250 bunches of grapes for the college fellows to enjoy when dining at high table – thick of skin but intensely flavoured (the grapes, that is).

There are several other gardened areas worthy of note in warren-like Wadham. There is a garden directly behind the dining hall, which faces the covered cloister that runs along the ground floor of the building. This passage has a subterranean quality and the garden beyond feels secret (indeed, as it is not open to visitors). A quiet and enclosed space, it is the site of a 1977 bronze sculpture by John Doubleday of celebrated 20th-century warden Maurice Bowra (his lower half intriguingly morphing into a chair), and is resplendent with bluebells under the horse chestnuts in spring, while a katsura tree lights it up in autumn. The college's splendidly avant-garde library (1976) overlooks this area.

Back Quad, also closed to visitors, is reached via the south-east corner of Front Quad, and was formerly the site of cottages and the warden's stables. It is now one of those piecemeal 20th-century amalgamations which tend to have an untidy and unsatisfactory air next to the relative unity of the typical pre-20th-century quadrangle. There are some fine old lime trees here and great efforts have been made with the planting, especially of shrubs and small trees, including a weeping silver lime, *Koelreuteria paniculata*, *Hydrangea aspera*, *Staphylea pinnata* (bladdernut), the corkscrew hazel, *Corylus avellana* 'Contorta', a loquat and rare Chinese gutta-percha tree.

The Barbara Naylor Garden, which adorns the college's new Graduate Centre, can be reached in dramatic fashion via a stairway at the western end of Back Quad. The visitor rises up to discover a delightful garden on the roof, with clematis and roses twining around the wooden pergola and a range of traditional English and dry-garden plants thriving in containers – penstemons, alliums, cistus, buddleia, pennisetum grasses, cordylines. The pergola was designed by Lee/Fitzgerald Architects and the planting by Mr Little. No wonder this has become such a popular spot in summer for all college members. Below here, Holywell Court is a tiny space where a variety of climbing plants and containers makes the most of it horticulturally.

The south-eastern corner of the college has seen a number of new developments in recent years, including the Bowra Building (1992) designed by Richard MacCormac, an accommodation complex realised in sandy coloured brick that has a serious landscape component at its heart: a narrow 'lane', focused on New College's bell tower, which evokes a medieval street. Descending the steps from this complex, one comes across a white-scented garden added by Mr Little, a delightfully realised space of yew hedges interspersed with white roses, malus, choisya and a number of different magnolias including M. *grandiflora* and M. *stellata*.

The 17th-century contrivances may be long gone, but Wadham today can boast gardens of distinctive character and quality, especially in terms of planting, which is considerably more original and ambitious than that to be found in many college gardens.

Wolfson College

I F SOMEONE WAS TO ask what the biggest surprise has been in writing this book, the answer would have to be: Wolfson College. The college's relative youth (it was founded in 1965), together with its status as a graduate institution, have served to make it something of a blind spot for many who feel they know Oxford quite well. I confess I had not visited it prior to researching this book. St Catherine's is well known as the university's 'modern college', and must take the laurels as an integrated architectural-landscape design. But Wolfson is probably easier to like than the uncompromising and occasionally austere St Catherine's. Nowhere else in Oxford captures better than Wolfson the sublime and somewhat other-worldly idealism of 20th-century architectural modernism.

Wolfson, though, surely had the most insalubrious beginning of any Oxford college. This was at 15 Banbury Road, a humble terrace house which was the college's temporary home between 1966 and 1968. The president (Sir Isaiah Berlin) had one room, the vice president an attic, and the cellar was fitted up as a common room. These quarters apparently bred a strong feeling of camaraderie but there must also have been an added urgency to the building plans for a permanent home. In 1967 the great British modernist architectural firm of Powell & Moya was commissioned to design the new college on a site next to the River Cherwell. The former residence of gaseous scientist J. S. Haldane was demolished to make way, though his name is commemorated by the Haldane Room within college.

The modernist elegance of Powell & Moya's 1967 design, offset by smooth green sward.

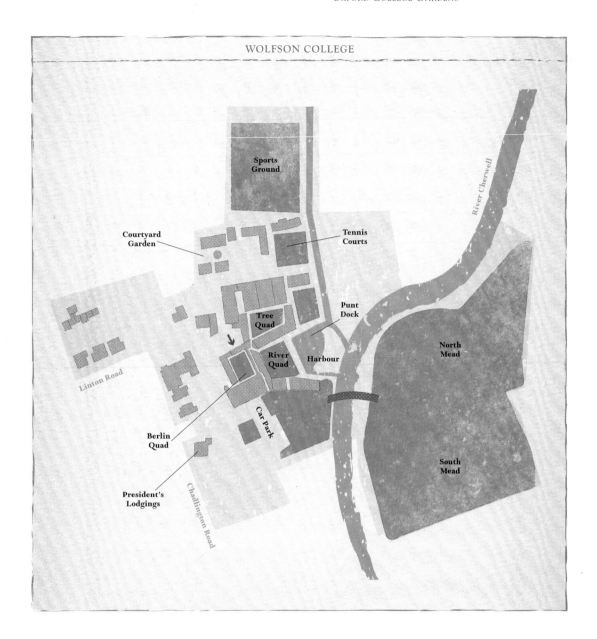

WOLFSON COLLEGE

Sports
Ground

Courtyard
Garden

Tennis
Courts

Punt
Dock

Tree
Quad

River
Quad

Harbour

North
Mead

Linton Road

Car Park

Berlin
Quad

South
Mead

President's
Lodgings

Chadlington Road

River Cherwell

RIGHT The college is some way
out of the centre but occupies
an enviable riverside position,
complete with 'harbour' and punt
dock. Every year the student body
elects its own 'Admiral of Punts' –
an egregious lapse in its avowedly
egalitarian principles.

In some ways Wolfson broke more decisively than anywhere else with the quasi-monastic tradition of Oxford colleges, in that family life was always integrated into the design and there was to be no hierarchy of common rooms, high table, academic dress and other ritualistic paraphernalia. But in the end, despite the modern style of architecture, the college's physical design was framed around traditional principles, with three interconnecting quadrangles, dining hall, library and porter's lodge.

Undergraduates as well as visitors can be forgiven for their ignorance of Wolfson College, as it is rather hidden away in the pleasant, villa-lined roads east of the Banbury Road in north Oxford. Fittingly, Wolfson does not announce itself in the grand manner of certain city-centre colleges. Perhaps it's a tad too modest, because it's not even clear which is the entrance lodge among the cluster of buildings that terminate Linton Road. The porter's lodge (to the right) takes one directly into Berlin Quadrangle, with thin pilotis (modernist columns) striding around the space at ground level, big glass

windows above and delicate horizontal bands of equally sized granite stones which at first glance resemble knapped flints. There is a simple lawn, but the overall effect of the quadrangle is not austere because of its relatively small scale. The addition of hanging baskets here, presumably in the name of colour to 'brighten things up', is to be regretted, because the unadorned Berlin Quad radiates optimism, somehow, of its own accord.

The transition from Berlin Quad into River Quad, via a corner passageway and past a marble staircase, is as masterful as any such episode in Oxford, as lawn, mature trees and river below burst into view. Wolfson is situated right next to the river and makes the most of it. There is a sizeable 'punt dock' at the centre of River Quad, an island reached via a bridge, and the sense of countryside beyond the river. In fact the college owns the flood meadows over the river towards Marston, which are designated as Sites of Special Scientific Interest (SSSIs) for their range of native flora and fauna.

There is a marvellous unity of design in these original parts of the college. The sweep of the buildings is complemented

by gently undulating, close-mown lawns, and it is all just as stylishly magisterial in its way as the neoclassicism of Queen's College. Mature tulip trees, swamp cypresses, willows and magnolias give the college an established feel within its proud modernity. There is a long herbaceous border along the southern (outward-facing) wall of the south range of River Quad, with shrubs and cottagey perennials. There is also a Gothic pinnacle from Merton set in a little formal enclosure near the car park, as a memorial to the long-standing amity between the two colleges. The third quad, known as Tree Quadrangle, has an intriguing mounded area at one end, and various trees dotted about, including a peeling-bark *Prunus serrula*. Perhaps there is a lesson to be learned here about placing too many trees in quadrangles, because now they are mature the space feels rather too dark and shadowy.

The original architectural ensemble of Wolfson College works triumphantly well in its landscape setting. But as so often in Oxford colleges, later work added 'in the spirit' of earlier design is, to be diplomatic, less triumphant. Wolfson's newer accommodation blocks simply do not compare with the original Powell & Moya work, though there is an attractive little garden associated, featuring a sundial and circular pool surrounded by low and herby Mediterranean plantings set in gravel. A feel for the landscape is integral to this college; Wolfson's coat of arms features three roses and two pears, and it is the only college, as far as I know, to offer its students allotments on site to rent.

OPPOSITE TOP LEFT A Gothic pinnacle, a gift from Merton, has been placed in the garden as a mark of the friendship between the two colleges.

OPPOSITE TOP RIGHT Bankside plantings in River Quad.

OPPOSITE BELOW River Quad, where it slopes down towards the 'harbour', with self-seeding *Lunaria annua* (honesty) growing beneath purple-leaved hazel on the bank.

ABOVE The meandering river forms an island directly in front of the college, the steps down to the punt dock visible in the background.

Worcester College

WORCESTER HAS A LAKE. It has an arboretum and sumptuous herbaceous borders. An Arts and Crafts rose garden. Velvety lawns, a 'hanging garden' and an orchard. It even has a cricket pitch. The Provost's Lodgings top it all off, an elegant and architecturally sophisticated facade benignly surveying the coddled acres. As dusk falls and light shafts through the leaves of sycamore and horse chestnut, the visitor, viewing this 'country house' on its apron of lawn from across the lake, might be forgiven for imagining for a moment they are in some rural vale as opposed to the western edge of Oxford's city centre, sandwiched between bus station, canal and railway line.

Worcester has created this confection entirely for itself out of rather unpromising circumstances. Inaugurated in 1714, this is not one of the oldest colleges in the university, though it grew out of a venerable house. Perhaps as a result, the college is not complacent about what it has. Worcester very nearly did not come about at all – it had to scrabble around to secure the bequest which paid for its existence, while the unfortunate man who had made it his mission to establish the college ended up in the Fleet Prison as a debtor. So beneath the tranquil surface of its pastoral environs, Worcester has had to paddle hard. The effort has paid off.

The bells have never stopped ringing in Oxford. In the 13th century this was a city of churches, monasteries, abbeys and priories: there were seven important monastic houses within a mile of the city centre. One of these was the Benedictine

'Queen of Night' tulips and camassias growing in the Nuffield Lawn, with the rear of the wisteria-clad medieval 'cottages' beyond.

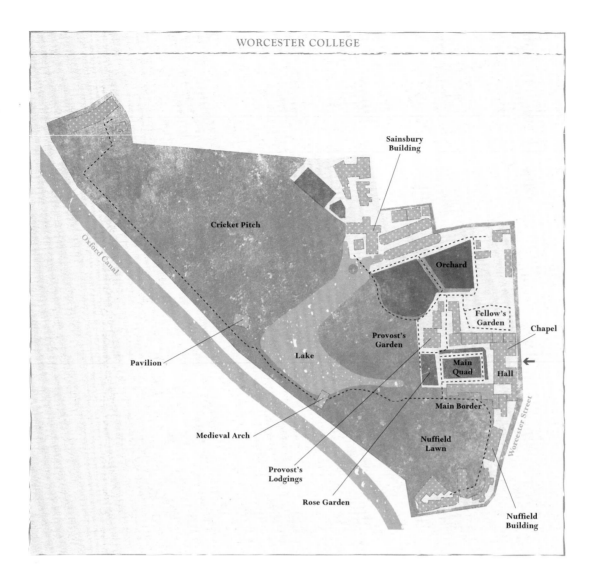

WORCESTER COLLEGE

foundation of Gloucester College, established in 1283 on the site of present-day Worcester College. This institution was established to educate the monks of the Southern Province of the Benedictine Order (15 monasteries), who would come for three-year courses of instruction just as today's undergraduates do – though the monks would have to study for more than a decade in all at various places. Each monastery leased its own rooms to accommodate its students within the college. We know, for example, that 30 monks were resident in 1537. A terrace of adjoining 'cottages' dating back to the 15th century and consisting of six of these rooms still stands, forming the south range of Worcester's Main Quad. Each doorway is emblazoned with the arms of a different house – it is Pershore Abbey at the far, western end of the range, for example.

There are no records until the mid 16th century, but it would have been unthinkable for a Benedictine institution to have done without a productive garden, especially if it was set in what was then the outskirts of the city. Of the older Oxford colleges, those which sprang from monastic foundations tend to be the ones with the largest gardens – Trinity, St John's, Magdalen, Christ Church – partly because of this gardening

tradition and partly because more land was available farther from the city centre.

As far as one can tell from the early maps and the way the site was later developed, the buildings of the monastery formed three sides of a square, with chapel and hall to the east and accommodation blocks north and south. The earliest gardening was pursued in two areas – a plot to the west which later became the Provost's Garden, and one to the north which would grow into the orchard and ultimately also contain Worcester's private Fellows' Garden. It is gratifying to find that the core of the modern college still follows exactly this basic layout. The land which today forms the greatest extent of Worcester's gardens, running west down to the River Cherwell, has been politely and romantically described as 'a water meadow', but might be less politely described as a marsh. This land was not in the possession of the medieval monastery (since the college acquired it only in the mid 18th century). Drainage dykes were dug at an early stage in an effort to make the land usable, but one of the reasons for the survival of this large expanse of open space in the centre of the city is the fact it was often waterlogged and therefore unsuitable for building upon. Oxford is a watery city and its people are under no illusions about what that means in practical terms.

Gloucester College was abandoned following the dissolution of the monasteries by Henry VIII in the 1530s, and rapidly fell into a state of disrepair. It was rescued in 1560 by the founder of St John's College, who converted the old monastery into an academical hall – a lodging house for students as opposed to a full college. A survey made at this point itemised 'The garden and orchard, 2 parcels of mead enclosed with water, whereof one containing 2 acres, the other 3 acres'. These are the two garden areas already mentioned – a substantial acreage already. The chambers on the north and south side of what became Main Quad were 'verie sorely decayed and withiut anie schollers or anie other person in the same', while St John's had been using the monastery's library as a corn store. The derelict shell of the chapel, with trees growing inside it, is depicted in David Loggan's 1675 engraving of Gloucester Hall. The fortunes of the hall waxed and waned, and by the 1660s there were only 11 students and

the principal in residence, and by 1701 no undergraduates at all. Gloucester Hall had deteriorated into an obscure and insalubrious place at the edge of the city – though that did have some advantages, as it became known as a lodging for Catholics who wished to live quietly. To judge from the Loggan engraving, the principal's garden was kept up as an enclosed garden of grassy compartments defined by hedges and trees set in orderly files, while an area adjacent to the old chapel is planted with cabbages. But the overall appearance is decrepit.

Everything changed in 1714, thanks to Sir Thomas Cookes, a landowning baronet who had attended Pembroke College. He bequeathed £10,000 in his will for the foundation of a new college at his old university, having already established two schools in the Midlands. There was a great deal of dispute and infighting about this rather open-ended bequest, with the Master of Balliol attempting to claim it and Magdalen Hall (the academical hall associated with that college) coming within a whisker of receiving the money. But Gloucester Hall triumphed and in the process was renamed Worcester College,

apparently in honour of the benefactor's home county. Four hundred years of continuous identification with Gloucester was wiped out at a stroke, but the institution had regenerated itself.

Fortuitously for Worcester, the notion of a brand new Oxford college presented a novel opportunity for George Clarke of All Souls, who with Dean Aldrich of Christ Church was an influential arbiter of architectural taste in 18th-century Oxford. Tired of political manoeuvrings and personal animus at All Souls, Clarke resolved to bequeath his library to Worcester instead and also made provision (amounting to £3,000) for new college fellowships and a brand new building for the fellows. Perhaps what proved irresistible to him, though, was the architectural *tabula rasa* that the college effectively presented. Clarke recruited his old friend Nicholas Hawksmoor on the project and between them over the next 20 years or so they constructed the north range of Main Quad and the noble east range, including chapel, hall, library and entrance lodge, with a wide and airy, nine-arched loggia overlooking the quad. The north range (enlarged in

the 1770s by Henry Keene) is directly opposite the medieval cottages, which it dwarfs, but in context the tidy Georgian facade seems restrained and polite as opposed to gargantuan and overbearing. Clarke would surely have demolished and rebuilt the medieval south range over time but the usual Oxford problem ensued: the money ran out. The result is a fantastically lopsided quadrangle which nevertheless has great charm and atmosphere. The key, perhaps, is the way the west side of the quad is bounded simply by a wall, with the trees in the Provost's Garden and beyond providing a sylvan backdrop and also an exhilarating sense of release and escape, as if one is in a large room with a full-width window. This is the least claustrophobic quad in Oxford. It compares favourably with Christ Church's Peck Quad, which falls headlong into the trap of superabundance, imprisoning the visitor in its architecture.

Clarke's and Hawksmoor's contribution gave the new Worcester College a strikingly up-to-the-minute architectural identity. The entrance arrangements seem urbane even today: an n-shape formed by the chunky protruding wings

Magnolia blossom (**RIGHT**), winter
aconites and crocuses (**BELOW LEFT**)
emerging on the Nuffield Lawn in
early spring.

of the chapel (on the right) and hall (left), with two perfect
rectangles of lawn occupying the recessed space between. This
ensemble constitutes a kind of miniature vestibule-quadrangle
that is open to the western end of Beaumont Street. The drama
continues as one passes the porter's lodge and emerges into
the loggia. It is not clear why or how the lawn of Main Quad
came to be sunk so low – or the terrace raised up so high – but
the change of level creates a moment of great drama which
is effective in every season. It helps that the lawn is kept in
immaculate condition.

In the early 18th century the extent of the college's gardens
was the same as it had been for centuries. There was the site of
the Provost's Garden, formally laid out in grass plats, and also
the garden area to the north of Main Quad, which was slightly
larger. (The Provost's Garden had been compartmented off
as early as the 16th century, but it was not officially given
over to the college principal until 1813.) A spirited young
lady called Elizabeth Sheppard wrote an amusingly facetious
account of her experiences of Oxford in 1737, entitled
'Shepilinda's Memoirs'. In it she describes Worcester, noting
how 'the Provost has one garden, & the Fellows another.' She
then describes the Main Quadrangle as 'most beautifully laid
out, in fine Gravell Walks', and also refers to 'a fine Rustick
Tempietto' at its centre – which is rather mysterious as there is
no other mention of such a structure. In context the reference
comes across as sarcastic, and the 'tempietto', whatever it was,
may have appeared ridiculous or pretentious.

The college had always owned a small portion of the land
south of Main Quad, behind the cottages, but in 1741 it

expanded in concerted fashion, acquiring the water meadow
(or marsh) there and to the west of the Provost's Garden, all
the way down to the River Cherwell – thereby increasing the
college's extent to something like the 10.5 hectares/26 acres it
is today. The college accounts of the late 18th century mention
the acquisition of numerous trees – 15 different species in 1787,
including 17 specimens of the fashionable Weymouth pine
(*Pinus strobus*) – and more trees in ensuing years. It is probably
the Weymouth pines which can be seen in an 1814 aquatint of
Main Quad looking west, with pines of one species dominating
the background. College tradition has it that the tree planting
in this part of the garden was pursued under the auspices of
William Sheffield, provost from 1777 to 1795, with the help
of two college fellows who were also serious natural historians
(one of whom was in correspondence with Gilbert White).
A map of 1789 shows straight walks and axial tree plantings
in this area, which is by now marked 'Gardens', but it was
probably not until 1817–20 that a serpentine path system and
island beds were introduced, very much in the Regency fashion.
The college accounts contain numerous bills and invoices for
garden work over these three years – about £1,500 in all was
spent – including payments for labour, turf, trees, shrubs and
roses, garden chairs, dung and gravel. There was another burst
of activity in the early 1820s, when plants such as box, laurels,
weeping willows, 'Scotch Firs', lilac, buddleia and azalea
were purchased. Some original specimens of *Aucuba japonica*
(spotted laurel) survive, near the service buildings by the canal
at the southern edge of the college garden; and there is also a
reference in 1813 to a swamp cypress – probably the one still

growing by the lake. The man credited with maintaining and improving Worcester's gardens in the early 19th century, and who conceivably also designed the new pattern of paths and island beds, is Richard Greswell, the college bursar.

One of the items in the 1817 accounts is fish for 'the pond'. This is the first mention of Worcester's artificial lake. It may have been dug partially to relieve the flooding problem which ensued after the college sold off part of its garden in 1788 to make way for the new Oxford Canal, so cutting off a corner of the garden, closing off access to the river and compromising the existing drainage-ditch system (the last entailing a lengthy lawsuit). The college's large, crescent-shaped body of water is shown for the first time on an 1837 map, in an area enticingly labelled 'Worcester College Walks and Gardens'. This map also depicts a number of large island beds in the area south of the cottages, with sinuous paths winding around them. Exotic trees and shrubs purchased by the college would have been displayed

in these beds, arranged in tiers according to height (with trees at the centre).

James Ingram's *Memorials of Oxford*, also published in 1837, includes an engraved view of Worcester's lake which reveals that the prospect across it to the Lodgings were decidedly open at this time, the building's elegant facade with double staircase framed by mature trees. Ingram writes approvingly: 'Much taste has been recently displayed here in converting at a considerable expense a mere orchard into a delightful garden; having pleasant walks interspersed with trees and shrubs, and terminated by a large expanse of water.'

Worcester's garden is often described as picturesque, which is a suitable epithet in many ways but also a little misleading. In garden history the term Picturesque relates to gardens created from about 1780 to 1820 that were specifically designed to create a frisson of mild terror and excitement in the visitor. The presence of books by Picturesque landscape theorist Richard Payne Knight in the college library is not a

clear indication that the garden would have been developed in this spirit. It is true there is some good general advice in Payne Knight about designing landscapes, and that this could have been useful to those planting trees or laying out new walks and vistas, but overall Worcester's gardens are too small, too domestic and too lacking in topographical incident (even with a new lake) to be considered properly Picturesque. They were realised much more in the Regency spirit of John Nash and Humphry Repton, which would in 1820 have been considerably more up-to-date than a Picturesque landscape. The way that the trees and walks in Worcester's garden are clearly arranged for ornamental purposes, and the composed views opening up at intervals towards the facade of the Provost's Lodgings, are evidence that this garden was conceived in such a manner. The provost's herd of dairy cows, which grazed the land on 'his side' of the lake until the end of the 19th century, would definitely not have been viewed as a contribution to a Picturesque atmosphere, if that is what

had been wanted. A certain delicacy of touch and a sense of the domestic are among the attributes of the Regency style of gardening. It is a tone which remains palpable in Worcester's garden even today, perhaps instinctively kept up by the garden team. (A celebrated garden made in this mode was close by, at Nuneham Courtenay, in Oxfordshire – it could have been an influence.) One of the best moments in the garden comes as the visitor approaches the lake for the first time, and must pass through a ruined arched gateway, a remnant of the old Gloucester College monastery. (Worcester and Christ Church harbour the last physical vestiges of Oxford's medieval monastic tradition.) There is something of the Picturesque about this gateway, it is true, but the theme of ruin is used

OPPOSITE The corner bed – here with tulips, orange pansies and deep-red velvety wallflowers – is one of the key horticultural moments at the college, with a completely different guise for each season.

ABOVE The orchard, with the Provost's Lodgings beyond. The college presses and bottles its own apple and pear juice.

RIGHT Horse chestnuts by the lake. This is one of the most elegant and tranquil walks in Oxford, less well-known and far less crowded than those in other colleges.

CENTRE Wisteria around the passageway that leads from the south-west corner of Main Quad to this spot in the college garden. It reputedly inspired the rabbit-hole in *Alice's Adventures in Wonderland*.

FAR RIGHT The north-eastern end of the lake.

here essentially for ornamental purposes – there is no attempt to make the visitor feel as if this is a portal into some quasi-medieval realm. Worcester might be described as a pocket landscape park realised in Regency spirit.

By the 1850s the island beds had been somewhat diminished and the garden took on a looser appearance, more in tune with Victorian fashion. The specimen shrubs and trees were still there, but arranged in a more informal way. By mid-century the present Fellows' Garden, north-east of Main Quad, had also come into existence, as a large area of lawn encircled by a path and mixed borders with trees. The insertion of the cricket pitch into the western part of the garden, beyond the lake, in 1900, will have altered the atmosphere somewhat, but it has proved a popular addition. As the college's gardens matured, they became a favoured haunt of members of other colleges, townspeople and tourists. But Worcester's garden was and is far less frequented than those of Magdalen, St John's or Trinity, for example – there has always been a special secret feel about Worcester. It is said that Lewis Carroll (Charles Dodgson) of Christ Church used the dark passage which leads from the south-west corner of Main Quad as his inspiration for the rabbit hole in his book *Alice's Adventures in Wonderland* (though admittedly a number of other subterranean passages have been credited as the prototype). There is another story about him giving permission for an outdoor charity performance of a play based on his book in Worcester's garden, and that he shyly watched rehearsals from a discreet distance. The stars of that performance were the daughters of the future provost, while their mother, Emily Daniel, was the artist who designed the

posters and programmes for the production. It was probably she who in 1903 suggested her cousin Alfred Parsons, the watercolourist and garden designer, as someone who might be able to make a formal rose garden in the Provost's Garden. The provost himself, Charles Henry Daniel, would also have been sympathetic: he had already collaborated with Parsons on illustrations for the Daniel Press, his own foray into 'fine printing'. Daniel had also been instrumental in the college's appointment of William Burges for the redesign, in remarkable fashion, of the chapel's interior.

For this artistic couple Parsons designed a rose garden in a self-consciously old-fashioned manner, quite in the spirit of the times, with the Arts and Crafts movement in the ascendant. There was a veritable cult around the sundial at this point, and one of these timepieces duly occupies the centre of the rose garden, surrounded by ten symmetrically arranged planting beds and a line of 20 clipped yew pillars as a permeable boundary on the west side. Parsons supplemented the roses with romantic 'cottage flowers' such as snapdragons, pinks, peonies and larkspurs; the idea was to create a quasi-Elizabethan, 'olde English' atmosphere. He also planted up the north terrace in Main Quad, adding climbing roses around the doorways to the staircases, and the entrance to the Lodgings, which faces east at the end of the terrace. Perhaps it was Parsons who established the romantic tone of Worcester's gardens, which persists so beguilingly to this day. Wisteria drapes itself splendidly over several facades, perhaps most effectively of all across the south front of the Lodgings.

The rose garden was comprehensively restored in 2007,

with 230 roses in 38 varieties supplied by rose breeder Robert Mattock. Roses of all sorts were used, mainly old-fashioned kinds of Damask, Gallica, Bourbon, Alba, Moss, Rugosa, Hybrid Perpetual and China in pinks and reds (all requiring slightly different methods of pruning) – the likes of 'Capitaine John Ingram', 'Cardinal de Richelieu', 'Charles de Mills', 'Ferdinand Pichard' and 'Great Maiden's Blush' as well as the striking violet rose 'Rhapsody in Blue'. The roses are underplanted with santolina, viola, aubretia and dianthus, in the spirit of Parsons, while an attempt to provide structure outside the flowering season by means of grasses (miscanthus and molinia) and tall plants such as veronicastrum and digitalis has met with mixed success, since they have proved too large in some cases and have been 'edited'. A decision was made to retain a lead statue of Mercury and two large heads from the front of the Sheldonian Theatre, all added to the scheme after Parsons' time, and this has perpetuated a sense of clutter in the garden. The southern end of the garden is bounded by a wall which extends the line of the cottages of Main Quad. There is an open walkway on top of this which is accounted Worcester's very own 'hanging garden', though it is hardly Babylonian. It is now largely left to its own devices (and there is no public access). The wall is old, but it is thought that the 'hanging garden' walkway itself was added in the early 19th century, as it offers views over Main Quad and the college garden.

But to return to the horticulture at Worcester College: head gardener Simon Bagnall previously worked at Lady Margaret Hall and Trinity – both good garden colleges – and today he aims higher than any other college head gardener. He has the resources to do this – a staff of eight including one volunteer – and the opportunity to expand and experiment in areas such as fruit and vegetable production, glasshouse plants, cut flowers, tree planting and aquatic gardening. All of this activity is regularly (at least weekly) recorded in the college garden blog, providing a good insight into the workings and requirements of a modern college garden.

It is probably the burgeoning herbaceous borders and perfect lawns that visitors and college members appreciate most. The lawn in Main Quad is titivated and even re-laid at periods throughout the year, and is the main responsibility of one member of the garden team. A decorative mowing regime has been developed almost into an art form in its own right. Rather than relying on simple stripes for the lawn, all kinds of circular or wavy patterns have been tried over recent years, each given a different name – Seeing Double, Change of Direction, Round in Circles, Triple Width Stripes and so on. Circular patterns have proved especially popular. These are created by means of two lengths of twine run at diagonals across the lawn, to discover its exact centre. The circles are then mown emanating from this midpoint, an activity requiring great precision and skill. The lawn is brushed of dew early each morning, partly to prevent the onset of grass diseases such as fusarium patch.

The top terrace in front of the north range is the scene of some of the most interesting gardening at Worcester College. Wisteria and climbing roses (including a huge Banksian rose) form a sturdy backdrop, bolstered by a vigorous *Campsis radicans* (with red trumpet flowers) and winter-flowering honeysuckle for the cooler months. But Mr Bagnall adds all kinds of interesting and unusual plants to the mix, such as *Cyphomandra corymbiflora* (hardy tree tomato) combining

with the tree mallow, *Lavatera maritima*, and *Indigofera pendula*, with its pendulous racemes of pea-like purple-pink flowers. Several of the tenderer subjects are raised under glass before being planted out. Here and across the garden (notably in the Provost's Garden) tulips feature heavily in the spring, a

ABOVE Purple asters, pink echinacea, white cosmos, purple-leaved ricinus and the strappy leaves of *Musa basjoo* are among the stand-out plants in the main border in high summer.

changing palette which typically includes rich-coloured varieties such as 'Apeldoorn', 'Black Hero', 'Black Parrot', 'China Pink', 'Labrador', 'Mount Tacoma', 'National Velvet', 'Paul Scherer', 'Queen of Night' and 'Shirley'. In high summer annuals also play a part in various areas – cosmos, cleome, antirrhinum, panicum and tagetes.

The west side of Main Quad, against the wall to the Provost's Garden, is the location of the 'bottom border', which is often themed in white and delicate pinks, incorporating annuals and biennials to create a delightfully blowsy and romantic atmosphere. The fresh whites might come from *Malope trifida* 'Alba', *Antirrhinum majus* 'Royal Bride', *Ammi majus* and *Panicum elegans* 'Frosted Explosion', while the pink tones are supplied by *Salvia* 'Penny's Smile', *Diascia personata*, *Nicotiana mutabilis* and *Cleome hassleriana* 'Colour Fountain Mixed', offset by the grey-green of *Plectranthus argentatus* 'Silver Shield'. Structure is provided by shrubs such as *Artemisia* 'Powis Castle', *Rosa* x *odorata* 'Mutabilis', *Cotinus coggygria* 'Royal Purple', *Hydrangea paniculata* 'Pinky-Winky' and *Indigofera heterantha* (the last making an interesting contrast with the *I. pendula* on the top terrace). In the south-west corner is *Actinidia deliciosa* 'Jenny', a kiwi plant that has successfully fruited in recent years. In the shade in front of the cottages the planting is quieter, with ferns, *Alchemilla mollis* and white Japanese anemones.

The best way to experience Worcester's main herbaceous border is to exit Main Quad by a passageway in the south-east (lower left) corner. This takes you past Pump Quad, an ancient part of college which is paved but not forsaken by the garden team, with a large grapevine trained along one side and dramatic summer flower displays in large wooden tubs. (There are similar displays in the Provost's Yard on the other side of Main Quad.) Emerging south of the cottages, the visitor enters the wonderland which is the main area today of Worcester's gardens. The setting is the pasture of the Nuffield Lawn (the large Nuffield Building of 1939 now overlooks the space from the east) with its mature trees, and bulbous flowers (notably *Camassia leichtlinii*) in spring, but the attention is grabbed by a fiery corner display tucked immediately to one's left. This introduces Worcester's signature plant: banana species, represented here by a trio of the red Abyssinian banana, *Ensete*

ventricosum 'Maurelii', partnered with cannas and the almost extra-terrestrial-looking *Aeonium* 'Zwartkop'. Varieties of *Rudbeckia hirta* are used to great effect in this corner display bed and also in the main herbaceous border: 'Moreno', 'Autumn Forest', 'Chim Chiminee' and 'Cherokee Sunset'. The yellow and orange theme is upped again by the addition of different marigolds: *Calendula officinalis* 'Candyman Orange', *Tagetes tenuifolia* 'Golden Gem' and 'Paprika', and *Tagetes patula*. There is also room for more subtle plantings, such as the delicately spotted orange flowers of the *Belamcanda chinensis* (now known as *Iris domestica*) given to the garden team by the head gardener at Merton College.

The main herbaceous border stretches from east to west along the back side of the cottages of Main Quad, the old wall providing a perfect backdrop. This is not an 'old English' border in the manner of Alfred Parsons but an exciting experimental space with all kinds of exotica. It is announced by a group of the statuesque white-flowered tobacco plant, *Nicotiana sylvestris*. Then come huge banana plants (including *Musa basjoo*) mingling with bomarea, tetrapanax, echinacea, persicaria, clematis, paulownia, *Arundo donax*, daturas, cannas, nepeta, echinops, eupatorium, calamagrostis, veronicastrum, galega and, in late summer, dahlias and asters. There is a lot in here but it is outstandingly well balanced, the mood changing palpably as the border progresses towards the lake and a shadier environment, with the likes of *Phalaris arundinacea* and *Persicaria virginiana*, and bigger grasses. A collection of tree ferns – *Dicksonia antarctica* and *D. fibrosa* – here and in other parts of the garden add a note of mystery.

The visitor walks beneath mature trees towards the lake and the old arch that marks the entrance to the 'broad walk' alongside it. As well as common trees such as holm oaks, copper beeches, planes, limes, cedars, yews and horse chestnuts, there are specimen trees including weeping beeches, tulip trees (*Liriodendron*), an old catalpa and a trio of Princeton elms, *Ulmus americana* 'Princeton'. White waterlilies adorn the lake and the multitude of ducks are pleasingly (most of the time) vocal. A recent planting of coral-bark willows, *Salix alba* 'Chermesina', in the Provost's Garden creates winter colour on that side of the lake; a few more willow varieties would

give the provost a salicetum, and no other college principal has one of those. The broad walk is edged with hand-woven hazel binders – one of those little touches which marks this out as a special garden – and climbing roses ('Cooperi', 'Wilson's Worcester') have been trained up rope swags on trees by the lake.

The lakeside walk takes one north-east around the curve of the lake and the Provost's Garden opposite, and eventually leads to the Sainsbury Building (1984) by Richard MacCormac, a remarkable and successful addition to the college, set quietly by the lake with wooden garden terraces, shallow roofs and black window frames. The original idea was that there should be individual gardens to each room, focused on a maple or juniper; the vernacular feel is still strong despite the modernity of the design. The Ruskin Lane Building (2009) beyond also has its own garden area set in the space between its ranges. It is known as 'The Serpentine' by the garden team because of the clipped box balls which

meander its length, set below four yellow-flowered *Magnolia* 'Elizabeth' trees. The blue of grape hyacinth (*Muscari*) offsets the box, while feathery pennisetum grasses provide a textural contrast. There are more accommodation blocks farther north, and the garden team have established a tradition on the first day of term, whereby they load the luggage of freshers (new undergraduates) into trailers and then take it to their rooms by mini-tractor. This is one of several areas where the garden team's work intersects with the daily life of the college. Another is the college orchard (just north of Main Quad), the fruit from which is harvested each year, pressed and bottled to make the college's very own apple and pear juice. The apple varieties include 'Newton Wonder', 'Spartan', 'Chivers Delight', 'Golden Spire', 'Blenheim Orange', 'Orleans Reinette', 'Peggy's Pride' and 'Laxton's Superb'; the pears are 'Conference', 'Winter Nelis' and 'Doyenné du Comice'. The college ducks love the apples and can be found each autumn in the orchard, gorging on windfalls. Cut flowers are another college tradition that is properly kept up at Worcester. Sweet peas are the mainstay – including 'Albutt Blue', 'Blue Danube' and 'Mars' – and these are made into posies which are given to members of college staff, presumably to their absolute delight. Tomatoes, cucumbers and peppers are among the produce grown under glass.

The Fellows' Garden, which only came about in the mid 19th century, has recently been enlivened by the addition of a wildflower meadow, that fashionable accoutrement of 21st-century gardening. A meadow was sown in 2013 with a mix of native and cultivated plants, such as betony, bird's-foot trefoil, bulbous buttercup, California poppy, cat's ear, cowslip, common knapweed, cornflower, hairy toadflax, lady's bedstraw, ox-eye daisy, salad burnet, selfheal, Shirley poppy, white campion and yellow rattle. (The last is something of a worry, as it has a tendency to take over.) Presumably the Fellows' Garden was enlivened even more in the late 19th century by the presence of 'a fine eagle…from Norway', which is mentioned by Provost Daniel in his history of the college.

The garden of Worcester College, with its lake and fine lawns, has the capacity to amaze visitors to Oxford perhaps more than any other college garden. It is currently flying high horticulturally and setting a standard to which others might aspire. It provides a fitting conclusion and climax to this celebration of the extraordinary hidden gardens of the colleges of Oxford University.

Floreant Horti Oxonia.

FAR LEFT AND LEFT Brugmansias, tree ferns (dicksonia), variegated hollies and other histrionic specimens are used for dramatic displays in the square wooden tubs of Pump Quad, an ancient area off the south-east corner of Main Quad.

BELOW The stream leading to the lake at the division between the Provost's Garden (the yew pillars of the rose garden can be seen in the distance) and the main college garden.

FOLLOWING PAGE The main border in late summer swing, with yellow-leaved cornus, tagetes (marigold), ricinus, tithonia and *Rhus typhina*.

The Trianon Adventure

WHO EVER HAS HEARD of the Trianon Adventure today? Yet this true Edwardian ghost story was a *cause célèbre* in the first half of the 20th century, something which every educated person would have instantly recognised and had an opinion about. The book on which the controversy was based, *An Adventure*, became a bestseller after its publication in 1911 and went into five editions (the last in 1955). Now almost forgotten, the story still exerts a fascination. It also has a curious resonance for anyone interested in gardens and their particular atmospheres.

The 'adventure' in question happened on a hot day in August 1901, when Anne Moberly and Eleanor Jourdain paid a visit to Versailles and the *jardin anglais* of the Petit Trianon – Marie-Antoinette's celebrated hideaway half a mile (0.8 kilometres) north of the main palace. This is an informal landscape of mazy paths, meandering streams, dark glades and small, evocative buildings, such as the Temple of Love (a neoclassical rotunda) and the Belvedere (an exquisite octagonal pavilion). Secreted in a cleft among the little knolls behind the Belvedere is the queen's grotto; it was here that she was reputed to have been found, deep in thought, when she was first told of the revolutionary mob's approach. The planting in the garden was restored in 2008 using a 1795 botanical inventory; but even today, perhaps the chief sensation this garden inspires is disorientation.

Miss Moberly was principal of the fledgeling all-female Oxford college, St Hugh's Hall, and Miss Jourdain was headmistress of a girls' school in Watford. The two were spending three weeks sightseeing in Paris, partly in order to assess their compatibility as potential colleagues at St Hugh's – though they had met before on a few occasions.

According to Moberly and Jourdain, that afternoon they encountered a succession of people in late-18th-century costume. At the time they thought little of it, though they later concluded they must have been ghosts. The first of these spectres was a servant woman shaking a sheet from the window of a building (later found to be non-existent), followed by a pair of ill-mannered 'gardeners' in uniform (identified by the ladies as Swiss guards), then a repulsive-looking man with a pockmarked face leaning on a balustrade beside a rocky outcrop. He was followed by a handsome, out-of-breath young man in a wide-brimmed hat who told them to go back to the palace immediately. The climax of this ghostly tour was a woman seen sketching, who could only have been Marie-Antoinette herself – at least, that is what the ladies claimed.

After much research in the archives, their eventual interpretation was that they had somehow entered a daydream of Marie-Antoinette's while imprisoned in Paris in 1792, as she remembered her final day at the Trianon in 1789. The ladies suggested that they had gone back in time and participated in this reverie, and at one point even occupied the body of the queen herself – why else would they have been urged by the handsome servant to return to the palace?

One of the many extraordinary features of the story was the ladies' later insistence that, at the time, neither of them remarked upon the fact that anything unusual was happening. They noticed the strange costumes, they said, but reconciled them to modern life in different ways. It was only several months afterwards that they began to suspect it to be a paranormal experience, and wrote down their testimonies. It transpired that they did not see exactly the same things at the same time, and a second visit to Versailles by Jourdain revealed that the topography of the place as they remembered it was in fact completely different: certain features had disappeared or been replaced by others; paths had vanished; distances seemed radically foreshortened. In addition, Jourdain had some more ghostly sightings: peasant labourers loading a cart, a tall man walking through the woods, and the sound of music.

These delays and discrepancies were to provide ammunition for sceptical observers, but they also lend the story a peculiar piquancy, a frisson of the random unexpectedness and odd detail of real life, that has proved irresistible to many readers. One cannot help but be carried along by the ladies' accounts, whether one believes they are true or not. The story's ambiguities paradoxically make it seem more not less credible, which is the heart of its enduring appeal. With their book, Moberly and Jourdain produced an accidental masterpiece of supernatural fiction.

An Adventure was not published until 1911, almost a decade after that spectral afternoon at Versailles. The ladies felt compelled to tell their story – albeit under pseudonyms – because of the short shrift they had received from the Society for Psychical Research, to whom they had sent their accounts in 1902. The society's scepticism infuriated the pair, and they embarked on a concerted, even obsessional campaign of research in the French national archives and elsewhere, aimed at positively identifying the various characters and buildings they had seen. This they did – and they believed triumphantly so – although in fact the evidence they present in the various editions of their book is, to put it kindly, far from conclusive. But the ladies continued to be taken seriously because of their social and academic respectability: no one could quite believe that they had simply made it all up.

Moberly, then in her mid fifties, was the daughter of the late Bishop of Salisbury, for whom she had acted as secretary for 12 years, before being selected as first principal of the new Oxford college. Jourdain, in her late thirties and also the daughter of a clergyman, was an equally powerful personality. What was not widely known was that they already had a mutual interest in visionary experience – not the still-fashionable doctrines of spiritualism or the new 'scientific' subject of psychical research, both of which they denounced as tantamount to blasphemy. Their sphere was visionary experience of a religious nature and they saw no contradiction between a Christian life and a visionary life; in fact, they felt it brought them closer to God. Although they did not advertise the fact later on, both had already experienced a number of visions of a religious nature before their 'adventure'.

So what was the truth? Of course, there is a chance that they really saw the ghosts, but it seems more likely that between them they embroidered their memory of events, then talked about them publicly, and finally found they had no choice but to justify the stories as they best knew how – through academic research. Once that decision had been taken, there was no going back: their own reputations, and also that of St Hugh's, were at stake. It is possible that the ghosts may have been real people wearing 18th-century costume, dressed up either for a *fête champêtre* or film, or perhaps as guests at one of the parties held around this time at the Petit Trianon by the dandyish Comte de Montesquiou. But there is no conclusive evidence for any of this.

There is a compelling contemporary evocation of the queen at the Trianon in *The Story of Marie-Antoinette* (1897) by Anna Bicknell: 'A weeping willow by the lake was planted by Marie-Antoinette, whose memory haunts the place. Her last happy days were spent under the trees of Trianon, where at every turn the visitor almost expects to see the bright vision of a past which is there living still and apparently so real.' There is no evidence that Moberly or Jourdain had read Bicknell's book, but Pierre de Nolhac's works were cited as a principal source. In *Marie-Antoinette the Queen* (1898), the Trianon gardens are referred to as 'dreams', a place of 'enchantment' and as resembling a ballet set – exactly the metaphors used by the ladies. Later, de Nolhac envisions the queen 'gliding' the paths of the garden, and his account finishes with a spectre-like image of the queen seated on the grass at the Trianon, remembering her happy time there, juxtaposed with a dramatic description of her execution. This is exactly the situation described in the final section of *An Adventure*.

The ladies claimed to have had no knowledge of the history of the Trianon prior to their visit, but in fact Jourdain had been teaching the French revolution to her pupils. Could de Nolhac's account have contributed to the substance of the ladies' visions at the Trianon? I suggest that it could, and that between the week of their adventure – when they speculated very briefly as to whether the *jardin anglais* at the Trianon was haunted – and the time when they wrote down their testimonies, exactly three months later, the ladies had in fact been conducting some light research related to the topic, and perhaps even talked about it.

I am inclined to believe that the ladies invented almost everything on the slenderest basis from actual experience, partly arising from their own readings around the subject, as a manifestation of their excitement and delight in each other's company. After their meeting in Paris, Moberly and Jourdain remained devoted companions and worked together for many years, referred to as 'man and wife' by the college servants. In the end, the Trianon Adventure is perhaps more of a love story than a ghost story.

Head Gardeners
of the Oxford Colleges (2014)

All Souls	Steve Brooke
Balliol	Chris Munday
Christ Church	John James
Corpus Christi	David Leake
Green Templeton	Michael Pirie
Jesus	Jeremy Dickson
Keble	Adrian Roche
Lady Margaret Hall	Ben Pritchard
Lincoln	Digby Styles
Magdalen	Claire Shepherd
Merton	Lucille Savin
Pembroke	Richard Markham
Queen's	Kate Knowles
Rhodes House	Neil Wigfield
Saïd Business School	Nick Bishop
Somerville	Simon Horwood
St Catherine's	Susan Kasper
St Edmund Hall	Philip Underwood
St Hilda's	Martin Brandom
St Hugh's	Phil Shefford
St John's	Peter Minns
St Peter's	Bob Washington
Trinity	Paul Lawrence
University College	Bruce Taylor
Wadham	Andrew Little
Wolfson	Michael Pearson
Worcester	Simon Bagnall

Several colleges engage contractors – in most cases a team from
the University Parks, headed by Parks Superintendent Walter Sawyer –
to maintain their gardens. These include: Brasenose, Exeter, Harris
Manchester, Hertford, Kellogg, Linacre, Mansfield, New College, Nuffield,
Oriel, St Anne's, St Cross and St Antony's.

Index

Acknowledgments

The author and photographer would like to express our thanks to all the head gardeners who have provided valuable information and also facilitated entrance to private areas of the colleges, especially Andrew Little (Wadham), David Leake (Corpus Christi) and Ben Pritchard (Lady Margaret Hall). We would particularly like to thank Simon Bagnall of Worcester College for his help in this regard and with introductions across the university. We would also like to thank the garden masters and other fellows at several colleges who have been helpful, notably Robin Lane Fox of New College. The author would like to thank Michael Symes and Tim Brindley for information regarding Worcester and Pembroke. Judy Dod has provided invaluable assistance with the organisation of photographs. For Frances Lincoln, Sarah Zadoorian has been an exemplary copy editor and Sarah Allberrey a sensitive designer. We would like to thank Jo Christian for originally commissioning the book and her successor Helen Griffin for ably steering the book through its various stages of production and into publication.

The publishers would like to thank the following for permission to include in-copyright material: Judith Curthoys of Christ Church College for the extract from *A Brief History of Christ Church*; Vikram Seth for the poem 'Fellows' Garden' © Vikram Seth; Oxford University Press for the extract from *Oriel College: A History* by Jeremy Catto (2013); Queen's College for use of the 'Behaviour in the College Quadrangles and Gardens' document from its website.

Picture Acknowledgments
All photographs by Andrew Lawson except: 65, 74, 90, 168, 189, 253, 258, 286 courtesy of Sanders; Endpapers © Daniel Crouch Rare Books - crouchrarebooks. com; the college maps were created and adapted using data from Open Street Maps © OpenStreetMap contributors; 29 © The Warden and Fellows of All Souls College, Oxford; all college crests courtesy of Oxford Unlimited.

Key

1 All Souls
2 Balliol
3 Brasenose
4 Christ Church
5 Corpus Christi
6 Exeter
7 Green Templeton
8 Harris Manchester
9 Hertford
10 Jesus
11 Keble
12 Kellogg
13 Lady Margaret Hall
14 Linacre
15 Lincoln
16 Magdalen
17 Mansfield
18 Merton
19 New College
20 Nuffield
21 Oriel
22 Oxford Botanic Garden
23 Pembroke
24 Queen's
25 Rhodes House
26 Rothermere American Inst*
27 Saïd Business School
28 Somerville
29 St Anne's
30 St Antony's
31 St Catherine's
32 St Cross
33 St Edmund Hall
34 St Hilda's
35 St Hugh's
36 St John's
37 St Peter's
38 Trinity
39 University
40 University Parks
41 Wadham
42 Wolfson
43 Worcester

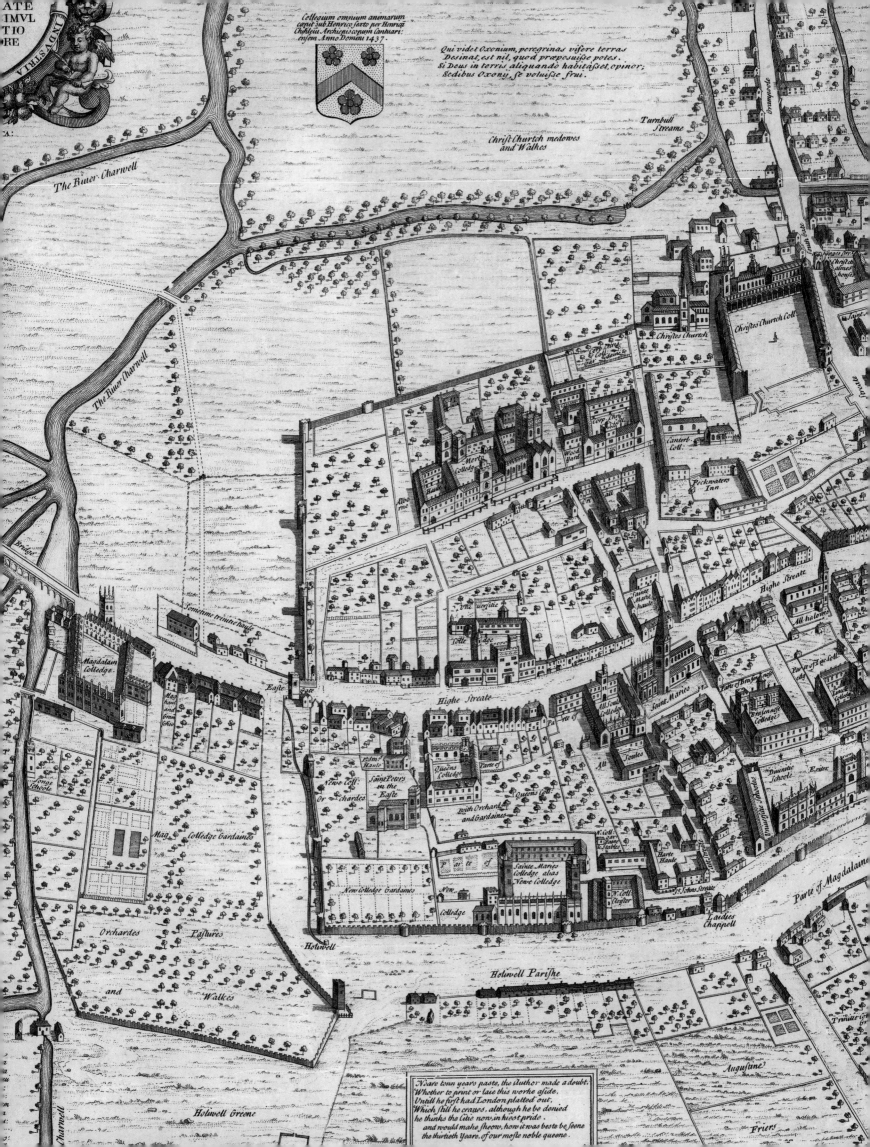